Language Mysticism

The Negative Way of Language
in Eliot, Beckett, and Celan

SHIRA WOLOSKY

Language Mysticism

The Negative Way of
Language in Eliot, Beckett,
and Celan

❧

STANFORD UNIVERSITY PRESS
STANFORD, CALIFORNIA
1995

Stanford University Press
Stanford, California
© 1995 by the Board of Trustees of the
Leland Stanford Junior University
Printed in the United States of America

CIP data are at the end of the book

Stanford University Press publications are
distributed exclusively by Stanford University Press
within the United States, Canada, Mexico, and Central
America; they are distributed exclusively by Cambridge
University Press throughout the rest of the world.

For my parents,
in gratitude

Acknowledgments

༚

This book pays homage to my teachers and colleagues over many years, and my gratitude to them is multiple and layered. I would like now to express my heartfelt thanks to Robert Fagles, Joseph Frank, and A. Walton Litz of Princeton University, who introduced me to cultural history as a frame for literary study; to Harold Bloom, Geoffrey Hartman, and John Hollander at Yale University, for a fuller grasp of figural language; to Jaroslav Pelikan of Yale, for theological information and suggestions; to participants in the workshop on literary theory at the Institute for Advanced Studies at the Hebrew University of Jerusalem for deepening the philosophical frameworks of my literary understanding: Gerald Bruns, Dan Pagis, Shlomith Rimmin-Kenan, Jon Whitman, and especially Sanford Budick, Stanley Cavell, and Wolfgang Iser; and to my friends and colleagues, for their generosity always: Gail Berkeley, Beverly Haviland, Susanne Wofford, and Emily Budick. I would also like to thank Daniel Boyarin for his encouragement and support of my work on this book, and Dina Makovsky, for her help in reviewing my English versions of Celan poems.

I want to thank Yale University for a Morse Fellowship, and the Institute for Advanced Studies at the Hebrew University for fellowship support.

I am grateful to my children, Talya, Elazar, Tamar, and Naomi, without whom this book would have been completed much sooner; and I wish to thank from my heart my husband, Ariel Weiss, and Mariska Perquin, who made finishing this book possible.

Portions of this book have appeared in earlier forms, and I wish to thank the following publications for permission to incorporate this material here: "Samuel Beckett's Figural Evasions," in *Languages of the Unsayable*, ed. Sanford Budick and Wolfgang Iser (New York: Columbia University Press, ©1989), pp. 165–86; "The Negative Way Negated: Samuel Beckett's *Texts for Nothing*," *New Literary History* 22 (1991): 213–31; "Paul Celan's Linguistic Mysticism," *Studies in Twentieth Century Literature* 10 (©1986): 191–211; "Mystical Language and Mystical Silence," in *Argumentum e Silentio,* ed. Amy Colin (New York: Walter de Gruyter, 1987): 364–74.

I wish to thank Deutsche Verlags-Anstalt, Stuttgart, for permission to reprint poems from Paul Celan's *Von Schwelle zu Schwelle*, ©1955; S. Fischer Verlag, Frankfurt am Main, for permission to reprint poems from Paul Celan's *Sprachgitter*, ©1959, and *Die Niemandsrose*, ©1963; and Suhrkamp Verlag, Frankfurt am Main, for permission to reprint poems from Paul Celan's *Atemwende*, ©1967; *Fadensonnen*, ©1968; *Lichtzwang*, ©1970; *Schneepart*, ©1971; and *Zeitgehöft*, ©1976. I would also like to thank Grove/Atlantic, Inc., for permission to quote from the following texts by Samuel Beckett: "All Strange Away," in *Rockaby and Other Short Pieces*, 1981; *Company*, 1980; *Disjecta*, 1984; *Fizzles*, 1976; *Ill Seen Ill Said*, 1981; "Imagination Dead Imagine," "Ping," and "Enough," in *First Love and Other Shorts*, 1974; *The Lost Ones*, 1972; *More Pricks than Kicks*, 1972; *Proust*, 1957; *Stories and Texts for Nothing*, 1967; *The Unnamable*, in *Three Novels*, 1958; and *Watt*, 1953.

Contents

ᘒ

Abbreviations

❧

General

AMC   *The Ascent of Mount Carmel.* In *Complete Works of John of the Cross.* Trans. and ed. E. Allison Peers. Westminster, Md.: Newman Press, 1953.

C   Augustine, *Confessions.* Trans. R. S. Pine-Coffin. Middlesex: Penguin, 1981.

DN, MT   Pseudo-Dionysius the Areopagite, *On the Divine Names and Mystical Theology.* Trans. C. E. Rolt. London: Macmillan, 1920.

DNS   *The Dark Night of the Soul.* In *Complete Works of John of the Cross.* Trans. and ed. E. Allison Peers. Westminster, Md.: Newman Press, 1953.

TR   Augustine, *On the Trinity: Basic Writing of St. Augustine.* Ed. Whitney J. Oates. New York: Random House, 1948.

Eliot Texts

All citations from Eliot's poems are to *The Complete Poems and Plays* (New York: Harcourt, Brace and World, 1971). Abbreviations for the *Four Quartets* are as follows:

BN	Burnt Norton
DS	Dry Salvages
EC	East Coker
LG	Little Gidding

Abbreviations for prose works are:

KE	*Knowledge and Experience in the Philosophy of F. H. Bradley.* London: Faber and Faber, 1964.
LPM	Letters to Paul Elmer More. Unpublished correspondence. Princeton University Archive.
OPP	*On Poetry and Poets.* New York: Farrar, Straus and Giroux, 1957.
SE	*Selected Essays of T. S. Eliot.* New York: Harcourt, Brace and World, 1964.
UP	*The Use of Poetry and the Use of Criticism.* London: Faber and Faber, 1975.

Beckett Texts

ASA	"All Strange Away." In *Rockaby and Other Short Pieces.* New York: Grove Press, 1981.
Com	*Company.* New York: Grove Press, 1980.
DJ	*Disjecta.* New York: Grove Press, 1984.
E	"Enough." In *First Love and Other Shorts.* New York: Grove Press, 1974.
F	*Fizzles.* New York: Grove Press, 1976.
IDI	"Imagination Dead Imagine." In *First Love and Other Shorts.* New York: Grove Press, 1974.
ISIS	*Ill Seen Ill Said.* New York: Grove Press, 1981.
LO	*The Lost Ones.* New York: Grove Press, 1972.
MP	*More Pricks than Kicks.* New York: Grove Press, 1972.
P	*Proust.* New York: Grove Press, 1957.
T	*Stories and Texts for Nothing.* New York: Grove Press, 1967.
UNN	*The Unnamable.* In *Three Novels.* New York: Grove Press, 1958.

Celan Texts

GW   Gesammelte Werke in fünf Bänden. 5 vols. Frankfurt
          am Main: Suhrkamp Verlag, 1983.

All quotations from Celan poems and prose are taken from this edition. Abbreviations refer to the title of each volume of poetry or prose work, followed by volume and page number in the collected works. The titles of the volumes of poetry are abbreviated as follows:

AW	*Atemwende* (Breathturning) (1967)
FS	*Fadensonnen* (Threadsuns) (1968)
LZ	*Lichtzwang* (Lightforce) (1970)
MG	*Mohn und Gedächtnis* (Poppy and memory) (1952)
NR	*Die Niemandsrose* (No one's rose) (1963)
SG	*Sprachgitter* (Speechgrille) (1959)
SP	*Schneepart* (Snowpart) (1971)
SU	*Der Sand aus den Urnen* (Sand out of urns) (1948)
VS	*Von Schwelle zu Schwelle* (From threshold to threshold) (1955)
ZH	*Zeitgehöft* (Timecourt) (1976)

Note on Translations

All translations of Celan poems are my own, but in consultation with available translations of Celan, especially *Speechgrille*, trans. Joachim Neugroschel (New York: E. P. Dutton, 1971), and translations by John Felstiner. Other collections of Celan's poetry in English include Michael Hamburger, trans., *Paul Celan: Poems* (New York: Persea, 1980), and Katharine Washburn and Margret Guillemin, trans., *Last Poems* (San Francisco: North Point Press, 1986). Prose translations here follow those by Jerry Glenn in "The Meridian," *Chicago Review* 29, no. 3 (Winter 1978): 29–40, and Jerry Glenn and Walter Billeter, *Paul Celan: Prose Writings and Selected Poems* (Carlton, Victoria, Australia: Paper Castle Mimeographs, 1977).

All translations from secondary sources available only in languages other than English are my own.

By homely gifts and hindered words
The human heart is told
Of Nothing
"Nothing" is the force
That renovates the world.

—Emily Dickinson

Language Mysticism

The Negative Way of Language
in Eliot, Beckett, and Celan

Introduction:
Beyond Inexpressibility

From that time forth she [Reason] found it
hard to believe that the splendor and purity
was sullied by the corporeal matter of words.
And just as what the spirit sees is always present
and is held to be immortal . . . sound, being a
sensible thing, is lost into the past.

—Augustine, *De Ordine*

᳁

The inexpressibility topos, which declares that words can never
adequately express ultimate meanings, is among the most pervasive
and least examined motifs in Western letters. It implies far more
than the rhetorical ploy E. R. Curtius identifies with an orator's
claim he can "find no words" fitly to celebrate his subject.[1] By making the inadequacy of language into the highest rhetorical praise,
inexpressibility raises meaning to a state beyond limit and formulation, into the infinite. But this is to appeal to hierarchies that are
fundamentally theological and, at their extreme, mystical. Inexpressibility is a literary device that carries with it a whole history of
metaphysics, a set of often unconscious but deeply entrenched commitments that continue to shape our imagination and understanding. In particular, it opens to view an ambivalence toward language
deeply embedded within the Western tradition, in which language
is seen as at best wanting, at worst profane, compared with the
truth it would express. But this ambivalence to language takes its
place in a broader ambivalence toward body, time, and toward difference, conditions for which language serves as image and with

which it is closely linked on many levels. Inexpressibility thus places language within a set of priorities and dualisms whose value-structure reaches back to Greek ontology, but which have now come under critical scrutiny and revision.

The writings of T. S. Eliot, Samuel Beckett, and Paul Celan show how far-reaching and immediate this history remains in its influence and consequences. In each writer, language is a central topic and inexpressibility a potent force. Their texts, however, explicitly place this concern with language, evident in so much modern writing, in the context of theological traditions that may otherwise seem remote. Their linguistic concern is not primarily aesthetic reflection on their own literary structures and processes—a claim often made for Beckett and Celan. Instead, the powers and purposes of language are framed by theological premises and judgments, suggesting how these continue to govern basic linguistic and literary stances. This in turn illuminates other modern works where language seems a subject in its own right but remains theological in implication and attitude.

Theology in the three writers nevertheless makes itself felt in quite different ways. The relevance of theology to Eliot's earlier work is a matter of controversy, but its importance for his later writings is self-evident. The later Eliot is a poet writing, with whatever complexity of intention, within the Christian tradition. In contrast, Beckett's work frequently invokes religious materials, but it resides within none of them. Though his writing treats, among other things, the Christian heritage, it does so in ways that are critical and parodic, not least by fulfilling Christian premises in macabre and perverse ways. In Paul Celan religious contexts are at times explicitly marked; their power and significance also extend well beyond the texts in which they directly appear. Celan's religious references, however, are Judaic rather than Christian and therefore differ significantly from those of Eliot and Beckett, both in content and in linguistic implications. The contrast and comparison help to make clear otherwise hidden aspects of the Christian metaphysic, while suggesting religious modes surprisingly different from those of the dominant Western tradition.

Eliot's work offers therefore a kind of paradigm within a mainstream Western tradition; Beckett's, a critical parody of it; and Celan's, an alternate version parallel but not identical to it. Despite these differences, the language-centered interest of each writer focuses on theologies that are mystical and negative. This tendency is not accidental. Language is a central issue in the negative theology of radical mysticisms. Or rather, silence is. In this sense, the term *language mysticism* is an oxymoron. Almost by definition, mysticisms demote and ultimately attempt to abrogate language. A negative approach to language is almost always central to the mystical desire for ultimacy, seen as a state beyond multiplicity, division, and dispersion—conditions closely associated with language. Exactly because mysticism longs to go beyond sequence and difference to unity, negation is an integral part of its evaluation of language, which is the site and sign of sequential difference. As the inexpressibility topos suggests, the assertion of what language cannot say is a traditional means for designating an ultimate realm beyond formulation. Negation and transcendence are thus closely allied.

Within mystical discourse, however, the problem of language is treated as tangential to prior spiritual or philosophical goals. Striving to resist differentiation in its spirituality and discursive reason in its epistemology, mysticism sees language as a dispensable means for accomplishing these ends. Its role is therefore often unexamined and apparently secondary. Whether language is indeed subordinate has recently been questioned. Steven Katz, for example, notes that despite disclaimers, mystical experiences have always necessarily taken linguistic form.[2] At issue, however, is more than inconsistency. Just why have mysticisms taken this stance against language? What basic commitments and values are revealed in their antilinguistic ideal? Mysticism's point of view on language dramatizes its fundamental attitudes toward experience in this world of time and difference as against a yearned-for unity. From this unity language is excluded. But excluded with it, no less, are time and the world. Language thus points beyond mysticism's metaphysical structure of ascent, into its axiological judgments concerning life in the temporal, material world, which language consistently represents and which mysticism aspires to transcend.

Here I attempt neither a sociology nor a typology of varieties of mystical experience, nor a general or systematic theological definition. Instead I examine mysticism as invoked by the three authors, especially in regard to their treatment of language. The chapter on Eliot is in many ways introductory, establishing certain Christian norms that Eliot both adopts and complicates. Beckett's work is then approached as a response to these norms, one which brings to light how decisive a place language has within them. Despite the accidental and even repressed position of language in the tradition, Beckett suggests how language establishes the very terms for the ideals that require transcendence of language. From this point of view, language is no longer a mere instrument for its own surpassing, but the very framework defining mystical conduct and goals. The basic terms of value within mystical discourse turn out to be inextricably linked to language terms, which serve as generative tropes or figures representing the very states mysticism posits: differentiation versus unity, temporal sequence versus eternal wholeness, materiality versus spiritual essence. In each pair, language acts as trope or image for the first term, and a silence beyond language represents the second. This doubling recurs in Beckett. But Beckett's work asserts the primacy of language as a figure within this schema, not its subordinate status as a means through it. And his work brings into question the metaphysical hierarchy such language tropes reenact.

The power of language as figure rather than instrument emerges most forcefully in Paul Celan's poetry. Language is the focal, pervasive image in his work, which explores the borders of language as they verge upon the limits of expression. In Celan, however, the territories of language and silence shift from metaphysics as such to more specifically historical questions. Celan's work directly poses axiological challenges to the values implicit in mystical scales of being. A Romanian Jew who lived through the destruction of European Jewry, Celan offers one of the great literary responses to the disaster of European culture represented by the Second World War.

His work poses a riddle that is reflected in critical treatments of it. On the one hand, his poetry is regarded as a radically self-enclosed linguistic world; on the other, Celan is treated as a Holocaust poet, whose work is deeply embroiled in history. This study, inspired by that riddle, explores how Celan's linguistic focus intercrosses with the profound historical and axiological involvement of his work. In Celan's case, language is expressly an image representing temporal, material experience. His figure of language accords in this way with Beckett's and Eliot's. But Celan's tradition gives it direct and devoted attention, and finally also different axiological weight. Judaic mysticism, particularly the Kabbalah, adopts language as the central image for the created world, including the world of historical experience. As such, language is fully exposed to the traumas and disruptions of history that Celan's poetry registers. Inexpressibility, conversely, has a double function in Celan. On the one hand, it reflects, as in Beckett or Eliot, claims of an ultimacy beyond language—an ineffability that does not so much transcend language hierarchically as act as the linguistic ground. On the other hand, it figures as the total collapse of all meaningful order into horror.

Celan's work thus situates language and silence within the specific context of Jewish mysticism, which presents a set of assumptions significantly different from those of Eliot and Beckett. Yet for each writer, and within each tradition, the figural status of language is central and impelling. My main purpose in this study is to illuminate these writers, each in his own way difficult and resistant to interpretation, by placing specific works within the theological and philosophical contexts they evoke. At the same time, I have kept in view topics that recur from author to author as these reflect basic attitudes to language within broader structures of value and commitment. Additional differences in interpretive treatment reflect the bodies of criticism each author has already attracted; I have tried not to reconsider issues fully treated elsewhere.

In the case of Eliot, since many religious and indeed mystical commentaries have been undertaken by others, I have not exhaustively reviewed every theological reference or issue. Instead I restrict my discussion to the *Four Quartets*, focusing only on how Eliot's theological commitments frame his linguistic ones. I trace the ways in which language serves as a focal topic and image in the poem, alongside and even situating the temporal structures that elsewhere have been made the central issue of interpretation. For although language is a frequent topic in Eliot criticism, it is rarely granted the priority it deserves as both shaping and reflecting Eliot's vision; in this, many commentators share the bias of both the poem and the tradition it resumes.

Beckett criticism has similarly lavished attention on philosophical issues or influences, often as seen through metaphysical, existential, or religious crisis. However, despite the imposing presence of theological play in Beckett, there has been little investigation of his specifically theological references. My own reading, moreover, sees Beckett less in terms of crisis than of critique. And while most Beckett criticism focuses on the long prose works and the drama, my main interest has been in the short prose texts, particularly the *Texts for Nothing*. My choice is partly due to the relative lack of comment on these prose works. I have also wanted to observe some constraint of genre: Eliot and Celan are both treated as poets, and while Beckett's short texts are not lyrics in any strict sense, they have often been called prose poems. Martin Esslin, for example, describes them as "some of the most beautiful pieces of Beckett's prose poetry, with sweeping rhythms, complex patterns of sound and imagery." [3] Their aesthetic value inheres in this beauty and mastery of rhetoric. Certainly they have no plot, no characters, no progressive structures. Lack of closure, of consistent formal patterning, of clear shape or direction, make them resistant to a traditional textual explication in which every element finds its place. But Celan's work also resists explication, as does Eliot's. Linguistic negation, that is, penetrates each writer in formal ways. Eliot's fuller integration into traditional literary and cultural expectations may make his language less apparently disjunctive. Yet in his work as well negativity undermines the foundations of utterance, although perhaps in ways he did not entirely intend.

Interpretations of Celan are rapidly approaching in volume those of Eliot and Beckett. Most critical writing on Celan, however, has been in German, and now also in French. Celan remains less known to the English-speaking reader; my discussions of him are therefore more introductory than those of Eliot or Beckett. Celan poses as well the nearly impossible task of translation. His texts are based rather than written in German, and the difficulty of making them available in English cannot be exaggerated. Neither do I attempt to situate Celan within the German literary contexts relevant to him, which are not my primary concern. Instead, I focus on Celan's tropes of language as figures for temporal and material, which is to say historical, reality. Celan's is a radically reified language of substantive, malleable material. The kabbalistic view of creation as made of the letters of language becomes in him a powerful, realized poetic. But this is directly to tie orders of language to the order of experience; language becomes a mode for investigating possible grounds for meaningful interpretation of experience. Such grounds also invoke what remains beyond language. The ineffable draws a boundary, sets a negative limit to language. But it does so in order to define a positive linguistic terrain—or else language's utter failure. Silence in Celan does not signal transcendence into suprahistorical, eternal realms. Linguistic failure is the failure to realize meaningful historical experience. On the one hand, the ineffable makes possible positive utterance; on the other, it may engulf it. Language trauma is historical trauma. And the possibility of positive utterance remains ever-threatened and vulnerable in Celan. Indeed, far from constructing enclosed aesthetic worlds, his language is invested with all the risk of temporal process and historical engagement. It goes ever in the face of inexpressibility; but beyond inexpressibility there is a commitment to language as the articulation of meaning within our immediate historical condition.

Celan's work is most directly situated within the historical ruptures of this century, which remain for him the impelling center of any cultural or literary undertaking. But all the works I focus on are situated by the Second World War. Eliot's *Quartets* directly refer to the war, during which all but "Burnt Norton" were written, and they are expressly concerned with evaluating temporal events. In Beckett there is little overt historical reference. Indeed, his evasion of history is so sustained as to suggest a deliberate project. Yet Beckett's own production is one demarcated by war. For example, a bombing early in World War II destroyed most of the London edition of *Murphy*, and Beckett described *Watt* as an exercise—"a game, a means of staying sane, a way to keep my hand in"—while hiding from the Nazis in Roussillon in the Vaucluse for his work in the French Resistance.[4] The arrest of his close friend Paul Léon in 1940 first led him to participate in Resistance activities; the occupation forced his publisher, Editions de minuit, to become a clandestine press.[5] Beckett's work is even routinely divided into pre- and postwar periods corresponding to his move from English to French—a shift that took place in the *Trilogy* and *Texts for Nothing*, written in the immediate aftermath of the war experience.

Each writer's approach to tradition takes place within the context of war and the challenge to tradition its catastrophe poses. In *Four Quartets*, as also in later essays, Eliot seems to see the crisis of European culture as due to its failure to be true to its central tradition, including a Christian metaphysic. Beckett's work, in contrast, seems to me to suggest not a failure to uphold the tradition, but rather a failure of the tradition itself. While declining to engage historical events directly, Beckett's work addresses paradigms of European culture that become, in his representation, modes of destruction. Not least among these is the ambivalence about language his texts obsessively enact. Beckett's work might be called the revenge of the inexpressibility topos. What he shows is how the question of language is profoundly a question of value; how our attitudes toward language both construct and reveal our attitudes toward historical life itself; and how our desire to transcend language may inscribe a failure in our culture to acknowledge and take responsibility for the actions we perform in the concrete conditions of history.

The image of language and the negativity in the three writers reflect elements of diverse traditions that each develops in diverse ways. Their work elaborates such differences, as well as projecting issues they have in common. In this study, I show how their uses of language and perceptions of its status and value draw upon and reflect religious traditions in which language has an often equivocal but always radically revelatory place. Yet I argue that their stances toward language show how metaphysics and history mutually implicate each other. The question of language is finally a moral one. Language is the sign of body, of history, of difference. The approach to language of Eliot, Beckett, and Celan inscribes the struggle to define and to locate the values that endow our lives with meaning, and to translate these values into temporal and historical reality.

CHAPTER 2

Linguistic Asceticism in "Four Quartets"

> Great simplicity is only won by an intense mo-
> ment or by years of intelligent effort, or by both.
> It represents one of the most arduous conquests
> of the human spirit: the triumph of feeling and
> thought over the natural sin of language.
> —T. S. Eliot, "The Post-Georgians"

ༀ

The Mystical Context and Inexpressibility

T. S. Eliot's journey of return to the tradition no less returned
him to some of the tradition's most problematic sites. Critical discussion, especially of Eliot's religious backgrounds, has usually
taken the form of exegetical comment and argued for his successful
recovery of traditional stances. When complications have been recognized, they have generally been referred to Eliot's personal religious and philosophical development, at times in a manner suggesting a religious court judging degrees of orthodoxy or heresy.[1] I
would instead like to accept Eliot's claim to the tradition, and
to argue that religious complications in his work in fact reflect
complications and contradictions often hidden within traditional
discourse.

This is especially the case regarding the status and treatment of
language. Language constitutes a fundamental trope throughout
Eliot's work, where it serves both as a subject and as a medium of
representation. But its place in his work is highly ambivalent, at
once prominent and occulted, asserted and negated. This ambivalence, however, is not Eliot's alone. It is deeply inscribed within the
history of Western metaphysics and theology. Eliot only makes evi-

dent the equivocal and even self-contradictory place of language within that tradition.

Self-referential language is present in Eliot's work from the outset. Prufrock's "I cannot say just what I mean," Sweeney's lament that "I gotta use words when I talk to you," the arcane reference to the "Word" as "*to en*" in "Mr. Eliot's Sunday Morning Service" all display Eliot's undercurrent of concern with linguistic issues, and specifically his sense of linguistic limitation. In "Prufrock" and "Sweeney Agonistes," language seems to be a kind of concession to others, a barrier that must be negotiated. "Mr. Eliot's Sunday Morning Service" projects, if only through its parodistic failure, a longing for a Word beyond mere words. "Ash Wednesday" displays this longing, now positively expressed without irony. Finally, in the *Four Quartets*, the Eliotic figure of language takes shape with greatest clarity and urgency. There the trope of language becomes the center of meditation, and urgently so in each quartet's culminating section. It is also in the *Four Quartets* that an ambivalence toward language is most pronounced, as is the Christian context for this ambivalence. Language appears as a necessary instrument, but one that is flawed and limited. It is this appeal to so faulty an instrument that emerges in Eliot as profoundly self-compromising, with implications not only for Eliot's own progress but for the Christian tradition as it becomes the final articulation and framework of Eliot's concerns.[2] Not only in Eliot, but in the tradition, positive claims for language come to undermine themselves, against the tradition's (and Eliot's) expressed intentions.

The negative, mystical theology that marks *Four Quartets* particularly situates the compromised position language has in this work. The *Four Quartets'* involvement with negative mysticism is self-evident in the material they directly cite and the variety of negative constructions they employ. Lengthy allusions to John of the Cross, references to Augustine and Julian of Norwich, extensive litanies of systematic negation, as well as figural patterns of lessening, descent, withdrawal, and emptying profoundly shape the poems in terms of a mystical theology of apophasis or negative way.

This of course has been long recognized in Eliot criticism. Besides numerous articles and reference guides, two book-length studies— by Eloise Knapp Hay and Paul Murray—are devoted to tracing Eliot's interest and education in mystical theology (starting with notes taken at Harvard on Pseudo-Dionysius and John of the Cross, as well as Eastern mysticisms) and thoroughly reviewing central points of Christian mystical theology as these bear on Eliot's stances, references, and texts.[3]

These studies, however, do not give special notice to the place of language either in mystical theology or in Eliot. In general, they remain exegetical and descriptive, rather than interpretive and critical, regarding the Christian material they assemble. They identify rather than analyze, review rather than investigate, the theoretical implications of the mystical material in Eliot's work. And language enters into discussion only as a subsidiary topic, not as a crucial figure that provides and even generates central images for mystical conduct. Yet it is exactly this priority of language that Eliot's work dramatizes. Ultimately at issue, then, are not specific mystical regimens such as Hay, for example, insists on charting, claiming that "it makes considerable difference in Eliot's poems to know which part of [John of the Cross's] negative way is in question."[4] Eliot does not intend his poem as a handbook for mystical progress (which John's works were for the [discalced] Carmelite monks and nuns he served as prior). The *Four Quartets* instead strive to appeal beyond technical regimens and sectarian affiliations to a truth Eliot regarded as essentially universal, although attaining its fullest revelation within Church dogma.[5] It is this universal truth, along with its negative character, that is central—the negative force and direction of such statements by John of the Cross as Hay cites: "All things of earth and heaven, compared with God, are nothing."[6]

This declaration of nothingness stands at the heart of the mystical project and situates its fundamental values and attitudes toward the things of this world, transcendence, and language. It accords with the basic definition of mysticism in Evelyn Underhill's study, which Eliot read at Harvard: "the impassioned desire to transcend the sense world, in order that the self may be joined by love to the one eternal and ultimate object of love."[7] The negative drive of such apparently positive transcendent desire becomes clear in the works of John of the Cross, himself reflecting a long mystical tradition. For John, the soul in its progress toward union with God must choose the way "not easy, but difficult; not pleasant, but unpleasing; not restful, but wearisome; not great, but least; not precious, but despised" (AMC, 56). It must be "stripped of all things created—of its own actions and abilities—of understanding, perception, feeling;—so that nothing remains in it that is not the will of God and thus it is transformed into God" (AMC, 76). "Through emptiness and darkness and detachment from all things," the soul must pursue its desire in "obscurity and annihilation of all outward and inward things, to build on that which it neither sees nor feels, to journey by denial of ourselves and of all things" (AMC, 180).

In John of the Cross, positive ascent becomes indistinguishable from negative asceticism. This is a way Eliot follows. Eliot's "dark night" differs in some degree from John's, as he himself notes in the Clark Lectures.[8] John of the Cross's darkness is never one of doubt of the divine reality, but only its temporary eclipse. Eliot, in contrast, does at times imagine a "negative" negativity of true alienation from spiritual experience—a descent into the "dark, dark, dark" of temporal motion without reference to a timelessness beyond it.[9] Eliot's "positive" negativity, however, has strong ties to John's, and especially with the Sanjuanist emphasis on asceticism. John's is a mysticism strongly marked by the affect and personal passion first associated in the Western tradition with Augustine.[10] In the earlier, Neoplatonist writings of Pseudo-Dionysius the Areopagite, the negative way more closely addressed the problem, or rather the impossibility, of defining God. This I would call a mysticism of negative definition. Negation is here mainly directed to the (un)naming of God as that which "exceedeth all Being, Deity, and Goodness." Its function is to point beyond form and language, "where the simple, absolute, and unchangeable mysteries of heavenly Truth lie hidden in the dazzling obscurity of the secret Silence" (MT 1). Dionysius's litanies of negation in the Mystical Theology are thus primarily devoted to the transcendence of God, paradoxically declaring the Divine to be that which, beyond all limit and form, surpasses all definition:

Ascending yet higher we maintain that It is not soul, or mind . . . nor can It be described by the reason or perceived by the understanding . . . nor can the reason attain to It to name It or to know It . . . nor can any affirmation or negation apply to it . . . in as much as It transcends all affirmation . . . and transcends all negation by the pre-eminence of its simple and absolute nature—free from every limitation and beyond them all. (*MT* 5)

While John of the Cross also pursues such negative definition, in his work emphasis shifts toward affect, in what I would call a mysticism of ascetic negation. Here negation focuses not only on the "nothingness" of divine transcendence, but on the "nothingness" of the self. In order to be assimilated to God, the self must be gradually stripped away. Negation is directed at the affective and cognitive states of the soul, which are thus progressively denied in a gradual emptying that alone paves the approach to the divine transcendence.

Such ascetic negation seems especially to mark Eliot's own highly psychologized writing ("distracted from distraction by distraction"). The call to the soul in "East Coker" III to "be still and wait without hope . . . / wait without love . . . wait without thought, . . . for the faith and love and the hope are all in the waiting" is strongly Sanjuanist. John of the Cross similarly urges the "emptiness of hope," the "detachment of will," and the "darkness of faith," for the "soul must be dark to its own light to have the light of faith" (*AMC*, 80, 89, 70). Eliot's negative way, that is, follows John's particularly in its ascetic emphasis, its concern with the mystical purgation of the self as an ascetic approach to ultimate things. This exceeds textual allusion to become extensive appropriation. When Eliot writes in "East Coker" III, "You say I am repeating / Something I have said before," he is in fact repeating not only himself:

> In order to arrive at what you do not know
> You must go by a way which is the way of ignorance.
> In order to possess what you do not possess

You must go by the way of dispossession.
In order to arrive at what you are not
You must go through the way in which you are not.
                                        (EC III, 138–43)
In these lines Eliot directly reworks one of John's poems:

In order to arrive at possessing everything,
Desire to possess nothing.
In order to arrive at that which thou knowest not,
Thou must go by a way that thou knowest not
In order to arrive at that which thou are not,
Thou must go through that which thou art not
                                        (AMC, 58)[11]

Still, the distinction between mystical (negative) definition and mystical ascetism remains one of degree and emphasis rather than of fundamental values. Before John, Dionysius applied his negative way to the mystic himself, who must "leave the senses and the activities of the intellect" and "by the unceasing and absolute renunciation of thyself and all things . . . shalt in pureness cast all things aside . . . [to] be led upwards to the Ray of divine Darkness which exceedeth all existence" (MT 1). Like Dionysius, whom he knew not least through Thomas Aquinas (Dionysius, with Aristotle and Augustine, are the authors the Summa Theologica most frequently cites), John also insists on negative attributions for God. Eliot was familiar with both, as well as with other mystical writers, as is amply attested in the Clark Lectures.[12] And despite Eliot's temperamental affinity with John of the Cross's ascetic mysticism of affect, his work also reenacts issues evident in Dionysius. Moreover, most crucial for Eliot as poet is the common ground in language to which both mystics point.

Language provides Dionysius with the fundamental trope, as well as the fundamental means, for the transcendence he is seeking. The characteristic and ultimate expression of his negative way is to arrive beyond language. This linguistic transcendence is moreover essential and not accidental to ultimate experience, informing the very conception of such experience. Dionysius's negations arrive finally and necessarily at speechlessness: it is even this speechlessness that defines his vision of ultimacy. For to be beyond form, limit, and thought in ultimate union is exactly to be beyond language. As Dionysius explains against those who "describe the Transcendent Cause of all things by qualities drawn from the lowest order of being," the divine in "a stricter sense" is "beyond all positive and negative distinctions." It is beyond form, beyond attributes, indeed beyond being, "possessing neither speech nor understanding because it exceedeth all things" (*MT* 1). Therefore, no representation can ever be adequate. Representation can finally only be misrepresentation.

Of the many motives and characteristics of this drive for linguistic transcendence, perhaps the most central, and most resonant in Eliot, is the exaltation of unity and simplicity. Dionysius repeatedly employs imagery of contraction, unification, and straitening for his vision of ascent. Thus he explains that "the more that we soar upwards the more our language becomes restricted to the compass of purely intellectual conceptions, even as in the present instance plunging into the Darkness which is above the intellect we shall find ourselves reduced not merely to brevity of speech but even to absolute dumbness both of speech and thought" (*MT* 3).[13] The condition of wordlessness is a condition of seeing in a way "restricted to the compass" of increasingly unitary conceptions, finally transcending these as well in its approach toward a "simple and absolute nature—free from every limitation and beyond them all" (*MT* 5). As Andrew Louth remarks, Dionysius, in urging withdrawal from the sensory world, is urging "withdrawal from the inevitable fragmentariness of our involvement in the world of the senses, to a more collected, unified state."[14] But language is by definition fragmentary. It is discursive and successive, partial in its unfolding. God, then, is beyond representation in language not only because he is beyond any category, but because his unity radically opposes the differentiations of language.

It is, I would argue, exactly in his own attitude toward unity that Eliot is most traditional, with the most important consequences for his linguistic stances. Unity is, perhaps above all others, the impelling motive in *Four Quartets;* and synecdoche, as the substitution of part for whole, is its master trope, as the poem's striking figures make evident. The vision of the dry pool, the still point of the turning world, the dance, the Chinese jar, the zero summer, and of course the moments of outright negation, of "meeting nowhere, no before and after" (LG II), are all points of contraction and unification, in opposition to the dispersions of world and time. Hillis Miller argues that such pursuit of unity is in fact the enduring impulse of Eliot's entire career: "Everywhere latent is the idea of a unified whole made up of a complex network of relations. The individual part has meaning only in the way it fits into the parts around it." [15] This same will to unity is displayed throughout Eliot's career as a critic, from the early "Tradition and the Individual Talent," with its image of the poet's mind as "always forming new wholes" (SE, 8–9), through the late "Frontiers of Criticism," which defines poetry as "an original way of assembling the most disparate and unlikely material to make a new whole" (OPP, 119). As he says of Dante, so we can say of him: "The vital matter is that Dante's poem is a whole; you must in the end come to understand every part in order to understand any part" (SE, 257–58).

Eliot's philosophical remarks similarly turn to and around this unifying vision. Thus, in a graduate school "Report on the Ethics of Kant" he writes that "truth becomes available as we embrace all views by elevation to the one standpoint." [16] His lifelong interest in F. H. Bradley, from his doctoral dissertation through later writings (in a letter to Paul Elmer More he refers to himself as "Bradleyan" [LPM, August 10, 1930]), also seems to center in Bradley's own conception of "the Whole which demands our devotion" (SE, 397). And in a late assessment of the function and status of poetry Eliot finally refers art to a unity that exceeds it: "For it is ultimately the function of art, in imposing a credible order upon ordinary reality, and thereby eliciting some perception of an order in reality, to bring us to a condition of serenity, stillness, and reconciliation; and then leave us, as Virgil left Dante, to proceed toward a region where that guide can avail us no farther" (OPP, 94).

But this will to unity poses immense problems for language, as the literature on mysticism indicates. This is already the case in the

Neoplatonist background to Christian mystical writing, as when Plotinus remarks of unity that its "expression [is] already touched by multiplicity."[17] John of the Cross, too, urges a marked suspicion against "all forms represented by bodily figures and images" (*AMC*, 103), of which the soul must rid itself along with "every stain of creatures" (*AMC*, 78). Fancy, imagination, even supernatural visions are "still based on external sense" (*AMC*, 105, 123), are still forms of "attachment" (*AMC*, 129). Echoing Dionysius, John emphasizes the ineffability of ultimate union with the divine as "beyond description, beyond form of imagination, transcending sense and speech" (*DNS*, 429–30).

Inexpressibility is likewise central to Eliot's mystical commitment. The ultimate moment language can achieve is its own transcendence. As Paul Murray insists, Eliot defines his mysticism as, first, the "path of negation; second, as an ecstasy of thought . . . ; and third, as an incommunicable vision." In his 1930 essay on Donne, Eliot himself describes the mystic's vision as the "assurance of experience incommunicable," just as he writes in the conclusion to *The Use of Poetry* that mystical illumination is characterized by "the realization that you will never be able to communicate it" (*UP*, 144).[18] Unity precludes its own expression.

The Way Up and the Way Down

It has often been claimed that in Eliot this negative, transcendent impulse against worldly attachment, which is also antilinguistic and antirepresentational, harmoniously coexists with a more positive vision. Helen Gardner, for example, citing Eliot's own epigraph from Heraclitus on how "the way up and the way down are the same," comments, "Christianity has always found room in itself for both types of spiritual experience: that which finds all nature a theophany, and that which feels the truth of . . . 'Deus Absconditus.' This deliberate descent into darkness out of twilight is 'one way.' It is the same, the poet tells us, as the other: the undeliberate ascent into the world of light which we read of in the first movement."[19] Gardner here refers to "Burnt Norton" III, one of several moments in the poem where Eliot himself invokes this ancient notion of "two ways":

> Descend lower, descend only
> Into the world of perpetual solitude,
> World not world, but that which is not world,
> Internal darkness, deprivation
> And destitution of all property,
> Desiccation of the world of sense,
> Evacuation of the world of fancy,
> Inoperancy of the world of spirit;
> This is the one way, and the other
> Is the same, not in movement
> But abstention from movement; while the world moves
> In appetency, on its metalled ways
> Of time past and time future.
>
> (114–26)

Eliot's witty reference to memories of the London subway, where the stairs offer a "movement" of descent while the elevator provides "abstention from movement," may disguise the more profound homology between them. These two "ways" are in fact the "same" in a quite literal sense. As in John of the Cross, whom this passage closely recalls, the negative way not only takes precedence over any positive one, but finally absorbs it. John, too, calls on the soul to divest itself of all "property" as attachment (AMC, 33), of all involvement in the "world of sense" (AMC, 360), and finally even of spiritual things: there is, he warns, also "spiritual luxury" and "spiritual gluttony" (DNS, 338, 350). The hope is to arrive at an "internal darkness, spiritual detachment" (AMC, 63) where the soul is "suspended" in a "loss of operation of faculties" (DNS, 358). Nor is the main issue the distinction between an "active" purgation of the beginner and a "passive" one of the experienced contemplative.[20] Active and passive, ascent and descent, are varying modes within a single, controlling ascetic vision of divestment.

What this Sanjuanist context dramatizes is how affirmative theology is in many ways inextricable from a more forceful negative theology of greater cultural impact. In either of Eliot's "ways," the movement is one of negation, figured in a series of direct denials, distributed through a list of words that lessen: *deprivation, destitution, evacuation, inoperancy.* Both "movement" and "abstention from movement" trace withdrawals, retreats that are as much inward as downward, toward a "solitude" removed from the exterior world—where exteriority is fundamentally rejected. The world, and all involvement in it, is figured only as imprisonment in the "metalled ways" of appetite and temporal process.

Where, then, is the "theophany" Helen Gardner cites? Where is the fullness of life, the "ascent into the world of light"? Eliot's two "ways" are the "same" because both are kinds of negative way. The "positive" way has no independent status. This is the case even in the apparent vision of fullness offered by "Burnt Norton" I. There the music is "unheard" and the eyebeam is "unseen." The vision of the pool is reached "along an empty alley," the pool itself is "drained" and "dry." Only against this emptiness does the "heart of light" come forth. And it does so to disappear at once, and in a way that emphasizes its contrast with the life of world and time it for a moment eclipsed. "Human kind cannot bear very much reality," the poet intones, where "reality" seems to refer to the vision achieved only by the emptying of the natural world, while loss of reality occurs with the return to the world of time, which has been less redeemed than unmasked. As "Burnt Norton" concludes: "Ridiculous the waste sad time / Stretching before and after."[21]

Despite promises to the contrary, the affirmative vision turns out to be negative. The relation between true fullness and the world proves to be one of contrast—the "positive" being formulated in terms that negate the world—and finally serves to underscore the world's emptiness. This contrast, however, is not due to a "split" between Eliot's aesthetic and religious intentions, between his "vision" and "doctrine," as Graham Hough, George Bornstein, and David Spurr argue.[22] Nor can heretical incursions unconsciously subverting Eliot's commitment to orthodoxy be blamed, as Sister Mary Gerard and Father William Lynch propose.[23] Paul Murray, writing in defense of Eliot as a Christian poet, insists that Eliot is quite orthodox, but in the tradition of the negative "doctrine of transcendence" rather than the affirmative "doctrine of immanence." It is not, he explains, Eliot's intention to "celebrate the presence of God in the temporal realm." Rather, Eliot's desire is to move away from "the illusions of the temporal world" and toward becoming "almost wholly absorbed into a world of transcendent Spirit." This tendency is already evident in Eliot's college notes on Evelyn Underhill's *Mysticism*, where he writes that "vision through the senses is imperfect, capricious, often a delusion."[24] It reemerges in such later writings as the essay on Pascal, where Eliot describes the three orders of nature, mind, and charity as "discontinuous; the higher is not implicit in the lower as in an evolutionary doctrine it would be" (*SE*, 368).

Eliot, then, is consistent in his commitment to the negative "doctrine of transcendence." What is odd and troubling is, first, the position and status this allows for the affirmative "doctrine of immanence"; and second, the implications of the negative doctrine for the language that conveys it. Inconsistencies in *Four Quartets* cannot simply be dismissed as failures either of Eliot's artistic competence or of his religious fidelity, as is often argued. The conflicts in the text are not merely Eliot's, but the tradition's as well. The *Four Quartets* illustrate how within the tradition the balance between affirmative and negative is unstable, how the negative theologically takes precedence over the affirmative. Nor is this precedence restricted to mystical writers. Thomas Aquinas, for all his insistence that within the limits of human power God is knowable with a valid knowledge, still opens the *Summa* by declaring, "We cannot know what God is, but rather what He is not" (1.Q. 3). Similarly, in the second part of the *Summa*, he concedes that "in the things of God . . . because of our inadequacy, negation has greater value than affirmation, as Dionysius says" (2.2, Q. 122, art. 2).[25] Thus, Etienne Gilson, whose work Eliot commends in the Clark Lectures, concludes that Saint Thomas agrees "in the end with Dionysius, [that] the fullest knowledge is that God remains beyond our knowledge."[26]

Dionysius himself makes this priority of the negative, or apophatic way, a central theme. Dionysius was no less an authority on "positive" or analogical theology—his book *Divine Names* was used as a textbook for analogical knowledge of the Divine in the medieval West. Yet Dionysius always reminds us that "affirmation . . . leads to a more fundamental negation" as the "path to a deeper knowledge of God."[27] Thus he writes in his treatise *Divine Names*:

> We know God in terms of the order of all beings which are projected out of it and which have some similarity and likeness to its divine paradigms . . . [but] we ascend step by step, so far as we can follow the way, to the Transcendent, by negating and transcending everything and by seeking the cause of all. . . . The most divine knowledge of God is one which knows through unknowing in the unity beyond intellect, when the intellect stands away from beings and then stands away from itself. (*DN* 7.3)

In Dionysian terms, *descent* technically denotes the "positive" movement of analogy as creation is "projected" out of God, while *ascent* denotes the "negative" movement of transcendence and negation of created things toward the God beyond them.[28] But both are finally negative modes. The goal of both is a vision of "unity beyond intellect," approached directly through "negating and transcending" step by step, but also, if less directly, by attention to the order of beings in their "similarity and likeness to divine paradigms." In either case, an opposition remains between the multiplicity of created things and the unity of the Divine. And in either case, the desire is to see beyond the multiplicity to the unity. This is obvious in the way of systematic negation of multiple forms. But it also obtains for knowledge by analogy, which rather than focusing attention on the multiple forms of likeness subjects them to what René Roques describes as a process of purgation:

> The analogic process corresponds to negative theology. . . . Through elimination, the symbols are progressively reduced to unity. And this unity is at the same time a unity of being stripped away and one of plenitude: stripping away of all spatial multiplicity and of all temporal distension; plenitude, beyond forms and things, in that the function of the symbol and of the intelligence are justified in their final and supreme destination, which is the meeting with the one.[29]

Positive analogy, too, is intended to direct attention away from the material embodiments it makes use of, and toward the spiritual reality they are meant to convey. Its conduct toward the "meeting with the one" beyond "multiplicity" must be one of "elimination," of purgation and unveiling, so that the analogy, rather than pointing to itself, serves to point away from itself. Forms and things are never immanently full. They remain instead modes of emptying, so that "by knowledge, by asceticism, by love . . . the intelligence can gradually rise to the principle behind all symbols."[30]

Strategies of Negation

In both the positive and negative ways, language has a defining and central role. In both, despite the apparent option of fullness of expression, this role is negative. Of the two ways, Dionysius writes:

> In the former treatises [on the affirmative way] the course of the argument, as it came down from the highest to the lowest categories, embraced an ever-widening number of conceptions which increased at each stage of the descent, but in the present treatise it mounts upwards from below towards the category of transcendence, and in proportion to its ascent it contracts its terminology, and when the whole ascent is passed it will be totally dumb, being at last wholly united with Him Whom words cannot describe. (MT 3)

Whether going down or up, the ladder of transcendence is a ladder of language. But it is a ladder that seeks its own abrogation. The descent from ultimate things to the "ever-widening number of conceptions" in the world is principally intended to pave the way of retraction, back up out of multiplicity to unity. This scale has specific linguistic corollaries: the world's multiple forms correspond to the partial, successive, multiple nature of words; unity ascends beyond them. Ascent here is an ascent toward silence—contraction until one becomes "totally dumb, being at last wholly united with Him Whom words cannot describe." Transcendence is linguistic transcendence; which is to say, linguistic negation.[31]

There are a number of strategies for achieving such linguistic negation, a number of negative forms it can take, as *Four Quartets* amply demonstrates. There can be systematic denials of positive designations; or reductions by elimination; or paradox; or negative designations; or direct meditations on the limits of language as fragmented, partial, and successive, always pointing to a unity beyond the multiple linguistic condition. Eliot uses all of these, which of course also flow into one another. Thus, the poem's central and controlling image of the "still point of the turning world" moves from systematic denial to negative designation to reductions (which are also paradoxical) to overt linguistic dismissal:

At the still point of the turning world. Neither flesh nor fleshless;
Neither from nor towards; at the still point, there the dance is,
But neither arrest nor movement. And do not call it fixity,
Where past and future are gathered. Neither movement from nor towards,
Neither ascent nor decline. Except for the point, the still point,
There would be no dance, and there is only the dance.
I can only say, *there* we have been: but I cannot say where.
And I cannot say, how long, for that is to place it in time.

(BN II, 62–68)

Such positive images as the "still point" or "the dance" are at once reduced by being denied any attributes ("neither flesh nor fleshless," "neither ascent nor decline"), denials which themselves take paradoxical form. A movement of exclusion ("except for the point") seems to assert positive presence. Yet this is a presence that evades all formulation: "do not call"; "I cannot say where." The image is finally of language as unfit, a betrayal of the vision that cannot, however, otherwise be conveyed: "And I cannot say, how long, for that is to place it in time."

These negative strategies recur throughout the *Quartets*, establishing important aspects of their rhythm and shape. Regimens of reductive release especially concentrate in each poem's third movement, as these pursue figures of descent and detachment. "Burnt Norton" III issues its call to "descend." "East Coker" III resumes the Sanjuanist call to the "soul" to "be still, and let the dark come upon you / Which shall be the darkness of God." There, negative descriptions ("what you do not know," "what you do not possess") become descriptions of negations ("the way of ignorance," "the way of dispossession"). That is, negations of something positive be-

come assertions of something negative. Or tautology further negates an already negative formulation: "where you are not," "what
you are not" become spaces of "no ecstasy," "the way in which you
are not."

Negative impulses are not restricted to the third movements,
however, but rather inform almost every movement, figure, vision,
and rhetorical sequence of the *Quartets*. To review every example
would be to recite most of the poem. There are repeated reductions
of the world of time to delusion and emptiness, as in the Sestine of
"Dry Salvages" III, where time is no more than a "soundless wail-
ing" and "drifting wreckage." "Little Gidding" II presents a litany
of death, in which air, earth, water, and fire all reduce to a state
where "last season's fruit is eaten and the fullfed beast shall kick
the empty pail." There are abrasive denunciations and deflations,
so that even the vision of the dance in "East Coker" I becomes mere
"keeping time," mere "feet rising and falling. / Eating and drinking.
Dung and death." "Dry Salvages" II reduces "the sense of well-
being, / Fruition, fulfilment, security or affection" to the same level
as "a very good dinner." Conversely, the poem's positive visions are
also framed in and through negation, as when "Little Gidding" I
offers its intense moment as "zero summer."

This disturbing figural negativity with regard to the world of
time, sequence, and materiality offers one of the poem's challenging
interpretive problems. Images of this life, of this world, of the sequences in which ordinary time unfolds, have consistently a negative figural valence in the poem. This negative figuration constitutes
a further level of negation. Yet it is based in one of the poem's most
fundamental claims: that negations are not merely negative, but
rather are ultimately positive. The poem promises to conduct from
negation to affirmation, from dispossession to paradoxical true possession. This conversion in turn is governed and guaranteed by a
further figure, that of concordance. The unity, the synecdoche, that
motivates the poem at so many levels does so here as well. The
poem proposes not to deny or deflate experience, but to restore it
within a totality of wholeness wherein each experience finds its true
place and significance.

What remains troubling, however, is how Eliot's images of fullness and wholeness finally fail to include and contain. These images
promise not exclusions, but inclusions; promise not to remove or
excise parts out of their sequence, but to gather together the sequence into a subsuming whole that will contain all of them. They
promise, that is, the synecdochic fulfillment that remains the poem's
governing trope and controlling desire. But instead, they generate
and entail further removals, excisions, denials, and deflations. Not
only is concordance couched in negative terms, it ultimately excludes exactly the conditions it sets out to embrace. This is so in
case after case. Thus, "East Coker" V seeks

> Not the intense moment
> Isolated, with no before and after,
> But a lifetime burning in every moment.

Yet the experience only emerges "when here and now cease to matter." The positive claim in "Dry Salvages" to "one action . . . which
shall fructify in the lives of others" is at once emptied: "And do not
think of the fruit of action" (DS III). In "Little Gidding," "midwin-
ter spring" contains every season, but only in that it is "suspended
in time" (LG I). The "gifts brought by age" finally consist of "bitter
tastelessness of shadow fruit," "the conscious impotence of rage,"
"the rending pain of reenactment" (LG II).

In each case, the figures that promise an ingathering of disparate
experiences and moments do so in fact by way of displacement and
elimination. The synecdochic "point of intersection" finally relies
on the negative representation of the parts that it is supposed to
gather, complete, and redeem. This devaluation of experience in
time has disturbed such readers as Graham Hough, who complains
of a "devaluation of ordinary human endeavour," and of "timeless
moments which are rare and fleeting, and seem to do nothing to
redeem the long stretches of insignificance in between."[32] F. R.
Leavis, in his sustained attack on the poem in *The Living Principle*,
similarly suspects the claim of the "still point" to "give us our apprehension of a real reality" while offering no more than "an escape
from transience." Against the claim in "Burnt Norton" to conquer

time within time ("Only in time can the moment . . . be remembered / Only through time time is conquered"), Leavis asks: "It has yet to be determined what value must be assigned to the conquered. Is it 'escaped from'?"[33] The whole redemption of history, a central thematic subject and goal of the poem, becomes problematic if time is not so much reordered as evaded. Yet this is the equivocal sense of transfiguration in the vision of redeemed history in "Little Gidding":

> History may be servitude
> History may be freedom. See, now they vanish
> The faces and places, with the self which, as it could, loved them,
> To become renewed, transfigured, in another pattern.
>   (LG III, 162–65)

This redeemed state has little resemblance to the world requiring redemption. Servitude or freedom, values of utmost importance to those living in time, become interchangeable from the vantage point of detachment. Faces, places, the self—all "vanish." History is abolished rather than reformed. Its transfiguration entails the negation of every condition that ordinarily defines it. This other "pattern" seems, in fact, to have very little relation to the one it transforms.

Critical discussion has repeatedly explored the poem's time-structures and its historical vision. Equivocation and self-subverting negativity take place, however, not only in the poem's treatment of history but also in its language. On one level, the poem's mysticism of time and experience is boldly announced in the culminating image, when "the rose and the fire are one"—a unity that only reconfirms the mystical strain informing so much of the text. Just such concord is the goal of mysticism and of its specific practices. On another level, the pressure and limits of unity are enacted not in the poem's temporal themes but in its linguistic practices. The wholeness it promises and seeks is, by definition, one the poem can never represent. The difficulty—indeed impossibility—of directly representing ultimate unity, a recurrent theme of mystical discussion, stems from the nature of representation itself. Unity stands beyond the multiplicity, differentiation, division, and succession that representation exactly entails. That is why attempts to represent concord must finally negate themselves, why negative strategies are intrinsic to figures of concordance.

Such defeat of language through negation not only is central to the progression of the *Quartets*, but is also a central topic within the poem. The problem of representation is something the poem both discusses and enacts: how to use the partial and successive medium of language to render a unitary wholeness that transcends differentiation and succession.[34] But the tension between the poem's positive claims to redeeming experience and its commitment to unitary wholeness as the redemptive figure is never resolved. Indeed, the negative representation of language only radicalizes this tension. Just how a partial, temporal language is to conduct to a unitary, atemporal representation that remains disjunct from it is a problem the poem's linguistic meditations dramatize rather than resolve.

Reflections on language as fragmented, partial, and successive, and therefore finally inadequate to the desired vision of unity, recur throughout the *Quartets*. "Burnt Norton" II complains, "I cannot say." "East Coker" considers its "way of putting things not very satisfactory," "leaving one still with the intolerable wrestle / With words and meanings"—adding, "The poetry does not matter," a dismissal that continues to annoy literary critics but is precisely what the poem is about. "Dry Salvages" II quietly frames the "approach to the meaning" in "something that is probably quite ineffable." In "Little Gidding" II, the life of language in time specifically disqualifies language: "For last year's words belong to last year's language / And next year's words await another voice."

Linguistic defeat is presented here and elsewhere in the poem as inevitable in two senses. First, language is itself subject to the incompletion and change that prevent temporal things from achieving fulfillment in inclusive stillness. Second, language functions as an image for succession, fragmented partiality, and incompletion. That is, in the poem language functions as both medium and trope. Itself a medium of differentiated parts, language also serves as an image for representing differentiation, division, and multiplicity. But in both senses it is faulty, in both senses it betrays the unity that inevitably escapes it, even as it remains the central means for attempting to represent just such unity.

In this context, the final movement of each *Quartet* offers a meditation not simply on language, but on linguistic failure. "East Coker" V emphasizes the faults of language as a medium. In its military imagery, language is "shabby equipment," leaving the poet to try

> to learn to use words, and every attempt
> Is a wholly new start, and a different kind of failure
> Because one has only learnt to get the better of words
> For the thing one no longer has to say, or the way in which
> One is no longer disposed to say it.
>
> > (EC V, 174–78)

Time passes away, and words pass away in time. As a medium, language cannot achieve the stability in which Eliot locates his "ineffable" meaning. But this linguistic condition has no solution, as "Dry Salvages" V implies. There the denunciation of language seems directed merely against misguided modes of discourse in their false attempts to penetrate beyond times past and into times future. Failed esoteric efforts to "communicate," "converse," "report," "describe," "haruspicate," "scry," "observe," "evoke," "release omens," "riddle," "fiddle," seem false kinds of divination. No better are more psychological efforts to "dissect the recurrent image into pre-conscious terrors— / To explore the womb, or tomb, or dreams." These are apparently problematic as false forms of linguistic activity. Yet the contrast offered as positive is one that transcends language altogether: "The point of intersection of the timeless / With time." This is an experience most suitable "for the saint," pursued through the ascesis of "ardour and selflessness and self-surrender." As to "most of us, there is only the unattended Moment, the moment in and out of time." And this is finally represented, not as language, but as silence and union: "Music heard so deeply / That it is not heard at all, but you are the music while it lasts."

Language in fact doubles as (faulty) dispersed medium and representation or trope of (faulty) dispersed experience. The relation between these two modes of linguistic negation emerges especially in the final movements of the two framing *Quartets*, "Burnt Norton" and "Little Gidding." Thus, "Burnt Norton" V opens:

> Words move, music moves
> Only in time; but that which is only living
> Can only die. Words, after speech, reach
> Into the silence. Only by the form, the pattern,
> Can words or music reach
> The stillness, as a Chinese jar still
> Moves perpetually in its stillness.
> Not the stillness of the violin, while the note lasts,
> Not that only, but the co-existence,
> Or say that the end precedes the beginning,
> And the end and the beginning were always there
> Before the beginning and after the end.
> And all is always now. Words strain,
> Crack, and sometimes break, under the burden,
> Under the tension, slip, slide, perish,
> Decay with imprecision, will not stay in place,
> Will not stay still.
>
> (137–53)

This passage has often been praised as the justification of time by eternity, the empowerment of words by the concordant silence that gathers in and informs them. And yet the passage finally undermines such continuities. Words move here not only "in" time, but also like time. Within the mutability of sequence, they "strain, crack, and sometimes break," and do so "under the burden" not only of expression, but as images of mutability. Like process itself, they "slip, slide, perish, / Decay with imprecision, will not stay in place, / Will not stay still." Words not only operate through succession, they represent succession as its trope. What they neither convey nor represent, except negatively, is what remains beyond succession in unity—the "stillness" or "co-existence" where "all is always now." This wholeness of time, this concord of moment, is represented not by language, but by its antithesis: the "after speech" that reaches "into the silence." Not language, but silence, is the ultimate sign for a transcendence that finally repudiates language as essentially other from its concord. In this, Eliot is not, then, confronting what Hillis Miller calls "the difficulty of putting named things in such a pattern that they will reach beyond time and space."[35] Nor is he offering language, in Hugh Kenner's terms, "itself as a transience on which sufficient form may confer endurance."[36] He is instead presenting language as transient, and ultimately as discontinuous with what endures beyond language. Words never reach beyond time and space; concord never fully descends into language. Only silence, linguistic negation, can act as figure for such transcendent unity.

Sign-Theology

Eliot's use of silence as transcendent figure, as sign of unitary vision, is perhaps the most traditional of his linguistic figurations. He himself places it in a traditional frame when, in "Burnt Norton" I, he goes on to oppose "shrieking voices / Scolding, mocking, or merely chattering" against "the Word in the desert . . . attacked by voices of temptation." The passage recalls the fifth movement of "Ash Wednesday," where its doctrinal context is even more explicit:

> Word unheard,
> The Word without a word, the Word within
> The world and for the world. . . .
> And the light shone in darkness and
> Against the Word the unstilled world still whirled
> About the centre of the Silent Word.

Against the "unstilled world" stands the "centre of the Silent Word," Christ as Logos. He is the "Word without a word" because in Logos language itself finds its transcendent fulfillment. Yet as "Word within the world" the Logos opens a way of transcendence— one that points beyond language and world to the "Word unheard."

Silence as an image of transcendence, and hence of Logos, is a trope for unbodied spirit beyond the shape of linguistic body; for an eternal moment beyond the temporal sequence in which linguistic body unfolds; for the wholeness or concordance achieved as a unity of what appears in language only part by part. As trope, silence recurs as a potent motif through centuries of theological writings, and not only mystical ones. For Dionysius the ascent finally must leave behind even "divine enlightenment and voices and heavenly utterances and plunge into the Darkness where truly dwells . . . ⟩ that One Which is beyond all things" (*MT* 1). The goal is to arrive at an "absolute dumbness both of speech and thought . . . being at last wholly united with Him Whom words cannot describe" (*MT* 3). John of the Cross similarly describes "locutions" as "parts," whereas Christ is the "single Word" as the "whole" (*AMC*, 164).

But it is Augustine who perhaps offers the fullest meditation upon and analysis of silence as figural sign for transcendence. In the *Confessions*, language and silence are primary images for the way in which the world of time finds its fulfillment in eternity. In the world of time, "not all the parts exist at once, but some must come as others go, and in this way together they make up the whole of which they are parts." Just so, "our speech follows the same rule, using sounds to signify a meaning. For a sentence is not complete unless each word, once its syllables have been pronounced, gives way to make room for the next" (*C* 4.10). In this analogy, language in its parts corresponds to flesh and the senses: "Whatever you feel through the senses of the flesh you only feel in part. It delights you, but it is only a part and you have no knowledge of the whole" (*C* 4.11). But silence acts as conclusion and concordance of all parts, beyond the flesh and sense of words: "You do not want the syllables to sound for ever in my mouth: you want them to fly from my tongue and give place to others, so that you may hear the whole of what I have to say" (ibid.).

In *Confessions*, book 11, Augustine further clarifies how this silence in turn acts as image for Logos. Language, he writes, unfolds "subject to the laws of time," creating "speech with a beginning and an end." But "the mind compared these words . . . with [God's] Word, which is silent and eternal, and said 'God's eternal Word is far, far different from these words which sound in time. They are far beneath me; in fact they are not at all, because they die away and are lost. But the Word of my God is above me and endures for ever'" (C 11.6). "For [God's] Word is not speech in which each part comes to an end when it has been spoken, giving place to the next, so that finally the whole may be uttered. In [God's] Word all is uttered at one and the same time, yet eternally" (C 11.7).

Augustine continues this analogy when, in *On the Trinity*, book 15, he more fully elaborates the meaning of Christ as divine Logos. There he aligns language with what is outward, temporal, and partial, while silence evokes what is inward, eternal, and whole. In doing so, he develops what is in fact a full-fledged theory of the sign.[37] Thus, the Logos is like the human word, in that "the word that sounds outwardly is the sign of the word that gives light inwardly." Like the human word, the Logos is incarnate. Just as the inward word takes on "that articulate sound by which it may be manifested to men's senses," so "the Word of God was made flesh, by assuming that flesh in which itself also might be manifested to men's senses." Yet the Logos also differs from "the word of ours that sounds in the ears, either when it is uttered in an articulate sound or when it is silently thought." The Logos, that is, is ultimately unlike the human word, whether spoken outwardly or inwardly, in that it goes beyond all shape, all form. It is instead like pure thought, "which is neither utterable in sound nor capable of being thought under the likeness of sound, such as must needs be with the word of any tongue." In terms that strikingly predict Saussurean sign-theory, the Logos is like the thought "which precedes all signs by which it is signified."

Jacques Derrida, in his critique of Ferdinand de Saussure, remarks that "the age of the sign is essentially theological," and Augustinian sign-theory certainly bears this out. It is, moreover, fundamentally dualistic, as Derrida underscores. The very notion of a "signified" thought given form and expression through "signifiers" reflects and relies on "the difference between the worldly and the non-ideality, universal and non-universal, transcendental and empirical, etc." These distinctions are also hierarchies. They assume a "signified able to 'take place' in its intelligibility, before its 'fall,' before any expulsion into the exteriority of the sensible here below." In this sign-scheme, a pure intelligibility stands above the exterior, sensible world, which remains, in comparison, a fallen one. But this hierarchy corresponds not only to the structure of the sign, where the "signified" is identified with the intelligible and the "signifier" is identified with the exterior world of sense. It corresponds to the structure of the Logos itself within the Trinity: "As the face of pure intelligibility, it refers to an absolute logos to which it is immediately united. This absolute logos was an infinite creative subjectivity in medieval theology: the intelligible face of the sign remains turned toward the word and the face of God."[38]

In Augustine, a clear linguistic hierarchy is established, corresponding to a hierarchy of theological values. There is in the mind, first, a disembodied thought prior to all articulation, a pure "signified." This is compared to the Logos. And, as the Word was made flesh, so too the "signified" can be expressed in "signifiers." Yet the distinction between signified and signifier remains essential. Only the thought as signified is "knowledge as it really is," whereas "when it is uttered by sound, or by any bodily sign, it is not uttered as it really is, but as it can be seen or heard by the body" (*TR* 15.11). This entry into linguistic body betrays the thought in fundamental ways, affecting its status as spiritual, immutable, and concordant. Therefore Augustine is careful to insist that although the Word became flesh, "far be it from us to say He was changed into flesh." As truth, the Logos must be entirely immutable. It can never be subject to change, for it is exactly in immutability that its truth inheres. Like the signified, and contrary to the signifier, the Logos is essentially unbodied and unchanging.

What this finally means is that the signified most truly corresponds not to linguistic signifiers, but to silence. As Joseph Anthony Mazzeo observes, for Augustine "true rhetoric culminates in silence, in which the mind is in immediate contact with reality. . . . True rhetoric, and thought itself were but attempts to reascend to that silence from which the world fell into the perpetual clamor of life as fallen men know it."[39] Margaret Ferguson concurs: "For Augustine, no sequence of words can adequately represent an atemporal and holistic significance. . . . Language is essentially inadequate . . . because its structural dissimilarity from its eternal referent is manifested by its inability to reveal except by a temporal process, not by an instantaneous unveiling."[40] This elevation of silence over language is amply confirmed by Christian mystics throughout the ages. Thus, Ignatius Martyr urges: "It is better to be silent and be real, than to talk and be unreal."[41] Thus, Thomas à Kempis proclaims that "the further [the soul] withdraws from all noise of the world the nearer she draws to her maker."[42] Thus, the *Cloud of Unknowing* declares, "I dare not take upon myself with my blundering, earthly tongue to speak of what belongs solely to God,"[43] while John of the Cross considers speaking to be an "attachment" that will prevent the soul from attaining "the liberty of union" (*AMC*, 51).

The priority that this model grants to signified thought, as opposed to signifiers which at best partially express it, also reflects a profound tension between the two terms. René Roques, writing of Dionysian analogy, describes the relation between "symbol" and "signified" as on the one hand necessary, but on the other hand suspect and compromising. There is in this sign theory a deep linguistic ambivalence: "The symbol, and this is an ambiguity often tragic, only offers the emblem of the message it carries. Only an intelligence already familiar with spiritual realities can hope to seize and comprehend it, on condition that its attention and search will always be oriented towards the realities without shadow and fiction." The symbol, or signifier, cannot in itself conduct to the truth beyond it; rather, some grasp of that truth must precede, in order properly to construe the symbols themselves. At the same time, the symbols pose a certain danger. They are not valuable in themselves ("the material universe does not interest Dionysius"). They must serve only as vehicles for the signified; and yet they always threaten to draw attention to themselves. This is why Dionysius himself preferred what he called "unlike resemblances," in which the signifier remains remote from the signified, lessening the danger of their confusion. Yet even unlike resemblances are "incurably faulty in that they always move on the plane of similitude and evocation rather than on univocity and identity."[44]

The relation between signified and signifier is, therefore, almost paradoxical: "What makes possible a certain revelation is also what covers it with veils; and what dares to disturb these veils in order to strip bare the Truth, can also destroy it."[45] Without the signifying veils, the truth remains inaccessible. But seen through the veils, the truth is ever obscured. What keeps the two incommensurate and at odds is, above all, the unitary nature of truth as opposed to the multiplicity of linguistic representation. As Thomas Aquinas puts it: "What is seen in the Word is seen not successively but at the same time. . . . Things seen in God are not seen singly by their own likenesses, but all are seen by the one essence of God. Hence they are seen simultaneously and not successively" (I. Q. 12, art. 10). Only the divine Word transcends the temporal succession of ordinary language; but that Word therefore remains beyond expression within ordinary linguistic conditions. Ordinary language can only point to what it would signify by pointing beyond itself. It must, that is, work against the very conditions that distinguish language from its ultimate object, but that also define language and make it possible.

The way for negotiating this antithetical and ambivalent state is finally what René Roques describes as purgation. The signifier can be employed, but in a way that constantly strives to diminish any attention to itself, insisting on its own transparency and on its role as mere vehicle to a truth beyond itself. And it must try to defeat the very conditions that both define it and distinguish it from the signified it attempts, paradoxically, to convey, as in a process of purification:

The symbol must be purified to rejoin the hidden significance that it envelops. Thus purification designates also exegesis. For it is also a question of disengaging in all its purity the element properly significative and anagogic of the symbol, and of rejecting all that can obscure that signification of the transcendent order, and all that can trouble it and pervert it in the intelligence, which can compromise the entire symbolic process.[46]

Value and meaning inhere in the transcendent order. This is something the signifier itself must assert. It does so by subverting its own status as a site of interest or importance, and by purging from itself the material embodiment, succession, and partiality that also, however, specifically define it.

Linguistic dualism ultimately accords with other dualisms fundamental to Western culture: mind and body, spirit and flesh. Just as ascetic religion directs purgation of body for mind, flesh for spirit, so linguistic dualism implies the purgation of word for idea, signifier for signified. Within this purgative process, the dual terms stand in a relation not only of duplication but of duplicity. They are distinguished in both kind and value, in a clear hierarchy where the (linguistic) body in order to serve the truth beyond it must ideally cancel itself in doing so. Linguistic body is placed in the paradoxical position of depending on a realm that promises to invest it with value, but that in effect divests it of value and demands its own erasure. In Eliot, such asceticism becomes an aesthetic. His is a purgative writing that strives, as he puts it in "Little Gidding" I, to offer "a husk of meaning / From which the purpose breaks only when it is fulfilled / If at all." In this ancient exegetical image, the signifier is a shell or husk that falls away once the truth it was its purpose to convey is achieved. Or, as Eliot writes in "English Poets as Letter Writers," the ideal of art would be a "poetry so transparent that in reading it we are intent on what the poetry points at, and not on the poetry."

Linguistic Dualism

T. S. Eliot's philosophical commitment to a proto-Augustinian language model has been variously argued. Leslie Brisman sees Eliotic language as "trac[ing] distances from what Eliot . . . presupposes as a fullness once there."[47] Paul Murray, from a very different standpoint, similarly identifies Eliot's mystical attitudes generally with Augustine's, and specifically with the mystical contemplation of the Word as opposed to articulate speech.[48] Walter Benn Michaels and Jeffrey Perl contest this interpretation, arguing instead that Eliot's philosophical position is closer to pragmatism. Citing

Eliot's statement in his dissertation on Bradley, "Without words, no objects," Benn Michaels proposes that "Eliot's conception of reference tries to avoid . . . the reification of the distinction between signifier and signified." Meaning must be referred not to a prior signified, but to a context of use: "A sentence, Eliot writes, is 'true and false or meaningless according to its context and bearing.'" And context, in turn, is finally social, relying on common reference: "A point of view is a situation, an intersection of habits or beliefs is social . . . 'Common Reference' is thus a function of what Eliot calls a 'community of meaning.'"[49] Jeffrey Perl likewise concludes that for Eliot "'reality' is a quality attributed to certain terms within a shared context of discourse."[50]

These discussions, however, address Eliot's (early) philosophical statements rather than his (late) poetic practice. The question of continuity from *Knowledge and Experience* to *Four Quartets* is a highly complex one, traversing, among other things, Eliot's conversion to Anglo-Catholicism. And even in the dissertation, there is a longing for unity that reemerges later, in the context of the Christian conversion. Thus, even the early Eliot discusses self-transcendence as "the painful task of unifying . . . jarring and incompatible [points of view], and passing, when possible, from two or more discordant viewpoints to a higher one which shall somehow include and transmute them" (*KE*, 146–48). In any case, my own concern is not the philosophical mind of Eliot, but the linguistic patterns in *Four Quartets*. These seem to me to imply a model of language based on the Christian hierarchy of values the poem also overtly embraces. In accordance with these values, the poem points to a state beyond language that finds fullest figuration in linguistic defeat.

In terms of sign-theory, the poem's negative strategies of denial, reduction, paradox, or tautology offer one course for taking a "signified" out of its imprisonment in "signifiers." The signified is instead asserted through negating all signifying attributes, or as the impossible-to-formulate space between paradoxical terms. Other well-recognized techniques in the poem contribute to the same end. Its mode of repetition, for example, of "repeating / Something I have said before" (EC III) so that "words echo / Thus in your mind" (BN I) serves to pull the poem away from temporal distribution toward stasis, a move toward "spatial form" that Joseph Frank was among the first to identify with Eliot.[51] Each repetition invites inter-reference through separate contexts, until some complete meaning is arrived at that intends and includes all of them.

This method may seem to confirm arguments for a pragmatist language-model. When Eliot asserts that a sentence "is true or false or meaningless according to its context and bearing" (*KE*, 138), Walter Benn Michaels construes this to say that "there is no literal, context-free meaning to a sentence, discussion of how or what any sentence means must always be as spoken and under-stood."[52] But Helen Gardner's discussion of the "music" of Eliot's words points in a different direction. She too writes that in the poem "the word itself, like the note in music, has meaning only in relation to other words." The word means, "not in itself, but in its relations to all the other words in the poem." Yet it is as total pattern emerging from these relations, the wholeness of their total representation taken together, that the words finally take on meaning. This Gardner emphasizes, using the poem's own figures of concordance to do so: "For the music and the meaning arise at 'a point of intersection,' in the changes and movement of the whole. . . . One must have some sense of the whole before one attempts to make very much of the parts."[53] Whole precedes part, determining and finally exceeding each disparate textual moment toward a formal "point of intersection" that is also the poem's theme.

This "point" itself resides outside and beyond the specifying words that together intend it—something that the poem also the-matizes through its pervasive use of tropes of dislocation. Any "there" in the poem is located it "cannot say where" (BN II). Any "here" or "now" becomes subsumed into an inclusive "always" that defies curtailment to specific place or time, a "here or there" that is equally "elsewhere" (EC I), a "here" that "is England and nowhere. Never and always" (LG I). In such additive lists, inclusion is really a mode of cancellation. The move is one beyond specification, to a no-place in no-time that only through its very negativity can signal the whole that bestows true significance.

What seems finally to govern Eliot's sign-theory is not pragmatist interrelationships among signifiers but a hierarchical sign-structure whose governing principle resembles purgation. As David Ward observes, Eliot seems to have "a distrust of emotion and of words as part of a distrust of all that is transitory." This Ward in turn compares with "the conviction of St. John of the Cross that the only true emotion is reached by a purgation of all that we normally think of as emotion."[54] At issue, really, are the nature and goals of purgation as such. Without embracing any radical dualism, any gnostic rejection of all temporal flux as illusory and all matter as demonic, the structure of purgation nevertheless adopts a strict hierarchy of values.[55] In this hierarchy, time and matter are not only lesser. They traditionally have, as Nietzsche was perhaps the first to expose, no value in themselves, but only in reference to a unitary, spiritual realm beyond temporal and material conditions. But this value is not directly mediated through them either. The temporal, material world cannot directly conduct to the other world of true value, which remains radically distinct from it. Rather, the movement from the one toward the other is a negative one, entailing the stripping away of the very conditions that define the temporal, material world.

Purgation, that is, envisions a redemption from, rather than a redemption of, the conditions it sets out to purge. It pursues redemption as gradual disengagement from earthly time and existence, into an otherworld distinct from and ultimately antithetical to it. While this is not simply negative with regard to immediate reality, it is hardly the positive redemption it claims to be. It does not accept the conditions of time, body, and multiplicity as growth, but as loss of an ideal unity; nor as creative production and possibility, but at best as ground for a transcendence into other conditions altogether. As Roque observes, there is a "dualism that is a fundamental characteristic of these doctrines, in which the created world can be considered as an obstacle to salvation, and qualified very pejoratively." Purgation in some sense acts to mediate this dualism, as a bridge between the sensible and intelligible realms. But it does so at the expense of the sensible. Through "asceticism . . . the intelligence can gradually rise to the principle behind all symbols."[56] But such asceticism ultimately does not assert the positive value of the created world, except as a negative means toward its own purgation.

Eliot's own language is in these senses ascetic. Negating every assertion, removing with steady determination every condition, pointing through all dispersed repetition to a center that will pass beyond all of them, the poem pursues its own linguistic undoing toward a signified unity it can never directly contain. In this, even moments of visionary fullness strain language and show how "words strain." Affirmation does not fill language, but instead dissolves it. Transcendence opposes immanence. This is the case in the final meditation on language of "Burnt Norton" V, where lyric form cracks and breaks the language it employs, even as it telescopes the tradition in which Eliot writes:

> The detail of the pattern is movement,
> As in the figure of the ten stairs.
> Desire itself is movement
> Not in itself desirable;
> Love is itself unmoving,
> Only the cause and end of movement,
> Timeless and undesiring
> Except in the aspect of time
> Caught in the form of limitation
> Between un-being and being.
> (159–68)

This synoptic lyric, at once Aristotelian, Neoplatonist, and Thomist, is structured around positive assertion: "Desire itself is movement," "Love is itself." But these at once modulate into negative designation, paradox or semi-paradox, and reduction through progressively exclusive qualification. Thus, desire is "not in itself desirable"; "love is itself unmoving." These negative constructions remove the desire and love from the movement and change they govern. They are the "timeless" reference point, the reduction out of time, outside love and desire in the life of time. Or, in the poem's mode of paradox and repetition that unites and displaces at once, they are "undesiring." It is not simply that these religious philosophical concepts strain language, but that such devices of inexpressibility themselves are signs of ultimacy. By being unable to say what Love is, Eliot confirms its absolute importance, playing on a valence and value in which language does not correlate with the Highest Things.

This way of linguistic remotion or removal is not neutral in value. "Between un-being and being" is not a neutral space. "Except in the aspect of time" at first seems to make room for temporal place within the poem's value system. But the construction only excepts; it does not include. The love that does move, that is in time, "caught in the form of limitation," is, exactly to this degree, un-being. Only the Love that "is itself unmoving" exists truly as "being"; and temporal love exists only as it points beyond itself to this true Love. The "detail" of the pattern may be movement. But the detail itself does not really hold Eliot's interest. It is in the pattern, not in the detail, that value and meaning reside. The "figure of the ten stairs," drawn from John of the Cross, strives to ascend above detail. The ascetic ladder does not endow, but rather purges, movement, temporal desire and love, and language itself, conducting to a stasis and silence beyond them.

The Axiology of Language

Eliot's commentators have sometimes noted that *Four Quartets* finally arrives at a linguistic position that is self-compromising. This, however, is mainly seen as due to accidental personal or aesthetic idiosyncrasies. For Ronald Bush, for example, it derives from a betrayal of genuine, poetic insight by ideology, so that what is asserted is "not feelings, but the pattern which we make of our feelings."[57] David Spurr similarly describes a contradiction between poetic and religious impulses, leading Eliot to "an artistically suicidal position that sees the poetic ideal as beyond thought and language and in fact beyond poetry itself." Graham Hough refers to "the antithesis that in one form or another lies at the heart of the poem, the antithesis between words and the Word," but sees it as private to Eliot and opposed to the tradition of faith to which Eliot appeals.[58]

Eloise Knapp Hay is, I think, truer to the poem when she argues that its aesthetic and religious positions do accord. She compares "the way of his poem" to a "spiritual discipline—the movement toward 'that which is not world.'" Language, too, is among the "discardings of all attachment" urged by John of the Cross. It too is subjected to "purgation as askesis, the discipline of purification, ridding the mind of all that is not ultimate." Hay, however, sees these discardings as issuing finally in the poem as an "icon of perfect presence," where "the time of the poem meets timelessness."[59] The poem, for her, thus makes good the Augustinian promise that parts find their ultimate fulfillment only in the wholes of their arrival.

To be rid of something, however, is not the same as to affirm it. Incompletion and fulfillment, multiplicity and unity, signifiers and signified: instead of being reconciled, these remain in Eliot's system ultimately discontinuous, and indeed at odds. They are differently valued—the parts depend on the whole, yet have in its light only the negative value of false attachment. And they are at odds in that to attain unity the multiple parts are "fulfilled" only in being dispensed with. There occurs not an ingathering, but a radical leap away from the partiality that defines them as parts to begin with. Fulfillment is in this sense a contradictory trope, one where the limiting particulars to be surpassed must be discarded: "And the fulfilled beast shall kick the empty pail." When "the past has another pattern, and ceases to be a mere sequence— / Or even development" (DS II), it ceases to be temporal altogether. It does not truly conduct to a moment where "past and future are conquered and reconciled" (DS V), for to reconcile and to conquer are not the same.

In this sense, Eliot's Mallarméan desire "to purify the dialect of the tribe" resonates well beyond a strictly aesthetic project. The poem is an ascetic discarding, a purgative process that also discloses the contradictions of Eliot's positions. The poem claims, in its numerous synecdochic tropes, to represent (necessarily only partially) "a lifetime burning in every moment," both

> still and still moving
> Into another intensity
> For a further union, a deeper communion.

But it inevitably does so only "through the dark cold and the empty desolation" (EC V). Those "united in the strife which divided them" are reconciled only when all "accept the constitution of silence."[60] Only by way of such constantly repeated descents, releases, darknesses and emptyings, rejections and remotions, calls to detachment and renunciation, does the poem assert a "fullness," which, however, can only be represented as emptiness. But this representation is not idle. It signals a reversal of value and a contradiction of means in ascetic ascent. Asceticism is affirmative, but only in its affirmation of an otherworld as superseding this one, which must be purged. It seeks things eternal through detachment from things temporal, unity through disengagement from multiplicity. Likewise the "affirmative" way itself is also fundamentally ascetic. It is no accident that a recurring image for Eliot's senses of transcendence proves to be martyrdom: a "symbol perfect in death" by the "purification of motive / In the ground of our beseeching" (or, in a manuscript version, a "purification of motive / which assent/consent to death perfects").[61]

Against its own claims, this vision of redemption as ascesis is fundamentally one where the relation between the eternal and mutable worlds is negative. The things of this world can never fully signify the world beyond; their inability to do so is a necessary condition for their proper functioning. Only their purgation, renunciation, and discarding can (negatively) "conduct" to what remains beyond and radically other from them. The two worlds—time and eternity, particulars and unity, or, in linguistic terms, signifiers and signified—are not continuous. The hope of what is to come not only rests in, but underscores, the incompleteness and dearth of what now is. "We had the experience but missed the meaning," Eliot warns (DS II). Experience does not construct meaning, but at best veils and at worst compromises it. And the restoration Eliot promises is instead utter transformation, an ascetic elimination of any term that defined experience initially, "experience in a different form, beyond any meaning we can assign to happiness."

This ascetic commitment finds its ultimate sign in silence. Both as representing and as subject to temporal division, language is to be surpassed, which is to say, denied. As the mystical descent of "Burnt Norton" III points away from "this twittering world"; as "words, after speech, reach into the silence" in "Burnt Norton" V; so the soul is enjoined to "be still" (EC III), and consummate experience is "quite ineffable" (DS II). It is only in this self-negating sense that there "is a voice descanting (though not to the ear, / The murmuring shell of time, and not in any language)" (DS III). Even supposedly positive images of voice thus prove to be contrastive—voice only as unvoice, as a trope for silence.

Both this positive promise and its subversion come to their finale in "Little Gidding" V, which at last and above all announces "the complete consort dancing together." Here words are apparently embraced and affirmed:

> And every phrase
> And sentence that is right (where every word is at home,
> Taking its place to support the others,
> The word neither diffident nor ostentatious,
> An easy commerce of the old and the new,
>
> . . . .
> The complete consort dancing together)
>
> (217–20, 223)

But here, as throughout the poem, linguistic goals prove to contradict linguistic means. Affirmation at once modulates into endings that, rather than embracing linguistic process, surpass it in ways that also deny it:

> Every phrase and every sentence is an end and a beginning,
> Every poem an epitaph. And any action
> Is a step to the block, to the fire, down the sea's throat
> Or to an illegible stone: and that is where we start.
>
> (224–27)

Eliot's "complete consort dancing together" promises union, harmony, reconciliation, mutuality. It offers a gracious gesture of synecdochic embrace. But the harmony proves to be founded on rigorous hierarchy in which parts serve wholes (in one manuscript version, each word does "its part / In subservience to the phrase")[62] finally to the sacrifice of their own differentiations. They come to an end, but inaugurate a condition that is altogether different, linguistically and otherwise. Thus the poem first becomes an "epitaph" at its own linguistic burial, and then ceases to be language at all: it is "illegible stone." The tropes inscribed within this sequence are those of rigorous subservience, sacrifice, and ultimately martyrdom, in which "any action" finds its fit conclusion as "a step to the block, to the fire, down the sea's throat."

But to renounce is not to have. To sacrifice may be to exchange one value for another, but this is not to embrace both. The claim to an ingathering involves a logical sleight of hand, for the whole only includes the parts at the expense of their own cessation and subsumption. Helen Gardner describes Eliot's "total subject" in "Little Gidding" as consciousness "by which man, living in time, transcends time, and stands outside process."[63] But to stand outside process is not the same as to live within it, affirming its value. Eliot's historical vision finally appeals beyond and outside history; and the same is true for his linguistic vision. The attempt to represent in language a unity that must overcome the very processes of language finally affirms not linguistic action, but the desire to dispense with it. As in the concluding image of sacrificial martyrdom, it is to seek "a condition of complete simplicity / (Costing not less than everything)." The oneness of simplicity does not embrace, but instead costs "everything." And since words move only within difference, the linguistic price to be paid is silence.

The severity of this exchange intensifies through the mystical crescendo that concludes "Little Gidding." Eliot now includes *The Cloud of Unknowing* and a repetition of Julian of Norwich—from what he calls "the other great [mystical] period, i.e. the 14th century"—along with references to Augustine and Dante.[64] Facing the trauma and cataclysm of the "History" of war that was "now and England," Eliot appeals to those who appeal beyond history in detachment: to "the drawing of this Love and the voice of this Calling" of *The Cloud of Unknowing*, which is not least a drawing and call to "try to forget all created things that he [God] ever made, and the purpose behind them, so that your thought and longing do not turn or reach out to them either in general or in particular"; to Julian of Norwich, herself devoted to the most severe rule of anchorite solitary enclosure (in a ceremony based on funeral rites), whose assurance that "Sin is behovely, but all shall be well" follows the recognition that "we shall be troubled [MS variant: denied], following our master Jesus until we are fully purged of our mortal flesh." [65] The historical world opens into eternity only through purgatorial negation—a way not of conduct but of contrast. As John of the Cross declares: "Only by voiding ourselves of all that is not God can we attain the possession of God; because the two are contrary. . . . The soul must rid itself of every stain of creatures to strip itself of all that is not God" (*AMC*, 23, 78). Or, as Augustine writes, between the "beam of light from that everfixed eternity" and "the times which are never fixed" there is finally "no comparison" (*C* 11). [66]

With regard to language, this stance is problematic, and not least for a poet. It suggests that language may not have access to the ultimate vision on which its signifiers depend, in this hierarchy, for their meaning. The radical discontinuity between signifiers and signified profoundly calls into question the value of language within a wider axiology, where language both represents and corresponds to the realm of historical world. In one sense, to say that Eliot rejects language as unable to represent wholeness is merely tautological: this is the very point the poem sets out to make. Succession, materiality, multiplicity, are by definition the conditions Eliot wishes to transcend as ways to represent the eternal timelessness that stands beyond and before them. They are exactly the conditions that asceticism seeks detachment from. But in another sense, Eliot's deflationary renouncings, negatives, and detachments raise questions about the relationship between the ideal of wholeness and the world on which it claims to bestow meaning and value. For it can be asked whether wholeness is a proper measure for partial experience; timeless eternity a positive ideal for time's productions in change and multiplicity; and totality an appropriate reference for the difference and division that condition time and language. We can ask, that is, whether another, antithetical world of unity is a proper, positive image and site for redemption of this world of change and difference, but also of development and growth.

The poem's own linguistic claims and conduct finally question its fundamental premises: whether the vision of unity and eternity indeed bestows positive value on the realm of time and multiplicity it is meant to redeem; whether silence, in surpassing language, indeed fulfills it. For to discard is not to redeem, if redemption means cherishing or even correcting. Transcendence instead becomes a mode of erasure—an erasure that applies no less to language than to world. Words themselves can never represent a transcendent signified beyond all signs. Only by negation can they indicate what remains forever beyond, and indeed opposed to, the conditions of representation.

But negation is hardly a positive use of signs to redeem language in the sense of endowing it with positive value. Contrary to mystical claims, the way of negation and the way of positive analogy do not coexist in harmony. Negation calls into question the very basis of analogy and can even deny the possibility of representation altogether, thus eliminating the claim of concordance between negation and affirmation, the ways up and the ways down. This potentially explosive implication haunts negative theology. As Steven Katz has recently noted, strictly speaking the commitment to apophatic nothingness makes "all language equally inappropriate," including analogical predication.[67] At stake is the very concept of analogy— the degree to which the world of becoming can be said to reveal any truth about the world of being. This had been a disputed question from the outset. Even in Neoplatonism, according to H. Dörrie, "it is an open question whether there is any relation (hence analogy) between Being and Becoming"; while a specifically negative theology developed among those "who eschewed any use of . . . the formula of analogy. . . . It was the adherents of a 'theologia negativa' who found no use for the analogy formula."[68]

Four Quartets was completed during the agony of the Second World War and finds perhaps its first motive in the effort to place the events of so dreadful a historical time into an eternal, redemptive pattern. While the historical vision has received meticulous attention, the linguistic vision that is its corollary has not. But in light of the poem's linguistic practices and contexts, the promise to redeem the time itself takes on a negative cast. The mystical frame of the poem may indeed derive from Eliot's ascetic temper—a "private necessity," in Grover Smith's words, that led Eliot to move from "affirmative" quest to "negative" renunciation.[69] *Four Quartets* nevertheless represents an axiological schema not merely personal to Eliot's temperament, aesthetic methods, or possibly heterodox misapprehensions. Eliot's treatment of linguistic issues firmly reflects theological tradition. But it raises troubling questions about the relation between affirmative and negative modes within it. A rupture emerges in the tradition itself, in its commitment to a unitary eternity as the final reference for time, multiplicity, and language. Especially in the ascetic disciplines of the mystical writers, the devotion to union with the beyond takes shape as a need to disengage from involvement in this world. *Four Quartets* realizes this metaphysical/axiological structure, not least in its linguistic stances. But in doing so it calls into question the very language that it must both accept and reject as means to a unity which, while claiming to bestow linguistic value, denies it.

Four Quartets inscribes an ascetic ambivalence in its negative treatment of language as both representing medium and representative image. In this, the poem resumes the tradition that frames it. But Eliot never directly confronts his linguistic positions as ambivalent. He never asks whether the ideal of Silent Union, rather than investing and endowing language with significance, instead demotes language and displaces meaning from this world into another one. Samuel Beckett, however, takes the ideal of Silence at its word, directly confronting the equivocal value it grants to language. No less a master of the tradition of negativity, Beckett makes its linguistic ambivalence an explicit center of concern and critique.

CHAPTER 3

Samuel Beckett's Figural Evasions

The antithesis of the apparent world and the true
world is reduced to the antithesis "world" and
"nothing."
—Friedrich Nietzsche, *The Will to Power*

᠀

Missing Figures

If Samuel Beckett's novels seem extended exercises in reduction, his late prose texts are reductions reduced. Despite an apparent absence of technique, however, Beckett's art of the minimal actually deploys complex strategies of apotropism—the turning away from figures. Such apotropism is pursued on every level, from a meticulously conducted language to entire textual structures. Yet it extends beyond technique. It evokes and fulfills a negative attitude toward representation in language that, for all the radicalism of Beckett's art, is profoundly rooted within the tradition. Beckett's figural negations invoke general theological frameworks and particularly negative mysticisms that his work repeatedly names and often implicates. What finally emerges is a rigorously critical rendering of traditional stances toward, or rather against, language, in part accomplished by assiduously fulfilling those stances.

Stanley Cavell offers one important avenue into the reductive methods of Beckett's language in his essay "Ending the Waiting Game," where he notes a tendency in Beckett to pure denotation. Beckett's words seem to demand "further, or other meaning when in fact their meaning was nearest" and "utterly bare." Cavell compares this "hidden literality" to positivism in "its wish to escape connotation, rhetoric, the noncognitive, the irrationality and awk-

ward memories of ordinary language, in favor of the directly verifi-
able, the isolated, the perfected present."[1] Such denotative or positivist use of language almost exclusively governs Beckett's late, short
prose texts, such as *Fizzles*. In "Fizzle 1," for example, a protagonist makes his way through what seems an underground labyrinth
of walks and turns and sudden sheer falls. The action consists of
this and only this activity; its plot, that is, becomes exactly plotting
a course through space: "He halts, for the first time since he knows
he's under way, one foot before the other, the higher flat, the lower
on its toes, and waits for a decision. Then he moves on" (*F* 1, 8).
Temporal succession is in turn entirely defined within the space the
protagonist traverses step by step: "But see how now, having turned
right for example, instead of turning left a little further on he turns
right again. And see how now again, yet a little further on, instead
of turning left at last he turns right yet again. And so on until,
instead of turning right yet again, as he expected, he turns left at
last" (*F* 1, 10). *Now, again, yet, until, at last*: these words of temporal measure here only mediate the stops and starts, the twists and
turns of strict, unmitigated spatial progression. Indeed, the "passage" seems constructed to explore just how curtailed and restricted the meanings of such terms can become when allowed to
function only within the limits of spatial context. As to the protagonist—if one can continue so to call a figure who himself seems only
a function of the labyrinth he traverses—his very life too becomes
a compilation of the space he crosses, in the time it takes him to do
so. In this way,

little by little his history takes shape, with if not yet exactly its good days
and bad, at least studded with occasions, passing rightly or wrongly for
outstanding, such as the straightest narrow, the loudest fall, the most lin-
gering collapse, the steepest descent, the greatest number of successive
turns the same way, the greatest fatigue, the longest rest, the longest—aside
from the sound of the body on its way—silence . . . In a word all the
summits. (*F* 1, 13–14)

In this passage—both as text and as action—what occurs is the
sustained elimination of any sense not confined within the spatial

motion that alone is admitted. Indeed, there seems a radical de-figuration of a whole tradition of literary journeys in which prog-ress is presented physically in order to re-present progress of a moral, emotional, religious, or psychological kind. Here the in-verse occurs. Terms of judgment such as "good" or "bad" are as-similated into the term "outstanding," which emerges in its physi-cally determined sense. Words that in other contexts open into metaphysical or psychical meanings—"the straightest narrow," "fall," "descent"—lose any sense but that of physical dimension and direction. And even words that retain some figurative us-age—"studded" with occasions, "passing rightly," "summits"—are turned back toward a physical, literal sense. Personal "history," then, is nothing more than a series of shifts in position. The inner life and the very terms for formulating it do not mediate the exter-nal world but are mediated by it. And yet, the force of this insistent physicality and literalism depends on the figural level that such a literary journey inevitably evokes.

Figuration has then not been so much eliminated as pointedly denied, a palpable evasion creating an absence within which this passage continues to resonate—and which accounts for its humor as well. Literal language need not in itself be funny. But here the literalism involves the kind of joke where "the normal implications of language are defeated"—here the norms of literary language.[2] Beckett's language is literal because it defeats expected literary fig-ures that it inevitably recalls. It is a humor of absences, of structures erased yet still shaping the utterance that has displaced them.

Humor, however, is not the main effect of Beckett's literalist reductions in his short prose texts. Whereas his dramatic works provide a more or less human context in which the dialogues of reduced exchange can humorously echo, it is exactly such human context that seems eliminated in the short prose works. These, to the degree that they suppress characterization, narrative or dra-matic action, and even humanly recognizable setting, also dissolve the arena for appreciating deflation in terms of something human enough to be funny. Thus most "Fizzles" are deadening rather than humorous, an emptying out of context that also empties of sense. "Fizzle 5," for example, offers a landscape stripped to "an arena and a ditch" with "room for millions. Wandering and still. Never seeing never hearing one another. Never touching. . . . See from the edge all the bodies on its bed" (F 5, 37–38). For all its populousness and activity, and despite the apparent exactitudes of description, such scenes portray a no-man's-land, an anti-community of non-relation: on its beds of dead leaves "no two ever meet" (F 5, 39). The method, in still other "Fizzles," penetrates from site to person. The apparent observer of "Fizzle 7" is figured only as a form of dismemberment: "Legs side by side broken right angles at the knees as in that old statue some old god twanged at sunrise and again at sunset. Trunk likewise dead plumb right up to top of skull seen from behind including nape clear of chairback. Arms likewise broken right angles at the elbows forearms along armrests just right length forearms and rests for hands clenched lightly to rest on ends" (F 7, 48). The armchair that could serve as comfortable support and frame for the body's repose instead proposes the inanimate terms by which the body, through description alien to its integrity, becomes a figure of contortion.

Marjorie Perloff, in her discussion of *Fizzles*, describes Beckett's as a process of decreation. Placing him within what she calls the poetics of indeterminacy, she argues that in Beckett the dominant feature is a difficulty of reference, in which "the process of specification is seen as urgent, and yet we do not know what it is that is specified."[3] This lack of clear referentiality serves, she argues, to dissolve the distinction between figure and ground so that the world is "emptied of human presence . . . only objects are left: the persons who have made the objects are missing."[4] But the appeal to referential obscurity somewhat misses Beckett's linguistic point. Beckett is not so much being ambiguous as intentionally negating human reference. And the issue is not an obscurity of extratextual reference, but the way words work to establish contexts in which they can mean—or fail to mean in humanly significant ways. Pure denotation here, as elsewhere in Beckett, subtly attacks the appeal to reference as controlling our language. If the human element is missing, it is the language we use that is responsible for the abdication—a language for which we must, in turn, take responsibility. In Beckett, our human worlds are exposed as fundamentally linguistic ("There is nothing but what is said. Beyond what is said there is nothing" [F 5, 37]). It is through our uses of language that we define the world we inhabit. Beckett's work offers, that is, an anatomy of discourse as the condition in which we live our lives and, above all, realize our values.

In *Fizzles*, this anatomy is directed toward a language-world in which the human is not merely lacking but revoked. Within such a domain of discourse, only certain modes of meaning are possible. The defining terms are inert physicality, remote from human forms of living, from human relationship and affect. A specific kind of language, that is, establishes the shape and meaning of action and utterance conducted within it. Such an investigation of language as establishing a restrictive, inert world is more extensively elaborated in *The Lost Ones*. *The Lost Ones* posits a complete cosmos, a cylinder-world constructed out of elemental forces and governed by their laws: light, which oscillates between darkness and a dim yellowness; heat, which rises and falls with the light; all timed in seconds. These physical conditions determine not only the space in which the lost ones live but every aspect of the lives they live there:

One body per square metre or two hundred bodies in all round numbers. Whether relatives near and far or friends in varying degree many in theory are acquainted. Seen from a certain angle these bodies are of four kinds. Firstly those perpetually in motion. Secondly those who sometimes pause. Thirdly those who short of being driven off never stir. . . . Fourthly those who do not search or non-searchers. (*LO*, 13–14).

Hugh Kenner has remarked that like Newtonian bodies, Beckett's are either in motion or at rest.[5] Inertia, resistance, and, in the text's apocalyptic end, entropy, when "the temperature comes to rest not far from freezing point" (*LO*, 62) and the last mobile figure's motion ceases, become life's governing forces. They determine all that takes place, making personal identity a function of the same degrees, measures, modulations, and oscillations that define the system's light and heat. The four "kinds" of inhabitants are thus defined by their relation to motion—perpetual, sometimes pausing, barely moving, immobile.

The timing of these movements in turn obeys the periodic, simultaneous rise of light and heat and their subsequent fall, which commands a "corresponding abeyance of all motion among the bodies in motion and heightened fixity of the motionless" (*LO*, 17). Placement within the cylinder's "three distinct zones" further defines its denizens: "an outer belt roughly one metre wide . . . favoured by most of the sedentary and vanquished. Next a slightly narrower inner belt [of] those weary of searching. . . . Finally the arena proper representing an area of one hundred and fifty square metres round numbers and chosen hunting ground of the majority" (*LO*, 43). Between the regulations controlling transit from one zone to another—"it appears clearly that from the third to the second and inversely the searcher moves at will whereas on entering and leaving the first he is held to a certain discipline" (*LO*, 44)—the set patterns of temperature and light, and the range of movement, the conduct of life of the lost ones has become not only subordinate to, but utterly indistinguishable from, physical conditions.

But more than the conduct of life is so determined: the conduct of discourse is determined as well—or rather, conduct *as* discourse. Physical conditions define not only *The Lost Ones*'s imagery and character, but also its modes of utterance, determining the significance of the text's words. The nature and indeed the very definition of such terms as "relatives," "in varying degrees," and "acquainted" become a matter of relation in space, of physical proximity and juxtaposition. What indeed can "man and wife" even mean when "man and wife are strangers two paces apart to mention only this most intimate of all bonds. Let them move on till they are close enough to touch and then without pausing on their way exchange a look. If they recognize each other it does not appear" (*LO*, 36)? *Intimate, bonds, exchange*: these words, in this context, can only register the relative distances of people moving and pausing. And of what, in this context, would recognition even consist? Just so, "passion" in *The Lost Ones* is the "passion to search"; the only emotion admitted here is the physical motion from place to place "such that no place may be left unsearched" (*LO*, 50). "What principle of priority," the text asks, "obtains among the watchers always in force and eager to profit by the first departure from among the climbers" (*LO*, 51). But the text's linguistic situation makes only one principle of priority possible, that involving exactly the order in which the watchers stand on line and no more.

Such carefully controlled linguistic resonance retains the exacting diction of Beckett's French versions—which helps explain the otherwise puzzling difficulty in translating them. What, one wonders, in texts so seemingly bare, should require such elaborate, lengthy linguistic negotiation that after repeated attempts at collaboration, Beckett decided to do his own translations?[6] The desire to "write without style," to "impoverish myself further," which he cites when asked why he chose to write in French, is something he then achieves again when retranslating into English.[7] For example, the passage from *The Lost Ones* analyzed above appears in the French *Dépeupleur* as follows:

Parents et amis sont bien représentés sans parler de simples connaissances. La presse et l'obscurité rendent difficile l'identification. A deux pas de distance mari et femme s'ignorent pour ne parler que du lien intime entre tous. Qu'ils se rapprochent encore un peu jusqu'à pouvoir se toucher et échangent sans s'arrêter un regard. S'ils se remettent il n'y paraît pas. Quoi qu'ils cherchent ce n'est pas ça. (*Dépeupleur*, 32)

"Connaissances" (acquaintances) only makes stronger the limits on knowledge possible here. "L'identification" (recognition) keeps even closer to relations as purely object-defined. The "lien" (bonds) of husband and wife disallows the word's emotional ties, transposing it to a spatial term. Their nearness of approach in French defies the kinds of reconciliations that "rapprochement" could mean. "S'ils se remettent"—translated "if they recognize each other"— plays against the recovery which the French *se remettre* especially suggests, denying even a past of possible different reference: what relation, here, could they even return to and begin again?

Beckett's late texts seem, at least in their art, meditations on such words, on how they mean, given the situations he imagines. In "Enough," a romance between "he" and "she" transpires by "podometer": "Total milage divided by average daily milage. So many days. Divide" (E, 59). The two lives accordingly take shape as "immediate continuous communication with immediate redeparture. Same thing with delayed redeparture. Delayed continuous communication with immediate redeparture" (E, 57), where communication can mean only stops taken side by side for so many moments in the course of covering average daily distances. Listening to sounds of crawling and falling, the voice of *Company* stops to wonder "what in the world such sounds might signify" (*COM*, 50). But in the world of *Company* they signify crawling and falling only, almost in a short circuit of signification akin to tautology—one figure Beckett retains in all its emptiness.

Some of this remains in a sense funny. When *The Lost Ones* describes movement from zone to zone as "one example among a thousand of the harmony that reigns in the cylinder between order and license" (*LO*, 44), introducing the language of political theory into a world without polis makes for a humorous discrepancy. It is as though a discourse has been displaced, with its original context felt as missing; or as if, in a palimpsest of language, usage recalls an ordinary sense now constrained within Beckett's strange contexts. Yet Beckett's textual worlds are not entirely strange. They are not simply "private, surreal fantasies of bizarre worlds," or descriptions of "fantastic objects, people, and images" registering the "nonrelation among the artist, his art, and external reality."[8] Beckett's world is in its own way representational. It is congruent, as has been recognized from the outset, with the physical reduction that abruptly redefined reality with Galileo, Descartes, and Newton. But even more, Beckett represents the language of this reduction. Beckett reproduces the mechanistic world of Cartesian extension not as physical law, but as a kind of discourse, a set of terms and their relation within a linguistic system. Beckett represents this in his linguistic design, reflected in restrictions of linguistic resonance to mechanized, physical significance—his delimiting of the

sense of his words to an unmitigated literalism while always including, as part of his intention, the "figurative" meanings the words
might otherwise convey but which he suppresses.

Evasion by Number

The reduction of language to the literal as sheer materiality
meets in Beckett another evasion of figure, almost opposite and yet
strangely converging. This second evasive strategy involves Beckett's puzzling and pervasive use of mathematical figures. Like his
literalism, Beckett's mathematics finds its source in his Cartesian-
Newtonian interest. As such, it has received extensive critical attention, beginning with Vivian Mercier's 1959 essay on "The Mathematical Limit," which resolves Beckett's plots into mathematical
configurations. Mathematical figures in fact control large portions
of such texts as *The Lost Ones*, "Ping," "Imagination Dead Imagine," "Enough," "All Strange Away," and "Ill Seen Ill Said." In
these texts, as in *The Lost Ones*, Beckett reduces space and any
activity within it to pure extension—not only as physical but as
geometrical and mathematical dimension. To such mathematical
treatment all other considerations are subordinated. Thus, "Imagination Dead Imagine" invites: "No way in, go in, measure. Diame-
ter three feet, three feet from ground to summit of the vault. Two
diameters at right angles AB CD divide the white ground into two
semicircles ACB BDA. Lying on the ground two white bodies, each
in its semicircle" (IDI, 63). The text goes on to devote itself to the
meticulous record of a rotunda, whose variations of light and heat
determine all motion, animate and inanimate: "All vibrates, ground,
wall, vault, bodies, ashen or deaden or between the two, as may be"
(IDI, 64). The assimilation of body to geometry in "All Strange
Away" extends from the mathematization of bodily position—"For
nine and nine eighteen that is four feet and more across in which to
kneel, . . . Arse to knees, say diagonal ac, feet say at d, head on left
cheek at b"—to the grotesque mathematization of sex: "Back of
head against face when eyes on cunt, against breasts when on hole,
and vice versa, all most clear" (ASA, 44, 43). "Ping" goes still further, if possible, in identifying dimensions of the self with dimen-

sions of space: "Bare white body fixed one yard ping fixed elsewhere white on white invisible heart breath no sound" (70). "All
Strange Away" formulates the principle, "A place, then someone in
it, that again," and then proceeds to give it flesh: "Five foot square,
six high, no way in, none out, try for him there. . . . Sitting, standing, walking, kneeling, crawling, lying, creeping, in the dark, in the
light" (ASA, 39).

In accomplishing the further reduction from physical to mathematical parameters, Beckett makes use of a method used by others
before him. Descartes in particular is a precursor in this as in other
of Beckett's commitments. Like Descartes, Beckett proceeds through
a programmatic elimination of all secondary qualities. Descartes,
puzzling in his *Second Meditation* over the ontology of wax, came
to eliminate all "that sweetness of honey," "that pleasant odor of
flowers," "that whiteness," "that shape," "that sound," until "only
a body, extended, flexible, and movable" remained. Only these are
its real attributes: "size, extension in length, width and depth,
shape; . . . location . . . substance, duration, and number." All other
elements, Descartes says, are unreal—"light, colors, sounds, odors,
tastes, heat, cold and the other qualities involved in the sense of
touch," complaining in his *Third Meditation* that these "occur in
my thought with so much obscurity and confusion that I do not
even know whether they are true or false or only apparent."[9]

Just so, Beckett bars from his later texts everything except
quantitative measure: number, figure, magnitude, and duration. All
other experiences—passion, hope, grief, pleasure—are either eliminated or reduced to mathematical terms as trajectories pursued,
paths demarcated, measures taken. The vision of love in *Company*
thus quickly becomes a calculation of "the height or length you
have in common [as] the sum of equal segments" (*COM*, 41). The
only interaction between the two white bodies of "Imagination
Dead Imagine" consists in the random spatial intersection of their
two gazes, when exactly once "the beginning of one overlapped the
end of the other, for about ten seconds" (IDI, 66). In "Ping," even
pathos is rendered through placement, omitting anything so vague
as emotion: "Head haught eyes white fixed front old ping last mur-

mur one second perhaps not alone eye unlustrous black and white half closed long lashes imploring ping silence ping over" (72).

Beckett's move into mathematical reduction actually begins with the novels. In *Watt*, characters succeed each other like terms "of a series" (131), and mathematical interludes repeatedly intrude. Watt, for example, extensively computes the intervals of leap years (34). An Orals examination unfolds through the multiple permutations of looks exchanged among its five committee members (their subject: a dissertation on *The Mathematical Intuitions of the Visicelts* [175–79]).[10] Watt's romance with Mrs. Gorman is conducted through "thirteen changes of position. . . . Which, allowing one minute for the interversion, gives an average session of fifteen seconds" per kiss (141), looking forward to the geometrized sex of "All Strange Away." The systematic starvation of a dog whose feeding is calibrated to the chance occurrence of household leftovers carries the subordination to number to still crueler, more grotesque, and more ominous patterns of anti-sense.

But while mathematical reduction remains episodic and occasional in *Watt*, it becomes in the later texts a systematic and governing program. The hands of a woman in "All Strange Away" shrink as they present "no real image but say like red no grey say like something grey and when again squeeze firm down five seconds say faint hiss then silence then back loose two seconds and say faint pop" until "they arrive though not true image at small grey punctured rubber ball" (ASA, 57). As the yellow light of *The Lost Ones* throbs until it reaches a lull and all activity accordingly ceases,

the fists on their way to smite in anger or discouragement freeze in their arcs until the scare is past and the blow can be completed or volley of blows. Similarly without entering into tedious details those surprised in the act of climbing or carrying a ladder or making unmakable love or crouched in the niches or crawling in the tunnels as the case may be. But a brief ten seconds at most and the throbbing is resumed and all is as before. Those interrupted in their coming and going start coming and going again and the motionless relax. The lovers buckle to anew and the fists carry on where they left off. The murmur cut off as though by a switch fills the cylinder again. (*LO*, 37–38)

Anger and love hover here. But they can only take place as geo-
metric figure in mathematical space: fists "freeze in their arcs";
climbing, carrying, crouching, or crawling, activities defined by extension, are equated with attempts at "making unmakable love"—
what the text elsewhere explicitly describes as a matter of "penetration" and "erection" (LO, 53). The light and heat, color and
sound, that govern these activities are themselves rendered, not as
the qualities Aristotle thought them, but as the mathematically
measurable phenomena established by Galileo's pulsometer and
thermometer and acoustical experiments, and Newton's optics.
They are, accordingly, admissible within the text's mathematical
rules, although only as restricted to periodicity and calibration. The
text's language, too, obeys mathematical conventions. When the
figures are once more set in motion, the "throbbing" of the light
that activates them cannot be distinguished from the "throbbing"
of life or of love; sexual partners then "buckle to," a pun both of
whose senses register only shape and momentum, while the fists
"carry on," but only in their arc.

Beckett's reductions here such that, as he writes, "little by little
all strange away" (ASA, 57), correspond to the reductions of his
literalist, denotative language. Yet the move into mathematics remains a radical one and represents nearly the inverse of literalism
in its relation to figuration. While radical literalism strives to eliminate any figurative level, mathematics strives toward the elimination
of the literal level. The two, that is, eliminate opposite poles within
the structure of figuration. But both register an assault on the structure of metaphor, in ways, moreover, that implicate a whole system
of representation that is ultimately metaphysical. Jacques Derrida,
discussing the structure of metaphor in "White Mythology," notes
that "metaphor remains . . . a metaphysical concept." Citing Heidegger, he elaborates: metaphor is a "transposition into the nonsensible of the supposedly sensible. The notion of transposition and
of metaphor rests on the distinction, not to say the separation, between the sensible and the non-sensible, the physical and the nonphysical, is a basic feature of what is called 'metaphysics,' and con-
fers on Western thought its essential characteristics." Metaphor

assumes a series of distinct levels, which the terms *literal* and *figural* themselves reproduce. The "literal" evokes a sensible, physical realm, which it is the task of metaphor to point and transpose into a nonsensible, nonphysical one. Thus, writes Derrida, metaphor attempts to pass "from a proper sensible meaning to a proper spiritual meaning through a figurative detour. [It] is nothing but a movement of idealization . . . [in] a schema that brings an opposition into play . . . between the sensible and the spiritual, the sensible and the intelligible, the sensible and sense itself (*sinnlich/Sinn*)." These, of course, are the terms of distinction inherited through Western metaphysics, which traditional analyses of metaphor echo and reproduce. As to mathematics, Derrida remarks, "It is difficult to see how . . . the text of mathematics . . . could furnish metaphors in the strict sense (being attached to no fixed ontic region, and having no sensible or empirical content)."[11] Mathematics at once evades and fulfills metaphoric transfer. It strives to assert only the "metaphysical" pole of figuration, the nonsensible, the nonphysical, "sense" (*Sinn*), by eliminating empirical content. In this, it hopes both to complete and to surpass metaphoric structure, accomplishing the ideal goal of metaphor as such, that is, transfer of meaning to a purely figural plane.

Beckett's mathematical figures pursue this program. They reduce the dual structure of figuration to one dimension of the nonsensible. But by doing so, they raise questions about the metaphysical structure that metaphor reflects. For Beckett's mathematical figures, precisely in attaining nonsensible ends, acutely call these ends into question. Accomplishing pure figuration is felt not as a fulfillment, but as an incompletion. In omitting the concrete level of human experience, Beckett causes it to be felt all the more, by way of its absence. The mathematical reduction thus fails to dispense with the sensible level, in that it fails to confirm the sensible as dispensable. Instead, a concrete level continues to haunt his texts, where it is felt as painfully lacking.

At stake, however, is not only a theory of representation, but the whole metaphysical scheme that supports it—a scheme in which mathematics has in fact had a significant and privileged place. From

Plato through Saint Augustine through Descartes, mathematics has been both trope and means toward the nonsensible as a higher ontological realm. In Plato, mathematical entities are among those placed in the intelligible realm, above the sensible realm of objects and their images (although below those "making no use whatever of any object of sense but only of pure ideas" (*Republic* 511B–C). Mathematics in fact has a special heuristic role, as a paradigm for philosophy's "turning away" from the things of daily life toward the realm of being and knowledge (*Republic* 518D).[12] Augustine, out of a Neoplatonist tradition, also proposes pure mathematical relation as distinct from, and above, all "images of things which the eye of [the] body has reported." "We know them simply by recognizing them inside ourselves without reference to any material object. . . . It is not an image of the things we count, but something which is there in its own right" (*C* 10, 12). And Descartes, whose figure haunts Beckett's texts and Beckett studies, similarly insists that mathematical vision reflects "my understanding alone"; that its apprehension is not in "a vision, a touch, nor an imagination, . . . but is solely an inspection by the mind . . . comprehend[ed] solely by the faculty of judgment which resides in my mind."[13] For, as he explains in Rule 12, the pure intellect is pure exactly as the "abstract beings" it represents are "free of all admixture of images or representations," "divorced from the aid of any bodily image." Rather, the mind beholds "ideas which are within itself," "simple things purely intellectual."[14] True numbers are bodiless.

Allusive Defeats

Beckett himself does not directly invoke any such history in his own use of mathematical figures. In this, in fact, we encounter yet another of Beckett's figural evasions—the evasion of allusion. Beckett's texts are full of allusive gestures, yet the allusions prove very difficult to ascribe. Beckett seems never to provide quite enough material to permit definite identifications for his allusive hints. These remain sufficiently vague to block attribution to any single source; or, if a particular source does seem indicated, there is just not enough elaboration to bring it into systematic relation with

Beckett's use of it. The whole procedure seems itself a comic allusion to Joyce, whom Beckett imitates by tempting readers and scholars to compile allusions lists—but then he leaves them with notations followed by question marks, with echoes that cannot be firmly identified.

Defeating allusions is in Beckett no minor affair. As the critical literature attests, there is ample opportunity to document borrowings. His works, from this point of view, may seem like textbooks of Western culture, including, in a list compiled by Ruby Cohn for *Proust* alone, "classical and biblical myth, Leopardi, Gide, Cocteau, Shadwell, Descartes, d'Annunzio, Shakespeare, Constant, Nietzsche, Racine, Calderon, Shelley, Stravinsky, Dostoievsky, Dante, Baudelaire, De Sanctis, Blake, Coppee, Hugo, Huysmans, Musset, Chateaubriand, Amiel, the Goncourt brothers, Curtius, Renan, Schopenhauer, Spenser, Keats, Giorgione, Leibniz, Montegna."[15] Like Joyce, Beckett even provided "keys" to his work: a saying by the seventeenth-century Cartesian Arnold Geulincx, "Where you are worth nothing, there you should want nothing"; and a fragment of Democritus, "Naught is more real than naught" (*DJ*, 113). But while these "nothings" do surface in the writings, their function is far less clear. Like the myriad other allusions in Beckett, they neither situate Beckett's own text nor fully conform it to any prior one. Despite critical effort, Beckett particularly resists constructions of his inconsistent and unsystematic references into a master system. Beckett's work is in the end less a cultural history than, in his own phrase, a "tattered concordance" (MP, 49), or, as he writes in *The Unnamable*, "its visions, shreds of old visions" (*UNN*, 405).

Even in the constrained spaces of the late prose, there are numberless instances of allusions, from single words to larger textual patterns. Yet they remain incomplete or cross-purposeful. *The Lost Ones*, for example, with its underground caverns and the vain wish to escape from them, seems to waver between Dante's *Inferno* and Plato's cave. Vague rumors "that there exists a way out" divide between "two opinions": "One school swears by a secret passage branching from one of the tunnels and leading in the words of the poet to nature's sanctuaries. The other dreams of a trapdoor hidden in the hub of the ceiling giving access to a flue at the end of which the sun and other stars would still be shining" (LO, 18). Tunnel or trapdoor, Dante or Plato; and a possible ascent to the sun and stars does little to resolve the matter—although, as the text adds, the choice between them has "so little effect on the comportment of either sect that to perceive it one must be in the secret of the gods" (LO, 19). There is in any case no hope for escape, since no one knows which is the right tunnel, and the ceiling is out of reach.

These bits of allusive material crop up throughout the *Texts for Nothing*, always tempting identification with references that are never certain. "Text 10," for example, invokes myths of souls waiting to be reborn that are at once Platonic, Neoplatonic, and Virgilian: "souls are being licked into shape, souls swooned away, or sick with over-use, or because no use could be found for them, but still fit for use, or fit only to be cast away . . . or it has knelled here at last for our committal to flesh" (T 10, 124). But the "Text" then makes nothing of them; and no specific source can be cited that would provide some stable context for interpretation. "Text 6" similarly inserts what seems to recall some gnostic myth: "Blot, words can be blotted and the mad thoughts they invent, the nostalgia for the slime where the Eternal breathed and his son wrote, long after, with divine idiotic finger, at the feet of the adulteress" (T 6, 103). But it is impossible to determine which gnostic myth and which gnostic figures—which father, which son, which adulteress— may be intended here, and again, the passage cannot sustain determinate extrapolation.

Thus Beckett's countless attributions never permit proper footnotes, while their systematic implications remain centrifugal. And yet, despite the defeat of any consistent allusive structure, Beckett's allusions cannot simply be dismissed, as they are by Susan Brienza; nor are they merely part of a "diversity of style" that, however, threatens a "pedantry . . . disdaining simpler formulations," as John Fletcher argues.[16] Beckett's allusive play forms an integral part of his figural strategies, with two particularly important functions. They are part of what Wolfgang Iser calls a general pattern of negativity in Beckett's prose; and they provide, in their sporadic way, background material for situating Beckett's whole negative project. Beckett's prose, as Iser describes it, pursues a "relentless process of negation . . . a ceaseless rejection and denial of what has just been said." This unrelenting process of retraction grips not only the narrators, but also the reader, who must ceaselessly undo his own readings. Every construction for interpreting the text must be constantly reviewed and revised: "The moment one tries to restrict [the texts] to a specific meaning they slide away in a new direction." This process finally implies an equivocal status for fiction-making itself. The constant retraction of the ordering structures we erect reveals them to be fictions, yet we can never penetrate beyond them. Our fictions emerge as inescapable, but also as necessarily false: "We cannot abandon our fictions, but nevertheless ought to realize that they are fictions, as this is the only certain knowledge we can hope to obtain. . . . [Yet] we are still searching for certainty where we know there can be none and . . . in spite of this knowledge we still take the image for the truth." [17]

Iser's description of the fiction-making process in Beckett applies as well to Beckett's use of allusions. We discover or uncover allusions, only to find them incomplete and unstable. They either dissolve into vague resonances, or twist out of established patterns, or recede back into obscurity after a momentary and elusive emergence. The reader's act is a constant self-undoing, a retreat from the frameworks repeatedly offered and no less repeatedly dissolved. At the same time, retraction is not mere dismissal. The allusions remain embedded in the texts, providing glimpses into the multiple layers of culture that Beckett's art uncovers and mines. In this sense they do situate his writing, as frame and ground for his retractions and erasures.

Metaphysics and Measurement

In keeping with his allusive practices, Beckett repeatedly but sporadically invokes the history of mathematics. Beckett's mathematical references prompt the reader to an endless and endlessly defeated effort to construct frameworks for making sense of highly resistant texts. Yet mathematics, both in its history and in the figural structures implied by it, retains a central place in Beckett's writing. It proposes structures of relation between fiction and truth, representation and the signified it presumably represents, fundamental to Beckett's whole self-unraveling fictional enterprise.

From the outset mathematics has had a peculiar status in relation to what has traditionally been considered the realm of truth. From Pythagoras through Plato through Neoplatonist theories of the One, mathematics has had a privileged position in defining an immaterial and ideal realm. The ancient elevation of theoretical mathematics over calculations applied to sensible things only underscores the idealization of pure numerical relation. Plato, for example, distinguishes numbers when applied to objects of sense from numbers as they are in themselves, grasped "by thought alone" (*Republic* 525C–D). Saint Augustine similarly distinguishes between "numbers as they are used in counting things" and the "principle of number by which we count" (*C* 10.12). Ancient mathematics, and, it has been argued, modern mathematics in its philosophical base, are profoundly metaphysical in structure and interest.[18] Mathematical notions of unity, identity, harmony, and pure relation closely ally with and provide central modes for defining the metaphysical realm of Being as unchanging unity and identity. These notions are especially crucial, for example, to Neoplatonist efforts to ascend from the multiple world of the senses to the absolute unity of the One.[19] Mathematics in fact provided the model for such ascent, as systematic abstraction. "The first method of forming a conception of God," writes Albinus, "will be the abstraction (*aphairesis*, literally, "taking away," "removing") of these [sensible predicates of God] in the same way we form a conception of a point by its abstraction from the sensible, namely by first forming the conception of a surface, then that of a line, and finally that of a point . . . [which] has no part."[20]

Mathematics, that is, in both its history and its structure, is fully involved in metaphysics, with direct application to problems of representation. It promises access to an ideal and nonmaterial realm, an ideal essence that it, above all, is privileged to represent. But it does so by eliminating material and sensible reality. Indeed, it offers a separate and higher order of activity. The tendency of mathematical figures toward the nonsensible pole of figuration is therefore firmly situated within a metaphysical system and tradition. In using them, Beckett at once reviews, examines, and challenges not only the mathematical ideal of representation but the metaphysic that underwrites it. This, I would argue, is the heart of Beckett's project. Mathematics is in fact only an extreme limit within a structure of representation that elevates as ideal a nonsensible realm. Such an intelligible world becomes the ultimate signified of any sign system. Beckett shows that this ideal signified is unattainable—but he does not therefore condemn the very possibility of representation; rather, he demonstrates how this particular metaphysical ideal makes representation problematic.

Mathematics is one mode in which Beckett conducts this project of exposure. But it is closely allied to the positivist language that so marks Beckett's work. *Watt*, for example, as Jaqueline Hoefer explains, pursues an extensive exercise in logical positivism in its effort to reduce language to near-mathematical system. The novel's language rigorously restricts itself to logical propositions, direct references, enumerations, and numerical relations. This proves to be, as Hoefer concludes, a language of failure. Yet Hoefer and the many critics who pursue similar arguments see this as a failure not only of positivism "when confronted with that which eludes rational analysis," but of language as such, which can never be adequate to a truth beyond representation.[21] As Raymond Federman concurs, *Watt* shows "the inadequacy of language, reason, and logic to reveal the failure of fiction as a means of apprehending the reality of the world."[22]

These critics, that is, accept the premise of some reality prior to language, and ultimately beyond its grasp. Mathematized language, like all language, is seen to suffer from a general incompatibility in Beckett between representation and its objects. As Hugh Kenner sums up, "All Beckett's writings bring some sustained formal element to the service of some irreducible situation round which the lucid sentences defile in baffled aplomb." If mathematics specifically offers an "impingement of system, and notably systematic forms of discourse, on experiences to which they seem inappropriate," there is generally in Beckett "some radical incompatibility between syntactic order and human nuance."[23]

But Beckett is calling into question this very structure in which representation attempts to equal a reality beyond it but inevitably fails to do so. *Watt's* reductive language, rather than failing in regard to some truth of experience, shows how the language we use constructs our experience. Watt is what he speaks: not in the sense of Wittgenstein's positivist *Tractatus*, as is repeatedly claimed, but in a sense more suggestive of the *Philosophical Investigations'* attack on positivism. Watt's world is exactly a function of his words— and its reduction is due, not to his failure to "express the true nature of the object,"[24] but to the fact that the language he uses is one that severely restricts his reality. Indeed, it is his desire for some absolute name that plunges him into aphasia. Wishing for some final, stable name for "pot" he exactly overlooks how "it answered, with unexceptionable adequacy, all the purposes and performed all the offices of a pot" (81). The peculiar comedy of the text works, as in some of the later "Fizzles," by the continued pressure on Watt's language system of all the words he steadfastly eliminates. Like Lewis Carroll's nonsense, words are interpreted only according to their logic. Their further resonances echo as a missing possibility, deflating and mocking Watt's narrow linguistic world—but only in the name of other language worlds he could, but does not, enter. In this, mathematical and literalist reduction conjoin.

Watt, then, neither relies on nor despairs of some realm of truth beyond linguistic meanings. Its logical conduct instead examines how language worlds set up particular limits of experience. In a text like "Lessness," on the other hand, a mathematized language more directly expresses traditional metaphysical longings for a realm of truth. This final Beckett text seems almost eerily to conjure meditative modes of abstraction. In repetitions that recall Beckett's earlier experiments with troubadour forms of poetry, Beckett pursues a reduction nearly frightening in its relentless purity. Here, the very syntax is in constant process of its own undoing. Each word requires a reconstruction of the one preceding it, as each interrupts and defeats any normal expectations of phrasing, grammatical relation, or sentences. The merciless lessening, however, carries with it echoes of absolute realms long defined by way of negation. "All sides endlessness earth sky as one no sound no stir" evokes the unity of unchanging, ideal intelligibility, beyond time, beyond difference, beyond language. "Never but this changelessness dream the passing hour" evokes age-old contrasts between a never-changing eternity and an illusive, passing world of time. Within these constantly repeated, constantly rephrased evocations of sameness, mathematical figures take their place: as reductions of "little body" to "grey face features crack and little holes two pale blue"; reductions of endless space to "blank planes sheer white eye calm," until "long last all gone from mind."

"Lessness" takes Beckett's mathematical, reductive language to its limit. And in this text, such language points toward what has always been held up as the metaphysical ideal. This ideal comes, however, through the rigors of Beckett's accomplishment, to look horrifying. "Ash grey all sides earth sky as one all sides endlessness." As every figure disappears into lessness, what emerges is not some achieved absolute, but never-ending erasure: "Little void mighty light four square all white blank planes all gone from mind." Indeed, the only bright impulse in the text, reversing all traditional hierarchies, seems tied not to what is unchanging, but to the passing world of time: "All sides endlessness earth sky as one no stir not a breath. On him will rain again as in the blessed days of blue the passing cloud." But this moment is soon swallowed by the mathematical and figural abstractions that traditionally conduct to metaphysical conditions long idealized. The Other World is there: but it is empty.

The (Non)essential Self

The question of representation, implicit in both mathematical figures and literalist reductions, finds its fullest expression in Beckett through what remains his central figure of evasion: the figure of the self. Beckett's texts relentlessly dwell in regions he calls the self, but whose boundaries he just as relentlessly dissolves. In the late texts, the evasion of the self in some sense governs both his mathematic and his literalist modes. The one assimilates the human subject into number, the other into matter. But the issue is engaged as early as the essay on Proust—in a manner opposite to its usual reading. Ross Chambers, for example, sees in *Proust* the desire for "the existence within us of some timeless essential being." But while Proust believes this "true self" can be attained "by gaining emancipation from the time-dimension" through art, Beckett despairs of attaining it. Life becomes "an exclusion from some timeless inner essence." The self, as "dimensionless, exists outside the world of space and time and is by definition unattainable within that world." Therefore, according to Chambers, for Beckett the effort to achieve this self inevitably fails, "establishing a basic image of life as endless exile from and pursuit of an infinitely unattainable self."[25]

This reading, in which Beckett is seen as desperately pursuing an idea of self as pure essence, yet always being defeated in his attempts to achieve it, is almost universally accepted as applicable to all of Beckett's works.[26] Yet Beckett repeatedly questions and critiques such a notion of essential selfhood, beginning with *Proust.* There the self is not portrayed as a stable, fixed identity, an unchanging subject that stands beyond the flux of time, enduring through different moments in some essential unity. Beckett instead describes the self as constantly modified through its experiences, existing in time—"the double-headed monster of damnation and salvation" (*P*, 1). Time is not an unreal or incidental condition, not a "milestone that has been passed, but . . . irremediably part of us." In some sense, this subjection to time is first seen as loss. Always "we are other, no longer what we were." As with Eliot's "time is no healer: the patient is no longer here" (DS III), so in *Proust* the subject in time is forever disappearing, defeating the very notion of accomplishment or satisfaction: "The aspirations of yesterday were valid for yesterday's ego, not for to-day's . . . What is attainment? The identification of the subject with the object of his desire. The subject has died—and perhaps many times—on the way" (*P*, 3).

By the time the object is achieved, the subject who desired it no longer exists; while the subject in time undergoes "an unceasing modification of his personality, whose permanent reality, if any, can only be apprehended as a retrospective hypothesis" (P, 4).

There is, then, "not only 'I' but the many 'I's" (P, 43). But this is not mere loss of true self. Beckett criticizes a unitary, self-identical self beyond time, and questions the Proustian ideal of one. For it is an ideal that imprisons the self in itself, making both love and communication impossible in any real sense. Love becomes "our demand for a whole" (P, 39), for a complete union between self and beloved beyond the differences and distinctions that take place in time. This makes love nothing more than "total possession" as "complete identification of object and subject" (P, 41).

But such total identification defeats, among other things, any possibility of communication, which becomes, in Beckett's analysis, either distortion or deception: "Either we speak and act for ourselves—in which case speech and action are distorted and emptied of their meaning by an intelligence that is not ours, or else we speak and act for others—in which case we speak and act a lie" (P, 46–47). Proust's ideal of a self beyond time reduces communication either to solipsism, in which discourse with others becomes empty masquerade; or to lies, in which discourse with others becomes self-betrayal. The position is not only deadly, it is also untenable. For it ultimately precludes discourse with the self as well, making itself, as addressed, exactly the betraying other it hopes to bypass. Thus any discourse becomes "tantamount to a sacrifice of that only real and incommunicable essence of oneself" (P, 48). The Proustian ideal, claiming to free "the essential reality" and reveal "the extra-temporal" (P, 55–56), Beckett finally rejects. Like Schopenhauer's notions of music as "the Idea itself, unaware of the world of phenomena, existing ideally outside the universe," it eradicates human circumstance. Its idealization of the Idea without phenomena or material body negates the realm of human experience, condemning human conditions as inessential, intrusive, unreal, fallen. Time is not redeemed, but annihilated. In his concluding line, Beckett equates Proust's Ideal with an "'invisible reality' that damns the life of the body on earth as a pensum and reveals the meaning of the word: 'defunctus'" (*P*, 72).

Thus Beckett, far from asserting an essential self as the ultimate if unattainable truth, instead treats it with pronounced suspicion. Essence in Beckett is not necessarily the object either of impossible desire or of nostalgic regret. Metaphysical essence seems, rather, to be what Beckett is disputing—and not necessarily out of defeated longing. But whether Beckett himself adopts or rejects Proust's essentialist premises, he at least displays their consequences. Beckett's enterprise is profoundly critical. He pursues Proust's premises to their conclusion, offering an anatomy of their assumptions, and above all a portrait of their effects. And these, indeed, point to the alternatives so often claimed for Beckett himself: either an insatiable longing for a truth beyond human attainment, or the renunciation of such truth as nonexistent, leaving in its stead only a meaningless void.

These alternatives consistently haunt Beckett's later ventures into, or rather away from, figures of the self. Especially from *The Unnamable* onward, his whole textual venture centers in selves that do nothing except seek themselves in some absolute, self-centered purity. Theirs is a relentless interiority, an ever-contracting stage on which Beckett rehearses, repeatedly, a search for self, essence, identity. Yet while it may be that the "heroes seek their essential selves," that the Beckett character is "obsessed with finding his true self," and that the fictions depict the "search for an underlying true self . . . one essential self, unnamable," heroes, characters, and fictions do so, finally, in ways that call this very project into question.[27]

Beckett indeed scrupulously adopts traditional notions of a pure, unitary self, one beyond time, space, and extension, essential, interior, and, as is often claimed, transcending "physical and material life" to "exist in nonmaterial dimension."[28] But his texts—through comedy, parody, tediousness, and the macabre—show this definition to be both quixotic and undesirable. The endless effort to attain the pure self is endlessly defeated. But this is not finally felt as either nostalgic or existential loss. Instead, Beckett shows how such purity of self, far from being true self, is itself unreal—no more than a fictional construction without basis in experience, commitment to which subverts our ability to experience, in positive ways, the reality we do in fact inhabit. What is habitually idealized as the "true" self, Beckett shows to be untrue, unreal, and finally not ideal.

Unnamings

The defeat of the pure self in Beckett takes shape, above all, as an endlessly failed attempt by the self to establish itself beyond figuration. Narrator after narrator, through page after page, asserts that he truly exists in a single and solitary selfhood. Yet narrator after narrator endlessly produces figures for himself, further projections and representations of his self. These, in turn, he endlessly retracts, only to produce yet further representations, which he again insists do not represent him. And yet, he can never finally extricate himself from the figures of the self that he never ceases to deny—his very selfhood becoming little more than the undoing of his own figures.

In *The Unnamable*, this self-undoing takes place over hundreds of tortuous pages. The text progresses as an endless production of figures of the self, coupled with an endless effort at overcoming them. Always insisting on himself alone, the narrator cannot cease from inventing characters, projections, speakers, which he then hurries to deny. Earlier fictional characters from Beckett's canon multiply into further apparitions, further figures: Malone, glimpsed in his "brimless hat . . . perhaps it is Molloy, wearing Malone's hat" (*UNN*, 292–93); followed by the "pseudo-couple, Mercier-Camier" (*UNN*, 297); then Basil who becomes Mahood who becomes Worm. All are denounced as empty fictions, mere self-evasions: "All these Murphys, Molloys, and Malones do not fool me. They have made me waste my time, suffer for nothing, speak of them when . . . I should have spoken of me and of me alone" (*UNN*, 303). To speak of the "me alone" is to be unnamable, extricated from all the false figures in order to emerge as a true self beyond representation: "Murphy and the others, and last but not least the two old buffers here present. . . . When I think of the time I've wasted with these bran-drips, beginning with Murphy, who wasn't even the first, when I had me" (*UNN*, 391, 390).

Yet these "others" continue to haunt the Unnamable. For they are also an inescapable part of his effort to express his selfhood. Even as he insists that they do not disclose but only disguise him, they remain his only avenue of self-expression. Thus the narrator laments the whole enterprise of self-representation as inessential self-detour, an unnecessary, superfluous betrayal of self: "If only I were not obliged to manifest. . . . Why did I have myself represented in the midst of men, the light of day?" (*UNN*, 296–97). Representations nevertheless recur in his very effort to seek himself, to discover himself: "But I just said I have spoken of me, am speaking of me" (*UNN*, 303).

The *Texts for Nothing* contract and intensify this antirepresentational regress. In many ways, they are like palimpsests of *The Unnamable*'s unending discourse. Like the Unnamable, the *Texts*' narrators attempt to turn away from figures, as though there were some pure, essential self independent of them, a self that would not dissipate itself in what the Unnamable disdainfully calls his "delegates" (*UNN*, 297). The *Texts*' speakers assume that somewhere prior to and outside of representation there is a true self, the signified that these representations merely signify, and in so doing distort and betray. As "Text 4" complains, "What am I doing, talking, having my figments talk, it can only be me" (*T* 4, 93).

Yet, like the Unnamable, the speakers, seeking their "me"s, endlessly do so via just such "figments." Each "Text" establishes its own scene of tension between these opposing and indeed mutually negating impulses—although "scene" may be an exaggerated term for the self-dissolving situations most "Texts" offer. Not that setting is utterly eliminated. There are characters and places—courtrooms and hospitals, hills and seas, park benches and waiting rooms and graveyards (but always, as we are reassured, "on earth, beyond all doubt on earth" [*T* 12, 133]; the attempt to evade ordinary reality is in Beckett a source of endless comedy). But these external settings finally retreat inward. They are claimed as mere projections of an overwhelming interiority, all contracting, like the jury of "Text 5," into "an image, in my helpless head" (*T* 5, 95), or, like the train's wheels of "Text 7," into "the wheel in my head" (*T* 7, 109).

But simultaneous with the retraction inward is an inevitable and irresistible impulse outward, beyond the interior self into external scene, beyond solitude into accompaniment. If the narrator of "Text 1" dissolves his setting into contradiction—he is at once on "the top, very flat, of a mountain, no, a hill," and also down in "troughs scooped deep by the rains, it was far down in one of these I was lying"—still he cannot desist from terms of location: "up here" and "down in the hole," "I'm up there, and I'm down here." And if he claims "I never much varied, only the here would some-times seem to vary," he also concedes that "we seem to be more than one," that "yes, I was my father and I was my son," until his very self-embrace divides himself into parts: "I'm in my arms, I'm holding myself in my arms."

In this way, every "no, I am alone" transforms into further fic-tional multiplicities: "I know how I'll do it, I'll be a man . . . a kind of man, a kind of old tot, I'll have a nanny" (*T* 3, 86). As in "Text 4," Beckett's speakers cannot help but generate scenes and then proceed to people them:

And all these things, what things, all about me, I won't deny them any more, there is no sense in that any more. If it's nature perhaps it's trees and birds, they go together, water and air, so that all may go on, I don't need to know the details, perhaps I'm sitting under a palm. Or it's a room, with furniture, all that's required to make life comfortable, dark, because of the wall outside the window. (*T* 4, 93)

As always, Beckett's writing seems to move in a realm of archetype and paradigm. "It's nature. . . . Or it's a room, with furniture," a romantic setting or a realist one. In either case, there is an irresist-ible urge to produce such settings, to surround the self with them and to step forward into them. Equally irresistible is the no less immediate retreat from them, retracting the fictional projections even as they are offered in an effort to turn back from creation to a true, originary selfhood. "Text 4" thus continues: "No point under such circumstances in saying I am somewhere else, someone else, such as I am I have all I need to hand . . . there I am on my own again at last" (*T* 4, 93–94). But at once and again erasure and retraction give way to invention, and the pure, simple self loses itself in reproduction at the close: "Then it goes, all goes, and I'm far again, with a far story again, I wait for me afar for my story to begin" (*T* 4, 94).

This trope of farness, reiterated throughout the *Texts*, asserts a distinction between a self that is remote, as opposed to a true self that is near. Such a "near" self must be distinguished not only from external setting, but also from external projection. The *Texts* seek continuously to render an inner self less and less encumbered by any representation divisible from it. Characters are therefore resisted even while they are inevitably produced. Though they are denounced as mere "derivatives" (*T* 2, 82), "pale imitations" of "number one" (*T* 10, 124), "various assumed names" (*T* 5, 97), there yet seems to be no other way to talk of the self. Thus, the narrator of "Text 7" insists, "It's not me in any case, I'm not talking of me, I've said it a million times, no point in apologizing again, for talking of me, when there's X, that paradigm of human kind, moving at will, complete with joys and sorrows . . . no, to talk of oneself, when there's X, no, what a blessing I'm not talking of myself" (*T* 7, 108). But the "Text" had opened with the injunction to "try everything, ferret in every hold, secretly, silently, patiently, listening? . . . I'd like to be sure I left no stone unturned before reporting me missing and giving up." To talk of X is not to talk of himself, is to protect his self from exposure, keeping his self to himself. But it is also his only means for searching for and discovering himself. Just so, the narrator in "Text 6" first insists that in talking of his keepers, he has been talking of himself. Yet in eliminating them, he eliminates himself as well: "There is no one here, neither me nor anyone else." Conversely, trying and trying to "find a way out, in my head," he discovers that "the world would be there again, in my head." The world, it seems, is inescapable, unless he finally escapes himself as well. His labor "all day long and, let me add, before I forget, part of the night" so that "with perseverance I'd get at me in the end" thus ends instead in a loss of self: "Leave it, leave it, . . . I'll never get anywhere" (*T* 6, 102).

The path of representation remains, so these selves claim, a detour. The self claims itself to be not only distinct from its representations, but at odds with them. Yet whether the speaker speaks of another as though of himself, or of himself as though of another, he fails to isolate himself, to define himself only in terms of himself, fails to achieve that ultimate and quintessential "me in the end." But it is not only projected characters that betray the effort to distill the self from all exteriority. One's own body equally betrays true selfhood, is merely an exterior, inessential representation. What the keepers in "Text 6" keep is nothing but "a little dust in a little nook, stirred faintly this way and that by breath straying from the lost without," a body that is merely "the tissues I was, I can see them no more, feel them no more, flaunting and fluttering all about and inside me, pah they must be still on their old prowl somewhere, passing themselves off as me. Did I ever believe in them, did I ever believe I was there, somewhere in that ragbag" (*T* 6, 102–3). But if in "Text 5" the speaker insists that his own hand has "no connexion with me" (97); if "Text 10" speaks of "our committal to flesh as the dead are committed to the ground" (124); or if "Text 8" dismisses its ghostly parade of Beckett properties, "white stick and an ear-trumpet," "bowler hat" and "pair of brown boots," as mere "insignia" that the speaker finally "would know . . . was not me" (114–15)—still, bodily dissociation hardly resolves the problem of identity. Thus, "Text 6" wavers: "Perhaps I'm still there, as large as life, merely convinced I'm not" (103). And the narrator of "Text 7" disclaims his body—"I am far from that heap of flesh, rind, bones and bristles"—but still searches for himself there, "in every hold, I mean in all those places where there was a chance of my being, where once I used to lurk, waiting for the hour to come when I might venture forth" (107). In the end, he is neither there nor not there, asking, "Is that me still waiting there . . . it's there, it's me. . . . This lump is no longer me and that search should be made elsewhere" (*T* 7, 109–10).

If the body is far, the head is no nearer. "Text 1" distinguishes the "I" from the body: "I say to the body, Up with you now, and I can feel it struggling"; but the "I" is no less distinct from the head: "I say to the head, Leave it alone, stay quiet, it stops breathing. . . . I am far from all that wrangle, I shouldn't bother about it, I need nothing" (75). The head, too, despite its claim to provide an interior place of selfhood, undergoes the rigors of denial. "I'll will it, will me a body, will me a head, a little strength, a little courage," only erases into calls to "leave it, no more of that, don't listen to it all, don't say it all" (*T* 3, 85–86). In fact, the self, to emerge at all, does so only against each of these locations and conditions. But where and what, then, is this self? "Text 4" opens with just these questions: "Where would I go if I could go, who would I be if I could be." But these questions are answered mainly in the negative. "I'm not in his head, nowhere in his old body, and yet I'm there, for him, I'm there, with him, hence all the confusion" (*T* 4, 91).

"Text 11" develops these nots. It desperately seeks to extricate an essential "me" from all else, asking: "Where am I, to mention only space, and in what semblance, and since when, to mention only time, and till when, and who is this clot who doesn't know where to go, who can't stop, who takes himself for me and for whom I take myself, anything at all, the old jangle" (*T* 11, 129). The taking of the self for that self in space and in time is in fact a mis-taking, a "clot who can't stop," "the old jangle." As to the true self, it is not these: not body, not even head, certainly not in time, but rather an eternal, internal, singularity: "This evening now that never ends, in whose shadows I'm alone, that's where I am, where I was then, where I've always been" (*T* 11, 130). The true self, the near self, the I "alone" that is, was, has always been, must be the self outside all mediation, all space of figuration.

But what exactly, we may ask, is finally left? What finally characterizes the self "alone," stable and self-identical? In the end, after all subtractions and retractions, what the self seems to discover is its voice. Beckett's *Texts* fill with voices that claim, after all else is removed, to be the self itself. The search for self-identity becomes in "Text 5" an effort to "strain for a voice not from without," an intimate "voice of reason," of "conscience" (95–96). "Text 12" places its self at least "under the sky, with a voice" (133). When all else is gone in "Text 13," there still remains "a voice without a mouth" (137). And "Text 11" pursues its reductions to arrive at last at "a head with a voice belonging to it, . . . or one head, or headless, a headless voice, but a voice" (T 11, 128).

And yet, voice too finally fails to provide the self with self-identity, for it also implies others than the self. What the speaker in "Text 5" discovers, instead of his own voice, is that "I'm haunted. . . . Theirs all these voices, like a rattling of chains in my head, rattling to me that I have a head" (98). "Text 11" finally reduces to the self alone with its voice: "I'm alone, that's where I am, where I was then, where I've always been, . . . and I speak, a voice speaks that can be none but mine, since there is none but me" (130). But in speaking, it discovers that it has no voice left either: "I don't speak to me any more, I have no one left to speak to." The voice too finally implies another than the self, without which the self itself cannot speak, cannot be. At the end of its purgation, the self in the *Texts* arrives at nothing but a "babble of homeless mes and untenanted hims." What it discovers, at the end of its self-search, is "this other without number or person whose abandoned being we haunt, nothing" (T 12, 134). The self, it seems, is essentially other.

Linguistic Selfhood

In Beckett, the identity of the self emerges not as some transcendent, unitary essence but rather as a scene of intrarelation between the self and its images of itself. This is the case both despite and because of efforts to evade such self-images. The Beckett scene of selfhood works exactly at cross-purposes. The more the self works to attain a pure self beyond multiplicity, the more it discovers that in doing so it cannot avoid images that are multiple. In the very act of expressing itself, it betrays its ideal of unitary selfhood. Beckett's quests for pure selves are, that is, purposely staged as failures ("to be an artist," he says in an interview, "is to fail as no other dare fail" [*DJ*, 145]). But in Beckett this failure is less tragic than parodic, because Beckett's quests for pure selves assault the very notion of the pure self. They set out to expose critically what Beckett sees as an untenable project.

This critique finally extends to language. But this is not to say, as is usually claimed, that Beckett's writing realizes a failure of language, a demonstration of its inadequacy in the face of a true reality that must always escape it. Critic after critic sees just such linguistic failure as the heart of Beckett's project. Beckett is forever said to display "a lack of faith in any form of expression"; "the impossibility of representation and the disengagement of language from the world"; "a region between the language which does not represent and a silence which is unrepresentable"; a "profound mistrust of the possibility of any real adequation between the word and the human actuality."[29] Or for Beckett "writing [is] mere deceit, a hollow dribble of inadequate words only approximating to what one knows is not even reality, and snatched at great price from the grudging, encircling silence." Or Beckett is engaging a "universal problem, . . . the dilemma of existence above and beyond all physical and linguistic limitations," which in turn reveals "the inadequacy of language as a means of artistic communication."[30]

Language, above all, is said to fail Beckett's selves. For the self is felt to represent a truth that language necessarily betrays. The true self is defined as beyond the divisions of time and space, as some ideal essence outside and prior to all material conditions. But language can never formulate this complete simplicity, because language takes place within a world exterior to the self, subject to conditions other than absolute, immediate unity. The "true" self, essential and interior, beyond time, space, and extension, is also beyond any representation. It is beyond language, which through discursive formulation can only raise a barrier to knowledge and access to the true inner self. Such defeat of language forms the central thesis in study after study of Beckett. Thus "the attempt to discover the fixed nature of the Self" is, according to Michael Robinson, "the constant search within all [Beckett's] work"; and this means that Beckett's characters must "escape from the prison of time and words into the timeless and changeless condition of Selfhood they believe was lost at birth." According to Ruby Cohn, the central relation between character and language throughout Beckett is one in which "the mind knows that it is limited to and by words, which falsify whatever they approach," yet defiantly seeks an "essence—call it being, self, identity—[that] defies verbalization." Judith Dearlove similarly speaks of a "formless narrator . . . who rejects all that is alien to the non-verbal core of himself," but who is condemned to inhabit "the fixed shaped and external orders of his spoken words." According to David Hesla, "the unnamable's goal is silence, and to achieve his goal he must stop speaking of fictions, and speak only of self." And Ross Chambers sees language in Beckett as given "a task it cannot fulfill, for the voice issuing from the soul . . . knows only the language of the outer world, of time and space." Only if the self were able "to invent a new language, of timelessness and spacelessness" would it be able to achieve a true "language of the self," one that in fact would become "the silence of eternal self-possession."[31] The list can be extended almost indefinitely. Beckett's critics are nearly unanimous on the default of language.

But in rushing to condemn language as inadequate, these critics are endorsing a notion of reality, truth, and selfhood that Beckett's work disputes. They assume metaphysical notions of essence and of essential selfhood as somehow extricable from time, space, matter, and multiplicity. This is, moreover, a metaphysic which, as the critical writing itself shows, has particularly negative implications for any linguistic project: only if language transcends its own fundamental conditions can it become a mode for representing essential selfhood. Regarding Beckett's fictions, such a commitment to linguistic transcendence is said to lead to a linguistic impasse in which fiction is caught in a language by definition opposed to the truth it would utter. Language is therefore denounced as failing, falsifying, and distorting an essence of self inevitably beyond expression. Only by ceasing to use language can the self be true to itself. As Dieter Wellershoff proclaims, "To talk means to stand outside oneself; he

who does not possess himself and remains concealed from himself
is compelled to talk. Only he who has attained to his own identity
can be silent."[32]

Alan Thiher restates this position in philosophical-theoretical
terms. Beckett offers a "separation of voice and language," in opposition to what he calls a "humanist" view where the "self possess[es] a voice unmediated by language." To speak is to fall into
plurality, "to force the voice to enter into an alterity that can be
only a form of alienation." Language inevitably "ensnares as it
transforms one into otherness." But the true voice of self must escape such "pluralized otherness." Only the voice as "divested of the
tribe's language would have direct access to itself." That is, the
voice and self can achieve true identity as union only in silence: "In
silence . . . the voice would be a pure self in which, as Derrida might
have it, consciousness would be fully present to itself as a plenitude unmediated by the alienating otherness of the tribe's linguistic
system."[33]

But unmediated self-identity as voice is exactly what Beckett
contests. Beckett, like Derrida for that matter, challenges Thiher's
claim of a "pure self" as "consciousness . . . fully present to itself
as a plenitude unmediated by the alienating otherness." But this
does not entail the failure of language as an instrument of selfhood;
rather, it shows pure selfhood to be a fantasy of the unreal, a fantasy that deceives the self into the impossible situation Thiher describes and Beckett dramatizes. For it is, as *The Unnamable* and
the *Texts for Nothing* especially show, impossible to defeat self-
expression without also defeating the self. Only in language does
the self, in Beckett, even exist; without linguistic expression, there
is no self at all.

But this fundamentally reshapes the very notion of selfhood.
The self is not, as it turns out, unitary, unmediated self-identity. On
the contrary, selfhood takes place in just those dimensions the es-
sentialists mistakenly seek to deny: in time and space, in intimate
relation to others, above all in language. In Beckett, this redefinition
is arrived at, however, in something like reverse, through an ardu-
ous process of defeating all efforts to achieve pure self-identity. In

The Unnamable it is conducted as a constant, and constantly failing, effort to reduce all others to the self. The unnamable narrator
repeatedly complains, "What I speak of, what I speak with, all
comes from them"; he complains that he cannot "open my mouth
without proclaiming them, and our fellowship, that's what they'll
have me reduced to." Wishing to speak only of himself, he finds
himself "having to speak and not being able to except of things that
don't concern me, that don't count, that I don't believe, that they
have crammed me full of to prevent me from saying who I am."
What the Unnamable wants is to eliminate the exterior "them" and
"their language." He wants to utter an "I am" without a language
that is by definition linked with others and shared by others:
"Within, motionless, I can live, utter me, for no ears but my own"
(*UNN*, 324–25).

Yet in struggling against language of and as the other, the Unnamable discovers that this language is the only avenue to himself,
that there is no himself without "them." The very voice he would
claim as full self-possession is not unmediated and utterly proper to
him. Each departure toward a single selfhood eventually returns on
itself, not as a unity but as a multiplicity. The more the Unnamable
tries to extricate himself from his figures, the more he discovers that
they are who he is. The "strange task which consists in speaking of
oneself," the "strange hope. . . . Possessed of nothing but my voice,
the voice," leads him on to "the admission that I am Mahood after
all," making up "these stories of a being whose identity he usurps,
and whose voice he prevents from being heard, all lies from beginning to end" (*UNN*, 311). Trying to extricate himself from all his
"predecessors," denouncing them as "vice-existers" (*UNN*, 315),
in the end only further entangles him, leaving him unable to assert
himself except as other. "There was never anyone but me, never,
always," becomes "he says I as if I were he" (*UNN*, 403).

Even the voice, that most intimate self-representation, proves to
be not self-identical, not unitary, but other. The Unnamable finds
himself filled with other voices, from which he cannot separate his
own. "They've blown me up with their voices, like a balloon, and
even as I collapse it's them I hear." But these voices that are "theirs"

are, despite himself, the voices proper to him, the language without which he himself does not even exist. The expression of the self as voice is finally also projected as figure: "It's entirely a matter of voices, no other metaphor is appropriate" (*UNN*, 325). Voice, too, is figural, a "metaphor" projecting a self; but in being so, it is "appropriate"—as fully the self as exists.

The Unnamable in this way is constantly asserting himself, despite his denials, in exactly the medium of language he would bypass. The *Texts for Nothing* only tighten this circle, contracting all discourse to the exchanges in which the self resides, even while denying discourse as the self's proper place. The narrators resist all self-representation, all self-expression as extension into a world other than pure self. They insist, as in "Text 8," that "all I say will be false and to begin with not said by me, here I'm a mere ventriloquist's dummy." Yet again and again the self proves to be no other than "that other who is me . . . because of whom I'm here . . . helpless to move or accept this voice as mine, it's as him I must disguise myself" (113).

Dualist attempts to distinguish essential spirit from accidental body undergo the same collapse. Reductions to "just the head and the two legs," then "just the head," and at last to "pure spirit," even the narrator concedes, "wouldn't work" (*T* 3, 89). Doing without any of these aspects of the self finally leads to self-erasure: "I should turn away from it all, away from the body, away from the head, let them work it out between them, let them cease, I can't, it's I would have to cease" (*T* 1, 75). In the end, "how you describe yourself, here or elsewhere, fixed or mobile, without form or oblong like man, in the dark or the light of the heavens, I don't know, it seems to matter" (*T* 3, 87).

Representation proves essential. Figures of body, self, spirit, even voice, establish identity by way of detour. Indeed, voice, too, for all its supposed interior privilege, fails without some form, some formulation. Emptying the self of all other voices empties the self of its own voice too: "That's how I speak, there is only me, this evening, here on earth, and a voice that makes no sound because it goes towards none" (*T* 4, 92). The loss of the other's voice leaves the self in the end voiceless, not as true self-assertion, but as loss of the self. Beckett's efforts in the *Texts* at reduction finally result exactly in that: not a reduction to essence, but mere reduction. No essential residue is distilled as beneath and before all self-representation. The more the self attempts to locate itself as a self alone, the less it exists.

Beckett, in his peculiar mastery of language, makes the effort to establish a nonlinguistic self a special mode of linguistic contortion. It becomes a comedy of language attempting to mean without the contexts that give words meaning. In the *Texts*, this emerges through precisely calculated puns that make dis-embodiment a kind of paradox. "What counts is to be in the world, the posture is im-material" (*T* 4, 93) restores "immaterial" to concrete and comic meaning. "How are the intervals filled between these apparitions?" makes interior shadows into actual ghosts who then "play cards . . . to recruit their spirits" and, in a pun linking entertainment to re-birth, are "entitled to a little recreation" (*T* 6, 101). Even renuncia-tion undergoes peculiar, paradoxical, and tautological wordplay, reversing itself toward strange recuperation. The multiple negatives of "give up . . . there was not, never anything, but giving up" (*T* 10, 123) makes reduction itself a positive activity: "He'll have done nothing, nothing but go on . . . giving up, that's it, I'll have gone on giving up" (*T* 10, 125).

In striving to withdraw from language, the narrators lose them-selves. But this, fortunately, proves impossible. The narrators con-stantly, in some sense comically, betray their own venture to a con-tinual, if resisted, restoration in the linguistic world. The final context of the self proves to be exactly the context of language. The self is a part of speech, taking shape through a linguistic body with-out which it simply disappears. Voice in Beckett is not interior, un-mediated unity against exterior language; and language, far from betraying the self, proves to be the self's essential medium. If lan-guage moves the self outside itself, this is not finally a loss of self. If it moves the self toward the other, this is neither intrusive nor dis-sipating. For the identity of the self proves not to be perfect self-identity. The self attains definition and reality only within multiple relations, through its shifting, multiply pointing, sequences of language. If, as Marjorie Perloff remarks, in Beckett "enigma is created by the 'fragility' of the words themselves, words whose meanings are constantly eroded and reformulated," this is because words *are* fragile.[34] Change, the passing away of old meanings and evolution of new ones through usage, is the very mode of linguistic life. However Beckett's narrators try to withdraw themselves and their words from this process, they are unable to do so. Indeed, the attempt to withdraw from process in the name of independent and fixed identity only threatens loss of meaning. It leads not to stability but rather to dissolution. Beckett's work points toward acknowledging and accepting fragility rather than attempting to escape it into absolute territories of solitary identity. Figures, self-representation, language do not oppose the self's voice but necessarily situate it. Without mediation through language and representation, there is neither voice nor self.

Therefore, the relation between language and the self is mutually confirming, just as the attempt to transcend this bond proves merely destructive. The self alone, beyond relation, beyond mediation, is finally merely empty. Mediation and representation are not intrusive, external conditions, but the very conditions without which the self does not even exist. As in Schopenhauer, so in Beckett, the effort to know and see ourselves as a "self-existing unity is by no means possible, for as soon as we turn into ourselves to make the attempt, and seek for once to know ourselves fully by means of introspective reflection, we are lost in a bottomless void. . . . And whereas we desire to comprehend ourselves, we find, with a shudder, nothing but a vanishing spectre."[35] Without the multiple figures constantly summoned in the act of self-assertion, there is no self to assert. Beckett's exercises in "introspective reflection," stripping away everything other than self, discover only "a vanishing spectre," and not self at all: "Now I'm haunted, let them go, one by one, let the last desert me and leave me empty, empty and silent" (*T* 5, 98).

Beckett, then, does not fail to attain some true self beyond time, space, and language. His writing instead shows the failure of this notion of the self. In this it reasserts expression and representation as exactly the conditions that make selfhood possible. Beckett confirms that the ideal of an essential self requires a move beyond figures, beyond language, in an effort to evade what the Unnamable calls "the fatal leaning toward expressiveness" (*UNN*, 390). But the drive to expression resists all attempts to defeat it. And the ideal, essential self emerges in Beckett as the product of a specific metaphysical program and definition, determined through a long cultural history, a metaphysic that assumes a realm beyond time, beyond space, beyond physical and multiple conditions, to be the realm of truth.

It is the nature of the essentialist self also to conceive of itself as transhistorical. This is consistent with the transcendence of all circumstances and conditions that it insists upon as its true condition. In Beckett, accordingly, history is glimpsed at most through hints and textual breaks within the accounts his narrators give of themselves: border crossings and frontier escapes, devastated landscapes and ash-filled skies, and what Hugh Kenner calls the "Gestapo theme" of interrogation.[36] All these suggest that Beckett's imaginative space is deeply structured by war. But Beckett's work more obviously conjures histories of culture: of science, of philosophy, of religion. These prove to be the contexts framing the very effort to transcend such contexts. Beckett's texts, that is, portray the desire to transcend contexts as in fact profoundly situated by them. His evasions reflect, as in a strange mirror, a whole tradition of values, ideals, and metaphysical commitments that, as he shows, themselves deeply involve modes of evasion. His texts finally pursue not only the logic of such evasion, but its metaphysical history.

CHAPTER 4

The Negative Way Negated:
Samuel Beckett, Counter-Mystic

> We told ourselves that this was only a quite
> special case of deriving, . . . which had to be
> stripped . . . if we wanted to see the essence of
> deriving. So we stripped those particular cover-
> ings off; but then deriving itself disappeared.
> —In order to find the real artichoke, we divested
> it of its leaves.
> —Wittgenstein, *Philosophical Investigations*

✑

Negative Theological References

Lucky's soliloquy at the center of *Waiting for Godot* dramatizes linguistic failure in ways central to Beckett's work as a
whole: "Given the existence as uttered forth in the public works
of Puncher and Wattmann of a personal God quaquaquaqua with
white beard quaquaquaqua outside time without extension who
from the heights of divine apathia divine athambia divine aphasia
loves us dearly with some exceptions for reasons unknown but time
will tell" (28). This apparent nonsense proves to be an exercise in
scholastic precision. "Apathia" and "athambia" are technical terms
for the atemporal Being of the Godhead ("outside time without
extension") who cannot, in classical theology, endure direct contact
with the world of time. But Lucky ties the divine as imperturbable
and impassible to aphasia, a linguistic breakdown that serves him
as both method and theme. No mere Fool, however, in this he acts
as spokesman for the central ontological tradition of the West, with
its implications for linguistic breakdown.

Here as elsewhere in Beckett, theological play is technically expert and premeditated. Beckett's texts generally evoke theological writing. In style and wording, in stance and subject, in specific allusion and general reference, Beckett's language repeatedly recalls the discourse of theology. Theology in turn provides one of Beckett's most pervasive sources of allusion. But his work's theological interest is not merely arcane. It fundamentally situates the negativity that, above all, seems Beckett's outstanding feature, even to the point of making his work seem one of linguistic nihilism. Beckett's negative practices are generally thought to extend beyond the world that language describes to a repudiation of language altogether. What Beckett offers, however, is an anatomy of the place of language within metaphysical and theological tradition. As he shows, language holds in this tradition a self-contradictory status and value. Beckett's becomes in this sense a work of exposure. It investigates the place and above all the axiology of language as deeply equivocal within a general system of values in which language's equivocal place and function are hidden from exposure.

Theological allusions, such as those pointedly embedded in Lucky's incoherence, pervade Beckett's work. They suggest an erudition difficult to gauge. Some are specific and direct citations of actual disputes or documents, such as Watt's exchange on the train with the editor of a Catholic monthly—a self-professed "neo-John-Thomist"—on the consequences of a "rat or other small creature eat[ing] of a consecrated wafer." ("Does he ingest the real body or does he not? If not, what has become of it? If he does, what is to be done with him.") This discussion, taken from the scholastic laws on eating the body of Christ (*Nomos Corpus Christi Edatur*), joins with Moran's question on the power of the eucharist if "taken on top of beer however light" to effect transubstantiation. And many of Moran's sixteen theological questions are similarly drawn from specific scholastic records.[1] Others restate classic questions: that of Mary's impregnation through the ear (by the angelic word); Moran's question whether devils feel the pains of hell (answer: not physical pain, because they have no body); the question of what God was doing before the creation (answer by Augustine: preparing hell for fools who ask this question); the problem in *The Unnam-able* regarding how hell can be both created and eternal. Still other theological references are too general to specify, such as *Watt's* distinction between "real reason and reason offered to the under-standing"—a concept standard to both theological and mystical thought.[2] Some are devious, as when Beckett names a character in *Watt* Arsenius, who happened to be a fifth-century anchorite re-ported to have said, "I am already dead."[3] And some are red her-rings, the most obtrusive example being the two thieves crucified with Christ. These two are repeatedly conjured from text to text, including *Murphy, Mercier et Camier, Malone Dies*—remarkably as two crucifixion earrings with a carved tooth of Christ between them (the strangest image ever of the Logos)—and of course *Godot.*

This persistent theological pressure never quite situates Beckett's work in a stable theological framework or even as a systematic criti-cal enterprise. Allusions resist consistent extrapolation; indeed, they often even resist being securely established as allusions. Regarding the two thieves, for example, Harold Hobson reports Beckett as quoting a phrase from Augustine—one "even more beautiful in the Latin": "Do not despair. One of the thieves was saved. Do not pre-sume. One of the thieves was damned." But, as Hugh Kenner con-cedes, this source of so much Beckett imagery cannot be traced.[4] A work devoted to despair and hope in Augustine does not contain it, nor does *Augustinus Lexikon*, the comprehensive concordance of Augustine now under compilation.[5] Yet this concordance does cite many Augustinian texts that balance despair against presumption, and the thieves are an Augustinian point of interest. Beckett him-self, in a letter to this writer, confessed only to having read *The Confessions*, yet *Godot* makes clear reference to Augustine's *Har-mony of the Gospels*.[6] And Augustine's treatise *On the Gospel of John* comes very close—but short of full allusive exactness—to Beckett's famous "citation": "From both, then, men are in dan-ger; both from hoping and despairing. . . . He who says, God is good . . . let me do as I please: these men are in danger of hope. And those are in danger from despair . . . [who] do say to themselves 'we are already destined to be damned, why not do as we please?' Despair kills these; hope, those" (Tractate 33.8).[7]

The quotation, therefore, while untraceable, also cannot simply be dismissed as Beckett's invention. It can serve as an emblem for the impossibility of tracing and systematizing Beckett's theological allusions, which is in turn part of the general pattern in his work of allusions that remain mixed and disparate, eclectic and confounding. Beckett does not so much work within or out of theological tradition as reflect back upon it—as Hamm in *Endgame* puts it, "The old questions, the old answers, there's nothing like them" (38). Yet the particular strategy of theological allusion has immense importance for the problem of language in Beckett's work. This is even more particularly the case with regard to the negative theologies that provide many of Beckett's allusions, not only as specific references but as fundamental to structures, patterns, and impulses in Beckett's entire project. The denials and negations of mystical practices—what John Fletcher calls the "ablation or abnegation of desire"—acquire in Beckett's work a particularly commanding persistence.[8] From the reference in *Dream of Fair to Middling Women* to Pseudo-Dionysius's "circular movement of the mind flowering up and up through darkness" (*DJ*, 45); through *Murphy*'s Nothing (Murphy himself was once a theology student [72]); through *Watt*'s constitutive structure, in which a Mr. Knott serves as the apathic, athambic, absent center around which all other characters revolve; to the very title of *The Unnamable*: the premises and practices of negative theology act as a generative condition of Beckett's books. *The Unnamable* openly parades this impulse: "First I'll say what I'm not," declares the narrator, "that's how they told me to proceed, then what I am" (*UNN*, 326). The way of negation—of passing to true reality by progressive denial and reduction—is here declared the Unnamable's very method. It is, as the Unnamable's name attests, Beckett's method as well, in his venture to deny all names, all utterance, all linguistic representation.

But while Beckett certainly invokes the methods of negative theology, he should not be mistaken for a negative theologian. He does not necessarily use mystical practices to achieve mystical goals. This distinction, however, is not often observed in critical discussion. The earlier novels, *Murphy* and *Watt*, for example, are consistently described as mystical enactments, endorsing quests for negative mystical realities. Thus, Murphy is repeatedly said, in the terms first proposed by Samuel Mintz, to follow "an asceticism" that requires him to "denounce the great world and withdraw into the life of his mind."[9] And indeed *Murphy*, like *Watt*, solicits through its allusive patterns and echoes just such mystical/ascetic reference. In *Murphy* it takes the form of Cartesian mind/body problems, which provide the basis for both plot and protagonist. As the novel puts it, Murphy's "mind was a closed system, subject to no principle of change but its own, self-sufficient and impermeable to the vicissitudes of the body" (109). Or, as Murphy puts it himself: "I am not of the big world, I am of the little world" (178). Throughout the novel, Murphy accordingly endeavors to withdraw from body into mind, and toward the novel's end succeeds in doing so. In emulation of a Mr. Endon—a catatonic whose name means "within" in Greek—Murphy penetrates through body and indeed all form into the state of utter inwardness he has been seeking: "Murphy began to see nothing. . . . His other senses also found themselves at peace, an unexpected pleasure. Not the numb peace of their own suspension, but the positive peace that comes when the somethings give way, or perhaps simply add up, to the Nothing than which in the guffaw of the Abderite naught is more real" (246).

Almost all interpretations of this text accept it as the positive fulfillment of the desirable venture to repudiate the body—a desire attributed not only to Murphy, but to Beckett as well. Starting with Belacqua, a still earlier Beckett character named for Dante's slothful friend, all Beckett heroes, and Beckett himself, are said to long for the "blissful condition" of learning "to exist beyond . . . physical and emotional needs, indifferent to the human body, exiled from the society of man." Again, "in the privileged and relatively rare experience of inner being Beckett finds his utopia, the beatific condition so prized by a succession of fictional surrogates." Murphy recognizes that the world's "aimless bustle distracts him from the attempt to enter this place of rest where, he is certain, the total freedom of the self is to be found." As Samuel Mintz first put it, despite qualifications and ironies "Beckett is committed to Murphy's doctrine." [10]

Even discussions of the novel in Cartesian terms of disembodied consciousness tend to adopt the terms of mystical asceticism. Thus, John Pilling speaks of Murphy's "fall into time" as betraying his "quest for the mystically timeless," while John Fletcher calls Murphy a "mystique raté." [11] Yet *Murphy*, far from being a mystical text, is, I would argue, a counter- and even antimystical one. Leaving aside the fact that throughout the novel the state of inwardness is identified with that of psychotics in an asylum, Murphy does not finally achieve a positive blissful state. [12] He is instead burned to death in an explosion of his gas stove. Nor is this failure simply due to his inability to be mystical enough, his failure "to detach physical from mental forms," his continued subjection to "certain passions which he cannot fully subdue" and which prevent him from "cutting himself off completely from the body," or his inability "to live entirely in his mind." [13] For Murphy in the end does not fail to retreat beyond body into inner mind; he succeeds. But having succeeded, he recoils from his vision in terror and revulsion: "It was his experience that this should be stopped, whenever possible, before the deeper coils were reached. He rose, hastened to the garret, now running, now walking" (252). This is no "peaceful experience of the Nothing." [14] It is instead a violent self-explosion that fulfills his ascetic desires only in gruesome parody.

Murphy does not fail to achieve a state of total inwardness; he rejects it. In arguing that in *Murphy* the inner world represents a distinct and superior realm, however, critics are assuming to be true what the novel seems to be trying to disprove. This assumption of priority for the interior world only asserts the strength of the tradition the novel is calling into question. What the novel does begin to explore, however, is how this tradition of interiority situates language, and in particular makes it problematic. For Murphy's final condition is also one of linguistic failure. Before his physical explosion, Murphy experiences a general dissolution of form. The vision of "accidentless One-and-Only, conveniently called Nothing" (246) is asserted against all formulation, a complete "colourlessness" (246) in which "scraps of bodies, of landscapes, hands, eyes, lines and colors evoking nothing, rose and climbed out of sight before him as though reeled upward off a spool level with his throat. . . . Murphy could not get a picture in his mind of any creature he had met, animal or human" (252). All shapes, images, differentiations, and boundaries dissolve into Murphy's Nothing, emptying him of everything, including speech.

Murphy's breakdown is proleptic of Watt's, for whom a similar interpretive pattern recurs. *Watt* exhibits the same skepticism toward mystical fulfillments that critics, however, similarly resist. Watt, too, is described as pursuing a mystical way toward Mr. Knott, who, as the name suggests, acts as the negative center of the novel's sequence. Watt, like Murphy, is seen as affirming "the desirable state sought in the sanctuary of mind by all Beckett's early protagonists." *Watt* follows a pattern of "service, obedience, renunciation of personal will" suggesting "the ascetic preliminaries to mystic experience." Watt's is a "mystical quest" for "infinity and nothingness," for Knott as a "negative God" requiring the "stripping of self as negative way [in] an essential detachment from things of this world" characteristic of all Beckett's work.[15]

Watt, even more than *Murphy*, makes such mystical reference impossible to miss. Watt's progress through the novel traces an asymptotic approach to the inaccessible Mr. Knott, who is defined in terms that almost tauntingly echo Aristotelian and Neoplatonist formulas. Against "anthropomorphic insolence," Mr. Knott is finally only defined as needing nothing "except, one, not to need, and two, a witness to his not needing" (202–3). Knott in his garden appears through terms pointedly drawn from the *via negativa* of mystical practice, "the longing for longing gone . . . the ways down, the ways up, and free, free at last, for an instant free at last, nothing at last" (201–2), achieving an "ataraxy" (208) that typically conflates pre-Socratic, Stoic, and Christian ascetic terms. This mystical language culminates in Watt's often-cited prayer, frequently claimed as a genuine expression of negative religious devotion: "Of nought. To the source. To the teacher. To the temple. To him I brought. This emptied heart. These emptied hands. This mind ignoring. This body homeless. To love him my little reviled. My little rejected to have him. My little to learn him forget. Abandoned my little to find him" (166).

This so-called "mystic poem" supposedly culminates Watt's "religious pilgrimage" in a "mystic language of madness that has seen the Godhead."[16] The madness of the language, however, is not incidental. This hymn to Knott's nothingness appears in the novel as an outburst of the radical aphasia to which Watt's quest has led him. It is a culminating moment of the linguistic dissolution which concludes the novel. Watt ends in a breakdown no less severe than Murphy's: if not bodily explosion, then linguistic insanity. And, despite differences in emphasis and degree, the linguistic condition of both heroes is strangely similar. Watt's breakdown, as specifically linguistic, clarifies Murphy's, and especially the link between language disorder and the nothingness central to Beckett's fiction as a whole. For it is in pursuit of Mr. Knott's Nothingness that Watt comes to speak (as Sam, the narrator of Watt's narration, recounts) from "back to front," first inverting "the order of the words in the sentence," then "the letters in the word," then "the sentences in the period" (164–66), an aphasia that the apophatic prayer illustrates.

Both novels, then, pursue the nothing to linguistic failure. Watt's "addenda" sum up the pattern as the attempt to "nothingness / in words enclose" (247). It is an attempt with a theological pedigree, which the novel graciously supplies. In a classic restatement of negative definitions of God, for example, Watt mocks the claims of positive analogy: "For the only way one can speak of nothing is to speak of it as though it were something, just as the only way one can speak of God is to speak of him as though he were a man. And as the only way one can speak of man . . . is to speak of him as though he were a termite" (77). All representation is finally a mode of misspeaking; unspeaking alone asserts truth.

Thus homage is paid to "what has so happily been called the unutterable or ineffable, so that any attempt to utter or eff it is doomed to fail" (62). But this makes ultimate expression into failed expression. The only good language is defeated language.

Linguistic Knowing

Mystical quest toward an ultimate nothing proves, in both *Murphy* and *Watt*, antithetical to linguistic representation. In *Murphy*, the issue is presented as specifically ascetic. In *Watt*, the mystical impulse is presented in more epistemological terms. Knott represents precisely what cannot be known, while Watt is in quest of an ultimacy that defies all modes of knowledge.

In such readings, the "ultimate reality beyond rational inquiry" that Knott is said to represent is construed in two guises.[17] Either it is the nihilistic meaninglessness of "an irrational and unrealistic universe," a "Void" signaling that the "correspondence between [man's] cognitive faculties and the nature of the world has broken down," or it is an ultimate, metaphysical, mystical unity, which Watt betrays "by reducing the mystical principle to the level of human comprehension."[18] In either case, however, reason fails. According to Ruby Cohn, "rational knowledge leads only to solipsism, the irrational defeats reason." For Jacqueline Hoefer, "Watt is forced to recognize the inadequacy of his weapons" of logic and empiricism "in the face of Knott's mystery." As Lawrence Harvey sums up, "The need to know destroys utopia."[19]

These two interpretive stances—nullity and unity—are not unrelated. It is Beckett's presumed rejection of a metaphysical ultimacy that grounds the argument for mere nihilism. But in either case language suffers. Mr. Knott—whether as an ultimate but irrational principle that resists discursive reason, or as an ultimate meaningless void—represents nothingness as beyond linguistic formulation. In the case of meaningless void, the result is tautology: an incoherence of existence that finds expression in the incoherence of self-destroying linguistic mimesis, a "language as close to it as possible, inchoate, groping."[20] In the case of an ultimate "mystical" principle beyond subject/object distinctions, the result is paradox: an ultimate meaning beyond articulation can only be expressed through the failure of articulation, a "mystical moment beyond subject/object distinction" that language can't express.[21]

Positivist language is particularly blamed for Watt's failure, because of its excessive commitment to rationalism. But the blame finally extends to language as a whole. Essentially sequential—a time-art, as Lessing calls it in *Laocoon*—language is inherently discursive, mediated through time and structures of differentiation. In this it opposes truth conceived as unity, which is assumed to be both the ultimate object and the source of linguistic meaning. Words accordingly become "a barrier between us and knowledge of ourselves . . . for language is necessarily a language of exile in time until the self is reached." Language is "of the outer world, of time and space"; it therefore can never resolve the problem of "defining the undefinable and naming the unnamable, of pinpointing a timeless, spaceless center" such as is posed by the "essential reality of Mr. Knott." Only "a new language, of timelessness and spacelessness" could do so.[22] But this "timelessness and spacelessness"— whether conceived as transcendent unity or as an ultimate, meaningless irrationality—contradicts the very conditions of language. Accordingly, either absolute unity acts as an ideal signified that the differentiated signifiers of language can never contain, or the lack of such unity deprives linguistic sequence of its object, leaving mere differentiation with no stable signified to ground it.

Beckett's own attitude toward the existence of an ultimate unity is more or less inscrutable. It may be that he believes in such a unity but feels he cannot achieve it. It may be that he rejects such a unity as an unreal philosophical construction. What is more clear is the way he shows the effect of the ideal of unity on linguistic order. In this regard, *Watt* seems much more a parody than an exemplum of linguistic limitation. The problem it poses is less one of a "Being beyond reason" and linguistic reach figured by Knott, than of how such notions of absolute meaning empty language of its ordinary meanings and condemn it to inadequacy.[23] Watt is indeed trying to know "the nature of Mr Knott" while "remain[ing] in particular ignorance" of it (199). In this attempt, Watt's language is parodic, even comic. His speech takes shape as a vaudeville of language, in which phrases themselves are the characters, changing places, miming each other, circling and missing in clownlike fashion. This linguistic vaudeville does not represent a failure to know absolutely; instead it questions the very idea of knowledge as of a unitary, prior signified that by definition must elude language's signifiers and transcend them.

Framing the linguistic problem in epistemological terms ultimately obscures the role of metaphysics in conceptions of both language and knowledge. This is the case not only in *Watt*, but in the traditional arguments concerning knowledge and language that Beckett in the novel evokes and recalls. The very term "Nothing" historically derived from discussions concerning the possibility of knowing ultimate Essences—or rather, the impossibility of doing so. In the tradition of the Nothing, absolute Being as perfect unity can never be grasped by the finite human intellect whose modes of knowing are discursive, partial, and sequential. And yet, these limits of human knowing are themselves derived from the limits of language. It is knowledge as expressed through the sequences of, linguistic process that fails. Describing the ultimate Essence as Nothing at once inscribes and tries to transcend this failure of language to apprehend Essence. But it also reflects a position that is circular, where language defines the possibility of knowing, and yet it is impossible to say what you know.

Language thus emerges as problematic within a structure that is at once epistemological and metaphysical. The notion of ultimate knowledge beyond naming is metaphysical. Two kinds of knowing are in fact assumed: a discursive knowledge inevitably and regretfully mediated through logical sequence, and an intuitive insight able to grasp the wholeness of its object, thus transcending discursive differentiation.[24] But these epistemological kinds in turn reflect prior metaphysical kinds, corresponding to different levels within an ontological structure.[25] Each differing mode of knowledge applies to a different mode of being that serves as its object, as an ontological level with which it correlates. In this hierarchy, the highest mode of knowledge is an instantaneous insight beyond discursiveness; its corresponding object is the highest mode of Being as eternal totality beyond spatiotemporal differentiation. The schema is of course that of Plato, who insisted that knowledge is the apprehension of unchanging Being. The highest knowledge occurs as intuition without dependence upon the changing sensible world that constitutes the lower ontological levels. Space–time differentiation conversely grounds the epistemological limitations of discursive understanding, exactly distinguishing it from the instantaneous intuition of "pure thought."[26]

Within such epistemological discussion, language emerges as an instrument of the discursive, allied with what makes access to absolute knowledge problematic. It is seen as a secondary term ideally to be excluded from a realm of Being that can be known without it. Yet this distinction between language as a merely instrumental way of knowing, as against a realm of Being constituted apart from its linguistic formulation, remains highly questionable. Breaches open within the system's careful alignments, which come to seem strained and even contradictory. Such strains emerge when Hans-Georg Gadamer, for example, discusses Plato's four levels of knowledge as each relies on a different means or medium of representation:

Each of these four means has a tendency to bring a reality of a specific sort to the fore instead of the reality of the thing itself which was supposed to be displayed in word or discussion, intuition or insight. They all have an intrinsic distortion-tendency, so to speak. In the process of bringing something else into presence they would assert themselves as whatever particular thing they are instead of fading out of view. For they all are something besides the thing they are presenting. They all have a reality of their own, a character which differentiates them from that thing. . . . Plato's thesis is this: all these means assert themselves as whatever they are, and in pushing to the fore, as it were, they suppress that which is displayed in them.[27]

Each mode of knowledge desires to grasp "the reality of the thing itself." But each can do so only by means of a representation that is not the "thing itself." Yet only the representation is available. Although the representations are merely meant to bring "something else into presence," they "assert themselves . . . instead of fading out of view." There is an inevitable incursion of the means of presentation themselves—"word or discussion," and even "intuition or insight." Far from offering an ideal transparency through which an ideal object of knowledge can be known, "they suppress that which is displayed in them."

Gadamer still refers to these incursions as "distortion," as though there remained some undistorted thing-in-itself apart from the modes that apprehend it so imperfectly. Yet knowledge of this signified Thing is only possible by way of its representing signifiers. The signifiers are all that we directly possess as the basis for knowledge of the Signified that is, however, claimed to determine them. As one commentator on Plato remarks, "It is extremely difficult to imagine how one can practise, independently of all words or symbols, the direct inspection of realities which Plato asserts to be the best way to attain knowledge."[28] The problem is already recognized in Aristotle's comment that "it is impossible even to think without an image."[29] The ideal Signified, presumably prior to and determining its representations, in fact depends on them to be known in the first place.

Just this recognition of an implicit contradiction between image-making and the Ideal beyond it marks the step into Neoplatonism—and into a specifically negative theology.[30] The Neoplatonic acceptance of Plato at his ambiguous word regarding the One ultimately led, in the quest for absolute Unity, to equivocation regarding its relation to Form. While this questioning of Form may indeed have its roots within Platonic metaphysics, it nevertheless represented a radical development, both with regard to the tradition of Greek rationalism and, perhaps more radically still, as a breach within its metaphysical systemization.[31] "In the tradition of classical Hellenic metaphysic," writes A. Hilary Armstrong, "being is the highest proper object of intelligence, and at least in the late Platonic tradition . . . identical with the highest divine intelligence."[32] The Greek "supreme god" is the intelligence as the "faculty which determines measurement, substituting fixed and mathematically expressible relations for the momentary and vanishing relations presented by sensibles."[33] But this apotheosis of knowledge presupposes that Being, which constitutes its object, is itself definite, knowable, limited, indeed unitary. "To be," writes Etienne Gilson of this tradition, "is to be its own self according to itself"—to be self-identical, eternal, a perpetual present, free from otherness, free from change.[34] And the more a thing in this sense is, the more it is knowable, where self-identity is the proper object of conceptual knowledge. As Armstrong remarks, "Forms are definite (Form can hardly be conceived as formless)."[35]

Yet the Neoplatonists discovered within the ontological doctrine of Unity and its epistemological corollaries the need for a principle denying a knowable Unity. "For a Platonist the world of Being is the world of stable and definite Form; for Plato the main point has been its contrast with the unstable flux of becoming that is the sensible world," writes R. T. Wallis. Accordingly, to assert that the ultimate source of "Form, Measure, and Limit . . . must itself be Formless, Unmeasured and Infinite" is "shocking for traditional Hellenic thinkers."[36] The Neoplatonists were thus led to take a position that contradicted the method and object of knowledge traditional to Greek philosophy. They came to assert an imageless, unmediated apprehension of the ideal, not as knowledge, but as a mystical experience beyond the modes of knowing.

The incompatibility between modes of knowledge and the unity that by definition transcends them becomes central to Neoplatonism. And there the linguistic consequence of this metaphysic emerges in all its contradictory force. For the elevation of the highest principle above all knowledge, above all mediation through image, representation, or sequence, finally repudiates language as well. This paradoxical outcome of the Greek search for simplicity and identity may derive from several sources: Pythagorean mathematization of the Forms, requiring an ultimate unit of measure transcending the things it measures;[37] the dissemination of the Judaic notion of an infinite God, particularly, as H. Wolfson proposes, by way of Philo; or perhaps simply the contradiction between the ideal of Unity and the multiplicity necessarily entailed in the modes of knowing it. As Plato objects in the *Parmenides*, our knowledge is always particular and never ideal.[38]

In any case, the transcendent Unity came to be defined only in negative terms, that is, as beyond all efforts to define it. As absolute unity, beyond space, beyond time, beyond all limitations and boundaries, the One was also beyond all representation, all language. Language, with its sequences, differentiations, and multiplicities, would not only distort the Unity, but fundamentally misrepresent and betray it. For the very claim to represent what can never be represented would be profoundly false, and indeed misleading. As Plotinus remarks, "Who, if he is able to contemplate what is truly real, will deliberately go after the image?" Indeed, because images may draw attention to themselves and away from true reality, they impede the pursuit of truth.[39]

Negative theology deeply reflects and affirms this equivocal status of language. The Neoplatonist One can never be adequately expressed in terms of spatiotemporal reality; therefore, all linguistic limitations and bounds must be regarded as inapplicable to it. Any description is suspect as an intrusion of limits and division, while discourse in general contributes to the unity's fragmentation.[40] The only possible mode of discourse that remains is the negative one of systematic denial, reduction, or negative definition. As Plotinus instructs: "If anyone attributes to [the One] anything at all, be it essence or intelligence or beauty, by that attribution one takes away from Him. Therefore, let us take away everything from Him and let us affirm nothing of Him." The One—"ineffable, unnamable, unable to be grasped by thought" in Plotinus's formulation—cannot be positively described; indeed, doing so detracts from him. Therefore, it is best to speak of the One, if at all, only by way of abstraction, stripping away, removal: "We say what He is not, but what He is we do not say."[41]

Language as Instrument/Language as Trope

Within the tradition of negative theology, the question of metaphysical ultimacy and the problem of knowing it remain central. Language enters the discussion only as a derivative problem, as the medium for a knowledge that can never accommodate the transcendent principle. Beckett in his work generally raises epistemological questions, specifically in *Watt*, but also in his later fictions. There, as Wolfgang Iser has argued, the self-reflexive obsession with writing about writing assaults any notion of a stable object of knowledge outside of the modes of representing it.[42] Yet the issue is not only, or even primarily, epistemological. The question of language remains distinct and (in ways that the tradition will not admit) prior to the question of knowledge that seems to generate it.

This is suggested by Beckett's terming the Nothing the "Unnamable," that which is specifically beyond linguistic formulation. The position of language does not finally derive from categories of knowledge. The reverse is more true. Language provides the crucially defining terms for knowledge itself, which is sequential, partial, dividing, differentiating. What is more, if attention shifts from knowledge of the Nothing to the status of language as such, the very issues at stake alter. The drive beyond language is traditionally situated as a problem of logic. Predication must be denied the One because it renders unity in terms of multiplicity. But language raises questions that are also axiological, and these ultimately control and give force to the negative project.

The problem of predication-as-division is essentially a logical one; but to see division itself as problematic is an axiological judgment. Determining the metaphysical hierarchy is a scale of values that asserts eternity over time and unity over multiplicity, and that excludes the body, externality, and temporality as alien to true, unitary, eternal truth, to which an inward self distinct from spatiotemporal expression alone has access. It is the suspicion of division and difference that in fact impels the whole effort toward unity—an effort "in the first place through and through axiological," as J. N. Findlay remarks, taking place within a metaphysic where "Unity is supremely good because it is the most absolutely restricted of all things, whereas Multitude is bad."[43]

These premises of metaphysical hierarchy have been assumed and asserted from author to author and text to text since at least the time of Plato. Augustine, for example, formulates the Neoplatonist tradition where the search for God is defined as leading from "exteriority to interiority to superiority" in Christian terms, declaring in the *Confessions*: "You were deeper than my inmost understanding and higher than the topmost height I could reach" (*C* 3.6). In *De vera religione* Augustine pursues the complex spatializations in which divine truth and interiority converge: "Do not venture at all outside, return into yourself; in the interior man truth resides." This text is one Meister Eckhart in turn repeatedly cites, making it the basis for his further mystical radicalization of the true self not only as interior, but as existing "neither in time nor in space but in eternity" in unity with God.[44]

The place of language within this metaphysic comes to the fore in a mysticism of negative theology such as Eckhart expressly practiced—although even then the problem is not directly posed or confronted. Language never emerges as an independent topic. But, as Beckett's work clarifies, traditional metaphysical hierarchies relegate language to the external and temporal realm. There it becomes an object of ambivalence, as disguise, distortion, and misrepresentation of inward, unitary, eternal truth. In this configuration, moreover, language not only acts as the medium and instrument of discursive knowledge, it also—and equally—has a figural value. As instrument, it acts as medium of representation. But language itself also represents representation—represents as trope the articulation, differentiation, and embodiment in images that the One transcends and that the mind in knowing and representing it is trying to go beyond. Not only is language a medium essentially sequential and temporal (and thus problematic for a theory of instantaneous, intuitive, undifferentiated knowledge), language itself represents these conditions, acting as figure for them. As sequential, as temporal, as articulation, as embodiment: language reifies the very conditions of existence which adulterate and exclude from Unity, and which it is the goal of the entire metaphysic to transcend.

If the logical problem of predication defines language's status as instrument, the axiological problem of fragmentation implicates language's status as trope. In a sense language remains caught between the two aphasias already confronted by Plato: the Heraclitean aphasia of the *Cratylus*, which denies the possibility of predication because everything is in flux and therefore cannot be formulated; and the Parmenidean aphasia of the *Sophist*, which denies predication as division of the One unchanging Being.[45] Plato himself in the *Sophist* attempts to open some territory for discourse between these two aphasias by insisting that even the realm of becoming has some partial reality.[46] But the Neoplatonists retreated from such temporizing, reiterating the *Parmenides*' logical concern with Unity as unpredicable, and above all, the *Cratylus*'s axiological implications identifying language with sense-perception and becoming, and their differentiations.

This metaphysic, in which the ultimate good is defined as totality, unity, identity, inevitably leaves little place for body, for temporality, for otherness and difference. And it leaves little place for the language that represents these, whether as instrument or as trope. In this axiology, "multiplicity is never a valuable addition to an initial unity, but connotes rather a fragmentation of that unity."[47] Whatever their necessity, multiplicity and differentiation essentially detract. And the goal of the system, both philosophically and religiously, is to return out of multiplicity and fragmentation, out of the definitions of time and space, even out of individuation and selfhood, to strip these away toward Union with the absolute.[48] In such a system, language stands for the life of the body, of space, of time, of division and individuation. It is both the medium and the figure of the difference from unity that must be stripped away, overcome, negated.

But while the metaphysical hierarchies have been more than expressly defined—indeed, they have been insisted upon as the value structure to be honored and obeyed—the position of language within them has been persistently obscured. For it is a self-contradictory one: an instrument that compromises its ends; the mediating structure that lacks validation and indeed invalidates; the posterior effect or accident that is indispensable. It even, in providing the terms for what is "beyond" it, constitutes the basis and prototype of a structure in which it must then negate and repudiate its presence and priority.

The question of linguistic mediation occurs at the border where epistemology and metaphysics meet, posing for both a problem of representation. But this problem raises problems of its own. Knowledge beyond all discursiveness is a questionable project, repudiating the very conditions that define and make knowledge knowable. In light of Beckett's presentation, stripping away all outward forms in the attempt to reach a truer, more essential Unity comes to seem a mode of self-destruction. And language appears not as mere instrument toward an understanding beyond its differentiations. Instead, it constitutes an understanding impossible and nonexistent without language. Doing away with it would then reveal not any ultimate Unity, but nothing at all.

Thus, the tradition according to Beckett is one that seeks to banish language to at best an equivocal status in its pursuit of truth, but in doing so compromises the mode of its own conduct and self-understanding. Inexpressibility is not self-transcending but self-defeating. The express wish is to repudiate discursive reason and language only at the height of ascent, as Plotinus would do; or, in the perhaps Wittgensteinian trope cited in *Watt*, to kick away the ladder of language at its top (44).[49] But through its every presupposition the system undermines the very means for its own accomplishment, repudiating the ladder at its first rung. Yet admitting language to be essential would no less undermine every presupposition and call the entire hierarchy into question.

Linguistic Divestment

If *Watt* raises the problem of language as instrumental within an epistemological framework, *The Unnamable* and the *Texts for Nothing* raise the problem of language as trope within an axiological hierarchy. These texts constantly meditate on linguistic mediation. They make representation their subject, not only with regard to figures of the self in characters and the scenes that frame them, but in terms of language as itself a figure of embodiment. Adopting the premises of interiority, of transcendence, and of unity as posed within mystical theology, Beckett treats them not as problems of knowledge only, as though language had only a secondary and merely instrumental role. *The Unnamable* and the *Texts for Nothing* instead expose this secondariness as primacy. Yet they do so less by contesting language's traditional place than by assiduously pursuing and fulfilling it. The conduct of both *The Unnamable* and the *Texts* is in great part the persistent denunciation of body, character, figure, voice, language, in the name of an interiority and essentiality before and beyond them. But in this it realizes Beckett's own peculiarly parodic genre, in which the relentless fulfillment of this metaphysical/negative project finally defeats itself. For it achieves a reduction that is revealed to be either impossible or empty.

To accomplish this, *The Unnamable* and the *Texts* each practice techniques of apophasis—that is, of linguistic divestment such as negative theology urges. Apophasis declares the need to abolish all form, all figure, ultimately all language. These are inevitably and necessarily inadequate to the ultimate truth, unity, identity—truth as unitary identity—which stands in its essence beyond form and utterance: that is, beyond time, matter, and difference, which linguistic process both articulates and represents. As the Unnamable remarks at the outset, "I shall have to banish them in the end, the beings, things, shapes, sounds and lights with which my haste to speak has encumbered this place. In the frenzy of utterance the concern with truth" (*UNN*, 299–300).

In *The Unnamable*, the negative way of language is both theme and plot. There are endless litanies of negation: "feeling nothing, knowing nothing, capable of nothing, wanting nothing" (*UNN*, 348); "bereft of speech, bereft of thought . . . feel nothing, hear nothing, know nothing, say nothing, are nothing, that would be a blessed place to be" (*UNN*, 374). These inevitably call to mind similar litanies from the Pseudo-Dionysius, Augustine, Basil, John of the Cross—all figures Beckett cites, or at least names he invokes. It is, of course, impossible as always to assign definitive source attributions; and the difficulty of distinguishing between Neoplatonist and Christian apophaticism has good historical reasons. The Unnamable more or less sums up the tradition as a whole, however, when he says, "That was always the way. . . . It's a lot to expect of one creature, it's a lot to ask, that he should first behave as if he were not, then as if he were, before being admitted to that peace where he neither is nor is not, and where the language dies that permits of such expressions" (*UNN*, 334).

The Unnamable invokes here a continuous tradition of linguistic evasion ("that was always the way") reaching through the philosophical development from pre-Christian into Christian tradition. In doing so, he affirms evasion of more than characters or action. Language itself is suspect, as the very realm in which character or action happens. "It all boils down to a question of words, I must not forget this, I have not forgotten it," the Unnamable insists. "I have to speak in a certain way, with warmth, all is possible, first of the creature I am not, as if I were he, and then, as if I were he, of the creature I am" (*UNN*, 335). He claims, in good theological fashion, that his attempt to extricate himself from self-representation is the very means for arriving at a true self. In a mode of repetition that eerily recalls Eliot's "shall I say it again," he affirms as a time-honored procedure ("that's how they taught me to proceed") the progressive negatives that ultimately turn against language altogether:

First I'll say what I'm not, that's how they taught me to proceed, then what I am. . . . I am neither, I needn't say, Murphy, nor Watt, nor Mercier nor—no I can't even bring myself to name them, . . . who I must have tried to be, under duress, or through fear, or to avoid acknowledging me, not the slightest connexion. I never desired, never sought, never suffered, never partook in any of that, never knew what it was to have, things, adversaries, mind, senses.   (*UNN*, 326)

To say what he is not, the Unnamable first denies every representation in characters; then their names, and the very act of naming; then any impulse, affect, or energy toward representation; and finally, with thorough apophatic flourish, all "things" and persons external to himself, and even attributes of himself: "mind" and "senses." This is rather comprehensive. One may ask what is left.

The Metaphysics of Representation

The Cartesian ring of these reductions is something Beckett himself insists on. "Perhaps that's what I am," the Unnamable muses, "the thing that divides the world in two, on the one side the outside, on the other the inside . . . I'm in the middle, . . . I'm the tympanum, on the one hand the mind, on the other the world, I don't belong to either" (*UNN*, 383). Cartesian terms have been made the center of critical discussion since Samuel Mintz's early essay on *Murphy* as "A Cartesian Novel." Hugh Kenner, for example, describes *The Unnamable* as the enactment of a Cartesian epistemological fantasy, rigorously realizing the "two Cartesian functions, movement and thought," until all that remains is "the serene confidence of the lordly Cogito . . . dissociated, in this last phase of the dream of Cartesian man, into a garrulity, vestigially logical."[50] An immense critical effort has been devoted to charting such Cartesian patterns, starting from Beckett's early, explicitly Cartesian poem "Whoroscope." And in general, Beckett is seen as embracing the Cartesian model and terms, but without accepting Cartesian solutions. That is, he is caught in "Cartesian problems but not for Cartesian purposes," an "anti-Cartesian struggling in Cartesian thought patterns."[51] Accordingly, Beckett is said to accept the mind/body split, but without the reintegrations sought by Cartesians; or, Beckett is said to adopt Cartesian doubt, but without using it as the first methodological step back toward certainty.[52] Finally, Beckett is said to reject Descartes's rationalism and its whole notion of the world as apprehensible to the human mind.[53]

And yet the substance of *The Unnamable*'s discourse—a discourse that remains the novel's only event—is concerned less with Cartesian epistemology than with questions of representation and language. What Beckett shows is how Descartes takes his place within a history and a typology of representation. Cartesian epistemology is strangely consistent with metaphysical hierarchies and assumptions antecedent to it, and which, for all its change of interest, it oddly reproduces.[54] These include the primacy of inwardness as opposed to externality; the assertion of ideal, eternal truths to which inwardness provides access and with which it is identified; correspondingly, the distrust of sensation, of temporally and extensively mediated experience, as opposed to inner and innate intuitions of pure reason (the Unnamable wonders whether his belief in the existence of other people is "innate knowledge. . . . Like that of good and evil" [297]).

Beckett's work underscores the way in which this metaphysical/ epistemological hierarchy demotes imagery and imagination. These are decidedly below pure intellect, outside the essence of mind, which can subsist without it. In Descartes, imagination can function positively as an auxiliary of understanding (Rule 14), but it is worse than useless in the effort to understand either true essence or God, because it is a way of thinking that relies on material sensation and thus cannot rise above sensible things. Indeed, in its confusing status between body and mind, imagination is itself in some sense the evil demon that proposes phantasms as real, the very mode that opens the way to radical skepticism.[55]

Beckett integrates the Cartesian presence in his work with the negative project that generally impels it. The Unnamable combines meditations on Cartesian identity with those against outward representation. Epistemological solipsism ("Anything is preferable to the consciousness of third parties and, more generally speaking, of an outer world") goes hand in hand with (ironic) dumbness: "Overcome, that goes without saying, the fatal leaning toward expressiveness. Speak of a world of my own, sometimes referred to as inner, without choking" (UNN, 390).

This retreat into inner Cartesian man proposes the mind/body problem as a problem of representation. And Descartes's suspicion of representation does not originate with him. It continues a Platonist tradition which, as Alexandre Koyre, for example, shows, informs Descartes's physics and mathematics as well.[56] This tradition, as Wesley Trimpi clarifies, is one that devalues representation in general and language in particular. In Plotinus, for example, "the fragmentation of reality which results from the discursive acquisition of knowledge is further intensified when that knowledge is represented in words. . . . What is true of spoken words will be even more true of written words which are their further image and reflection." In the chain of descent here assumed, discursive knowledge is itself a rung down, a concession to the realm of material and temporal embodiment: "Reasoning begins with the descent of the soul into the body." And below it still is imagination and language, imagination as mediated by body and expressed through language's sequences and figures: "Because imagination is inside the body, when it draws its objects out of the undivided center of its life, it expresses them in the medium of division, extension, figure."[57]

Trimpi here traces Neoplatonist descent from Reality to knowledge to language as embodiment; from the signified to signifying body and words. Yet the reverse order may be more true. Language provides the terms not only for embodiment, but through self-negation, for the world "beyond" embodiment as well. This of course is a point Nietzsche repeatedly insists upon. Asserting the inextricable and essential link between reason and language—"we cease to think when we refuse to do so under the constraint of language"—Nietzsche goes on to reduce the categories of reason and its ontology to linguistic modes and constructions:

> The metaphysics of language, in plain talk, the presuppositions of reason. . . . Everywhere "Being" is projected by thought. . . . These categories could not be derived from anything empirical—for everything empirical plainly contradicted them. Whence, then, were they derived?
>
> Indeed, nothing has yet possessed a more naive power of persuasion than the error concerning being, as it has been formulated by the Eleatics, for example. After all, every word we say and every sentence speak in its favor.[58]

De Man, writing on Nietzsche, describes "this entire process of substitution and reversals [of origins and causation] as conceived by Nietzsche as a linguistic one. . . . Language is the medium within which the play of reversals and substitutions . . . takes place."[59] J. Hillis Miller similarly remarks that while "things below are copies, that which is copied can come into language only by way of the transfers of metaphor. In that sense, things above are copies of what is below."[60] Above all, Jacques Derrida pursues the originary place of language and especially of writing for the whole notion of the figural as opposed to literal meaning; of posterior expression as opposed to an essential signified. What these dualisms inscribe is "the difference between worldly, the outside and the inside, ideality and nonideality, universal and nonuniversal, transcendental and empirical," indeed the very "distinction between the sensible and the intelligible with all that it controls, namely, metaphysics in its totality." Derrida calls these orders into question. For language and writing do not in fact reflect these distinctions. They determine them, beginning with the very notion of sign and signified, literal and figurative: "It is not therefore a matter of inverting the literal meaning and the figurative meaning but of determining the 'literal' meaning of writing as metaphoricity itself." [61] The "literal" is exposed as a figure, the founding metaphor for Western dualism.

Language, then, is not a mere instance, but is rather the master trope for the problem of embodiment in time and matter. As master trope, it provides the very terms and structures of the metaphysical system that aspires to transcend it. This is especially evident in mystical elaborations in which the continuity between Christian metaphysics and Platonist and Neoplatonist ontology is also strongly felt. Especially in mystical theology, language provides the terms and tropes for the entire mystical project. The lower ontological levels are defined as linguistic embodiments of higher levels, while the higher realms are also defined, albeit in increasingly negative ways, as "beyond" language. In this negative sense, even the relation to the ultimately transcendent is conducted and defined linguistically. It is as "Unnamable Name" that God is designated in his utter transcendence of all temporality, multiplicity, and exteriority by Pseudo-Dionysius, by Augustine, and by Thomas Aquinas as well, although each to be sure intends this title quite differently. Conversely, it is as language that temporal, spatial, exterior, multiple creation is portrayed. As against the anonymity of the ineffable and transcendent "Unnamable Name," there is the "polynomie," in Pseudo-Dionysius's terminology, of names derived from created effects of the transcendent source. [62]

The degree of radical separation between these divine names derived from the created world as against the ineffable transcendence beyond them marks the difference between mystical and natural theology. The negative, apophatic way differs from the cataphatic, positive way in just this emphasis on opposition and discontinuity between immanence and transcendence, which the "positive" way admits to be in some degree analogous. But the created world of space and time is aligned with language even more directly and literally: God's originary creative act took place through his Word, the Logos, so that creation is, in Vladimir Lossky's terms, a "kind of exteriorised word in which the Father, without saying perfectly what he is, nevertheless allows something of himself to appear."[63] The divine Reality remains, in Augustine's formulation,

> neither utterable in sound nor capable of being thought under the likeness of sound, such as must needs be with the word of any tongue; but which precedes all the signs by which it is signified, and is begotten from the knowledge that continues in the mind when that same knowledge is spoken inwardly according as it really is. . . . For when it is uttered by sound, or by any bodily sign, it is not uttered according as it really is. (*TR* 11.14)

The divine Word is one that can never be fully apprehended by man in its perfect indivisibility. Rather, it can only be "heard" partially and in fragments by man, who himself resides in the plurality and division of the created world (*C* 10.6). Indeed, the "silent Word" is only "audible at all because of its imperfect manifestation into exteriority and its imperfect reception by a created ear."[64]

Within Neoplatonism the poles distinguishing sensible language and the nonsensible truth it would represent became increasingly remote from each other, and the apophatic way becomes ever more strained as it attempts less to negotiate this gap than to emphasize and insist upon it. Damascius, for example, came to feel that even a negative relation remains a relation and therefore compromises the utter transcendence of the One, so that neither affirmative nor negative expressions could be adequate to the ultimate principle.[65] Gilson insists that in the Christian Neoplatonist tradition such extremes tend to be mitigated by a positive identification of God with Being.[66] But the Neoplatonic One is similarly ultimate Being rather than nonbeing—a "hyperessentiality" rather than a "nonessence," as Derrida observes; while the "Being" of God in a writer such as Pseudo-Dionysius can be difficult to distinguish from the Supra-Being of his Neoplatonic antecedents.[67] Thus his *Mystical Theology* concludes: "Nor is It a Spirit, as we understand the term, since It is not Sonship or Fatherhood; . . . nor can the reason attain to It to name it or to know It; nor can any affirmation or negation apply to It" (*MT* 5, 200).[68] But even for so normative a figure as Augustine the Word of God contrasts absolutely with human words. It is not "subject to time and change" but rather is "silent and eternal," and as such is "far far different from these words which sound in time. They are far beneath me; in fact they are not at all, because they die away and are lost. But the Word of my God is above me and endures forever" (*C* 11.6).[69] There is an absolute distinction and indeed mutual negation between the language of utterance and the immutability of God.

The Call to Silence

Beckett's texts, in the status they accord to language, reflect these theological premises and play upon them. In *The Unnamable* and the *Texts for Nothing*, language is a place of exile, from which the self must try to escape to the unity of self-identity. This central task of discourse is also the central topic. As the Unnamable puts it, in a rhetoric with distinct Neoplatonic resonance, there is the "One alone," "feeling nothing, knowing nothing . . . who having nothing human, has nothing else, has nothing, is nothing. . . . Who seems the truest possession because most unchanging" (*UNN*, 346). Only as "unchanging" is this One truly self-possessed. But, as the text continues, "we" remain "outside" this one, exiled in thought and in language: "The one outside of life we always were in the end, all our long vain life long. Who is not spared by the mad need to speak, to think, to know where one is" (*UNN*, 346).

But language represents the world—historically through theological usage, instrumentally as conveying worldly contents, and tropologically as image for the sequences and multiple divisions that above all characterize our human existences in time and space. The retreat from language is therefore no less than a retreat from the world itself. It is an effort to escape from inhabited creation. The darker implications of this logic surface in "Text 11":

And I let them say their say, my words not said by me, me that word, that word they say, but say in vain . . . vile words to make me believe I'm here, and that I have a head, and a voice, a head believing this, then that, then nothing more . . . or headless, a headless voice, but a voice. But I'm not deceived, for the moment I'm not there, not anywhere else what is more, neither as head nor as voice nor as testicle, what a shame.   (T 11, 128)

To say words at all—even the word *me*—is not to say the self: self and saying are antithetical here. All words are "vile words" of existence, "vile words" *as* existence, correlating with head and voice and body, which are all to be negated and denied. Reviling words is but another form of reviling world. The tirade becomes increasingly gnostic as it rejects and denigrates all organs of reproduction (and recall Question Twelve of *Molloy*'s sixteen theological questions: "Is one to approve of the Italian Cobbler Lovat who, having cut off his testicles, crucified himself" [167]).

Here as elsewhere, language and creation are corollary, so that rejecting and denouncing the first is both means and image for rejecting and denouncing the second. Language, on the one hand, clearly aligns with those conditions alien to true selfhood. It is multiple rather than unitary, external rather than interior, other rather than identical. Indeed language partakes in exactly the conditions against which the self must contend, out of which the self must escape, from which the self must distinguish and purify itself in order truly to possess itself. But this is to wish to escape from human existence, from the world as such—a world become antithetical to truth. Thus "Text 2" prescribes, "Better be silent, it's the only method, if you want to end," urging erasure of both creative linguistic act and created, flawed world: "Here at least none of that, no talk of a creator and nothing very definite in the way of creation" (83). "Text 9" similarly urges, "Let there be no more talk of any creature, nor of a world to leave, nor of a world to reach, in order to have done, with worlds, with creatures, with words, misery, misery" (118). And "Text 10" launches into incantatory malediction: "No, no souls, or bodies, or birth, or life, or death, you've got to go on without any of that junk, that's all dead with words, with excess of words," all a "guzzle of lies" (125).

The gnostic rejections of language and world that these *Texts* exhibit recall the fuller demonic mythology of *The Unnamable*.

There the Unnamable claims "the devil . . . showed me everything here, in the dark, and how to speak, and what to say, and a little nature, and a few names" (*UNN*, 405). He moves toward the antinomian wish to "banish from my vile mouth all other utterance, from my mouth spent in vain with vain inventions all other utterance but theirs, the true at last, the last at last" (*UNN*, 308). But to reject language is to reject worldly existence. The impulse finally issues in an apotheosis of apocalyptic destruction, immolating both the world and its words:

> Let them be gone now, them and all the others. . . . There, now there is no one here but me, no one wheels about me, no one comes towards me, no one has ever met anyone before my eyes, these creatures have never been, only I and this black void have ever been. And the sounds? no, all is silent. And the lights, on which I had set such store, must they too go out? Yes, out with them. . . . Ah yes, all lies, God and man, nature and the light of day, the heart's outpouring and the means of understanding, all invented, basely, by me alone, with the help of no one, since there is no one, to put off the hour when I must speak of me. There will be no more about them. (*UNN*, 304)

What is most shocking about this apocalypse of language is the way Beckett's critics have rushed to embrace it. Almost all concur that what Beckett seeks is an ascetic disengagement from temporal reality in the name of an essence beyond it: whether this essence is considered secular, against a reality that is ultimately an existential void; theological, in the name of a transcendence that may nevertheless be unachievable; or violent, as a gnostic repudiation of the material world. Beckett criticism has generally adopted one of these antiworldly positions, resulting in four patterns of interpretation: (1) Beckett's nothing designates a transcendent fullness opposed to the material world from which ascetic withdrawal is urged, making Beckett a kind of Christian mystic; (2) the nothing signifies an ultimate transcendence that cannot be attained despite ascetic withdrawal from the material world, making Beckett a failed Christian or a "mystic manqué"; (3) the material world is utterly repudiated in the name of a transcendent nothing absolutely antithetical to it, making Beckett a gnostic; and (4) at the core of reality, when all appearances have been stripped away, there is only an existential void, making Beckett a secular nihilist.

As to the first option, few critics go so far as to declare Beckett simply a Christian in the face of so much evidence against it (Beckett once said of his religious education that "at the moment of crisis it had no more depth than an old school tie"); yet there are those who do so, as when Helene Baldwin claims in *Samuel Beckett's Real Silence* that "Beckett's stripping of self is a negative way of mysticism to break the bonds of time and place, comparable to T. S. Eliot's still point."[70] More critics adopt the argument for gnosticism, calling Beckett a proponent of "Manichean dualism" that "rejects the creator God"; a "Manichean" along the lines of the Catharist heresy that rejects all procreation; a "gnostic" whose obligation is "to separate light from darkness without any union or compromise between them"; or a "Catharist choosing annihilation."[71] The most common argument presents Beckett as a kind of failed mystic—an "ascetic without beatitude," a "mystic without God," enduring "John of the Cross's dark night but without end."[72] And this shades into the argument for existential nihilism, which sees Beckett's work as a "secular dark night," presenting "Christian man trapped however in the temporal world and unable therefore to attain his true selfhood . . . rejecting the world but also rejecting God," so that he is left "alone bereft of God and world, suffering the unreality of reality."[73]

For all their differences, these various interpretations accept to an astonishing degree the structure of mystical axiology, even when questioning mystical goals or their fulfillment. Moreover, they all assume the negative valuation of language implicit in the mystical value-structure, whereby to attain essence is to be unable to express it. That is, all accept Beckett's silence as a positive ideal. The result is a choral denunciation of language, in which Beckett strives for "an ineffable ultimacy of Being that had necessarily to be betrayed by the concretions of verbal discourse"; his "ideal is to speak and say nothing," to try to "annihilate time and space with their own weapon, language, by freeing the latter from all meaning and context"; to him "language is inadequate to convey the truth of timelessness," for "language betrays true self . . . like all absolute reality. . . . To name is to distort."[74] As Jean-Jacques Mayoux sums up, "All speech is lying. The quest is for immobility, silence, complete reabsorption [into an] interiorized world [that] resembles the universe of the gnostics, where perfection is represented by the unity that precedes the fall into the multiplicity of creation, to be ceaselessly sought again through this multiplicity and through the imperfection of all existence."[75]

All thus assume that language masks true reality, whether as a defilement to be denounced, a delusion to be pierced, or merely a seduction to be resisted, in accordance with the various notions of the essence language at best conceals and at worst betrays. And Beckett does repeatedly appeal to silence as the ultimate and only genuine expression of truth, of self, beyond their linguistic misrepresentation. Silence is invoked as a longed-for relief from the deceptions and travails of the world of utterance. In "Text" after "Text," there is a longing for "the next silence," for the end of "this farrago of silence and words" (*T* 6, 104). Words are denounced as opposing the self that they represent. "I'll speak of me when I speak no more," as the Unnamable puts it (*UNN*, 392); "I've shut my doors against them, perhaps that's how I'll find silence and peace at last" (*UNN*, 390–91).

Silence, then, is for the Unnamable the "only chance . . . of saying something at last that is not false," the only way "to get back to me, back to where I am waiting for me" (*UNN*, 321). Against representation, against language, against world, the Unnamable finally refuses to "utter me, in the same foul breath as my creatures" and will instead be "me alone. Impassive, still, mute" (*UNN*, 300). Muteness is the ultimate expression of self, seeking in the "end" a "true silence," a "real silence," "the one I'll never have to break any more, . . . the one I have tried to earn . . . the real silence at last. . . . That gives me the right to be done with speech, done with listening, done with hearing" (*UNN*, 393). This is the silence which some have praised as the very union with truth beyond speech that mystical transcendence seeks.[76]

Such negative judgment of language, however, finally reiterates a profound and deeply rooted axiological ambivalence regarding the phenomenal world itself—the world figured as created through and represented by language. It is an ambivalence deeply inscribed within the tradition. "In all Platonism, a kind of sliding or fluctuation in the valuation of the material world, and a corresponding variability of feeling about our own embodied presence in it, is always inescapably possible," A. H. Armstrong concedes. "For Pythagoreans and Platonists there is much evil in this lower material cosmos which we are compelled to occupy in this life, and a very strong sense of alienation from it is possible."[77] This ambivalence need not necessarily lead to the extremes of gnostic dualism, utterly condemning the material world. Christian Neoplatonism certainly resists such extreme dualism; instead of seeing the material world as evil, it defines evil as privation or negation of existence. And yet, there is a range of dualistic positions, in which gnosticism represents a most extreme pole. Orthodox systems, while resisting this extreme rejection of the world, yet remain highly ambivalent regarding the world's positive value. E. R. Dodds even goes so far as to consider Saint Paul's Devil "who rules this world" and Saint John's "the whole world lieth in evil" as essentially gnostic.[78] In any case, any system that elevates unchanging unity ultimately judges multiplicity, individuation, and differentiation as problematic. Even if these are not seen as independent "evil forces within this lower world of space-time separation," the very conditions of that separation are considered to be fundamentally compromised.[79]

Beckett's texts are in many senses harsh in their judgment of this world. He makes suffering, emptiness, deterioration, inability, and failure his peculiar subjects. His works, as he explains in one interview,

deal with distress. . . . At a party an English intellectual asked me why I write always about distress. As if it were perverse to do so! . . . I left the party as soon as possible and got into a taxi. On the glass partition between me and the driver were three signs: one asked for help for the blind, another help for orphans, and the third for relief for the war refugees. One does not have to look for distress. It is screaming at you even in the taxis of London.[80]

In the *Texts*, the quintessential human product, besides language, is tears: "Stop talking and get on with your weeping," "Text 6" enjoins, to tell "a little story, with living creatures coming and going on a habitable earth crammed with the dead" (105). Beckett's bums, tramps, and amputees, his dispossessed of belongings, of body, of sanity, of love, give his compassion shape in character.

But Beckett's stance toward the suffering of this world is not that of traditional theodicy. His work disturbingly questions traditional assurances of divine justice and mercy. The courtroom fantasy in "Text 5" reduces the relation between these central attributes of the divine to (almost) comic paradox: "Perhaps I'll appear before the council, before the justice of him who is all love, unforgiving and justly so, but subject to strange indulgences" (97). "Text 8" acknowledges the force of justice, but sees its punishments as far exceeding any possible cause: "If I'm guilty let me be forgiven and graciously authorized to expiate. But whom can I have offended so grievously, to be punished in this inexplicable way" (113). In interview after interview, Beckett insists, "I can't see any trace of any system anywhere"; "It is not a mess you can make sense of." Even the two thieves, who keep popping up like a vaudeville team, in Beckett represent not an image of the larger good as balanced against a particular evil, but how redemption of one does not answer for damnation of the other: "One saved and the other damned. How can we make sense of this division?"[81]

But granted the indictments of earthly conditions and human suffering ("'It must be dead.' 'No more weeping,'" he writes in *Godot*), can we then say of Beckett, as he says of Watt, "If there were two things that Watt loathed, one was the earth, and the other was the sky" (36)? Beckett I think does not reject the world, although he does reject explanations that try to justify its suffering. He rejects traditional theodicies that try to offer solutions for this world of passing away and of passion in terms of an Other World of transcendent unity. He rejects transcendent solutions to immanent problems, rejects a totality of Being removed from the transient world and above it as its source of value and compensation. For Beckett, as far as I can see, suffering defies justification. And while there may be, nonetheless, ways for living in a world in which so much suffering remains inexplicable, these will not point beyond the world to some other realm as redemptive.

The other world is figured, both in tradition and in Beckett, by silence. But Beckett insists on the present world of language as the framework for either hope or despair. His ongoing stream of words contests rather than culminates in silence. Words do align with the world's traumas: as "Text 8" puts it, "It's an unbroken flow of words and tears . . . . I confuse them, words and tears, my words are my tears, my eyes my mouth" (111). Words, like tears, are the stuff of this world. But the call to silence does not resolve the theodicean problem, what "Text 8" calls "a new question, the most ancient of all, were things always so" (111).

If silence does promise an end to this flow and this confusion, it does so neither as ideal release nor as redemptive accomplishment. The release it offers proves instead to be a kind of defeat. The narrators may dream of reduction as an avenue to true self-knowledge: "As if to grow less could help. . . . Hoping to wear out a voice. . . . Or the breath fail better still, I'll be silence, I'll know I'm silence." But in the end this abolishes the very conditions of knowing: "No, in the silence you can't know, I'll never know anything" (T 8, 112). As to silence's promise of true being—"Watch out for the right moment, then not another word, is that the only way to have being and habitat?"—every effort to achieve it fails: "But I am silent, it sometimes happens, no, never, not one second."

Far from representing ecstatic transfiguration, silence in Beckett is a final descent, a "black silence" leaving the self "helpless to move or accept this voice as mine" (T 8, 113). It is a repudiation of the world. Language, conversely, may provide no final answer, but represents ongoing life—in protest, in hope, in despair, in tenacity.

Pro-nomination

Silence and nothingness evoke in Beckett a transcendence that, even if it could be accomplished, would fail to redeem the human world of time and change. Beckett's negative language is in one sense traditional. He shows how the absolute of transcendence be-

comes radicalized into nothingness, as occurs within negative theology. But his use of negative designation does not then convert
paradoxically into an ultimate Reality that measures the world
where human beings reside and suffer. Indeed, he casts doubt on
claims to such conversion. His texts exhibit how the more radical
the mysticism, the more negative its terms, the more the transcendence it seeks as goal and redemption of temporal life is removed
from and antithetical to that life. Instead of providing positive terms
for interpreting, structuring, or evaluating the human world, it becomes a ground for condemning it.

As to language, Beckett's texts exhibit not the negation of utterance, but rather the consequences of devaluing language in the
name of what would supposedly surpass it. In Beckett, the effort to
strip away all external form to achieve an inward, unitary essence
beyond it ultimately takes place as a double impossibility: the impossibility of accomplishing it, and the emptiness of attempting to
do so. It is impossible to accomplish not only because within the
very act of utterance—even an utterance that attempts to be self-
escaping and self-effacing—there is an inescapable multiplicity that
compromises the unitary, ineffable essence. This is an objection
that negative theology would no less insist upon, and is one basis
of that tradition's hostility to language. Rather, it is impossible because outside of such multiplicity there is in fact no essence at all.

Beckett, quite properly, makes this point above all within his
own play of words. "In the beginning was the pun" (65) is *Murphy's* substitution for Logos. *The Unnamable* and the *Texts for
Nothing* unfold in tortuous but also teasing, masterful, multilay-
ered wordplay. Essentialist words especially, instead of providing
stable, fixed reference, dissolve into self-undoing puns. In "Text
12," the "other" as true and absolute self leads only to equivocal
theological juggling as an "other without number or person whose
abandoned being we haunt, nothing. There's a pretty three in one,
and what a one, what a no one" (134). "Nothing" and "no one"
are here closer to pun than to paradox. They may represent an
absolute existence, but they may not. The text makes it impossible
to tell, except to the degree that these very terms remain transfixed

by a language from which they can never withdraw, and which supplies the only experience of them we have.

Pronouns especially prove unstable and tenacious. In the Unnamable's very act of unnaming himself, the words he uses to do so give him linguistic body, and impel him ever back into the persons and the discourse he would forsake. The Unnamable may insist: "I've always been here, here there was never anyone but me"; but the chant of "never, always, me, no one" serves to displace one into the other in a never-ending pronominal series. He may wish to say "I never spoke," but instead says, "I seem to speak, that's because he says I as if he were I" (*UNN*, 403). That is, his efforts to extricate himself from words into pure unity inevitably involve ever more words, with ever more intricate multiplicities. The pathway out of words proves never ending, ever reproducing, a process that "drags on by itself, from word to word, a labouring whirl," but in which the self, in its desire to withdraw, only becomes more involved: "You are in it somewhere. . . . It's I, here it's I, speak to me of him, let me speak of him" (*UNN*, 402).

Him, I, me, no one, anyone: in such texts, pronouns acquire a peculiar stature. They assert the very grammar of selfhood, the self as inherently and integrally grammatical. And they show how, whatever the desire for unity, the language needed to conduct it ever refracts into multiplicity, into pronominal splittings no unitary "I" can contain. The self exists not as absolute, inward essence, but as multiple, sequential linguistic event. "Text 4" may ask, "Who says this, saying it's me" (91) as though the "me" and its voice were distinct. The whole "Text" tells the struggle of the "me" to disengage from "him" in order to establish its own originary and absolute unity. But the "me" in its struggle constantly generates the "him," "the same old stranger as ever, for whom alone accusative I exist, in the pit of my inexistence, of his, of ours." To exist is at once a state of grammar and of questioning, "accusative"; indeed, even inexistence becomes intra- and interpersonal, at once "m[ine]," "his," and "ours." And delving into the self leads into ever more intricate wordplay, twisting parts of speech and levels of sense: "He has me say things saying it's not me, there's profundity for you, he has me who say nothing say it's not me" (*T* 4, 92). The meanings of *me*, *him*, and *nothing* become exceedingly difficult to parse. Does "me" say "nothing" as its true self-expression? Or is to say "nothing" the same as to say "not me," an occlusion of identity? And is "nothing" an empty place-holding pronoun, a silence that speech betrays into the "not me"? Or is it "not me" to say nothing?

In this equivocal grammar, the pronouns do not reproduce identities, but instead disperse toward a reformulation of identity's claims: "That should have been enough for him, to have found me absent, but it's not, he wants me there, with a form and a world, like him, in spite of him, me who am everything, like him who is nothing. And when he feels me void of existence it's of his he would have me void, and vice versa" (*T* 4, 91). The text here hovers between paradox and tautology: The "he," in an oxymoron, has "found me absent." This absence he rejects, insisting the "me" give "form and world," paradoxically, to "his" nothing. But this "everything" still remains "void of existence," as "he" does.

The quest of the "I" for simplicity founders in a multiplicity of address and of tense. Saying "answer simply, someone answer simply" (*T* 4, 91), "I" institutes, in the act of asking, a doubleness of person and of time. Beckett's sentences seem to follow no more than this path of conjugation and declension: "All mingles, time and tenses, at first I only had been here, now I'm here still, soon I won't be here yet" (*T* 1, 78); "I'll speak now of the future, I'll speak in the future. . . . We were, there we are past and gone again" (*T* 3, 87–88); "I'm alone, that's where I am, where I was then, where I've always been—it's from them I spoke to myself." (*T* 11, 130). "I" is, after all, a form figuratively inflected through past, present, and future, a grammatical tense.

Beckett characteristically treats his *I*s and *me*s not as shifters or indexicals but as objects in structures that always already imply self-multiplication. In a sense, his pronouns are nonreferential, underscoring their grammatical function rather than pointing beyond themselves as though to some fixed, extralinguistic identity. This intransitive play emerges as one reason for his writing in French: "pour faire remarquer moi," to point at the "me."[82] Just so, when

"Text 7" asks, "Did I try everything before reporting me missing and giving up?" (107) "I" splits from "me" in grammatical play between subject and object. "It's they murmur my name, speak to me of me, speak of a me" (*T* 5, 98) makes it impossible to extricate a "me" from "they" who speak, while "me" exactly is an object in syntax. The desire to evade the "other" becomes its internalization as "that other who is me . . . because of whom I'm here . . . it's as him I must disguise myself" (*T* 8, 113). The very act of separating the "me" from its speech turns back against itself, so that self-denial becomes self-assertion, as the "me" becomes a "who" against itself: "Who's this speaking in me, and who's this disowning me" (*T* 12, 134).

Beckett seems to be examining pronouns rather than merely employing them. He probes how they, like other words, mean only within a web of syntax that the self can never finally evade. The "I" would resist all pronominal representation, existing in a supralinguistic solitude. "It's I who am doing this to me, I who am talking to me about me," he will say. But at once "there's someone there, someone talking to you, about you, about him, then a second, then a third . . . these figures just to give you an idea, talking to you, about you, about them" (*UNN*, 394). On the one hand, "me" insists that it is indeed only "me" who is talking, who is; on the other, this "me" at once multiplies, becomes his own audience—"talking to me about me"—and then another's: "someone talking to you." The self is none other than this multiplication, none other than this procession of figures, both as numbers—a "second" and "third"— and as multiple persons: I, me, you, someone, him, them. And the more "he" attempts not to be implicated by his figures, the more "he" cannot but keep producing them.

In Beckett, the attempt to achieve an essence beyond words constantly founders, for the effort must necessarily be conducted with words. The effect is to reverse the traditional role of this defeat as showing the inevitable failure of language. Instead, it is the supralinguistic essence that fails. Each time the speaker embarks toward his solitary "me," he inevitably finds himself accompanied. The road to the self proves impossible to chart except by detour. No quintessential self seems even to exist except by way of the multi-plication of figures. Such seems the consequence of the Unnamable's interminable efforts to distinguish himself from all others. As *The Unnamable* sums up, "Someone says you, it's the fault of the pro-nouns" (*UNN*, 404).

Texts Against Nothing

The *Texts for Nothing* concede—indeed insist—that language immediately plunges the self into multiplicity and exteriority. But the *Texts* no less question whether this need "compromise" the self—indeed, whether outside of this linguistic multiplicity there is any self at all. Beckett's texts offer not the performance of asceticism but its display; not the effort to attain to essence beyond all human conditions but the anatomy and exposure of this very notion. *Nothing* and *no one* remain terms designating true selfhood and essential truth. But in Beckett's texts, such truth becomes suspect—not only as nonexistent, but as commanding a dubious structure of value. Within Beckett's linguistic experiments, the structure itself is re-vealed as wanting.

The attempt at reduction to the pure "I" proves to be both self-contradictory and self-defeating, in the most literal sense. Having divested the self of everything, every figment, every figure and voice, one finds no center, no unity; instead, one is left with nothing at all, no self at all. For beyond these pronouns, characters, names, there is no self. If the I resists this multiplicity, the I itself disappears. One is left then not with nothing as truth, but with truly nothing.

But it is a nothing at which Beckett's selves anyway never arrive. However much the I twists and turns, insisting that all figures of speech are falsehoods, it is always to a grammatical selfhood, with its pronouns and cases, that the I returns. The self that in the end emerges is not beyond linguistic body, but exists exactly and only within it. The dance of pronouns within which this self is inextri-cably caught in fact *is* the self, is all the self that is. The self is in Beckett ineradicably linguistic, "in words, made of words, others' words. . . . I'm all these words, . . . I am they, all of them, noth-ing else."

And yet, the Unnamable also equivocates: "Yes, something else, . . . a quite different thing, a wordless thing in an empty place, where nothing stirs, nothing speaks" (*UNN*, 386). In Beckett the language of the self never loses its ambivalence. On the one hand, this formulated, linguistic existence is all the existence there is. On the other hand, such formulated existence may itself be nothing as well. Words themselves are then denounced as empty gestures: "As if there were two things, some other thing besides this thing, what is it, this unnamable thing that I name and name and never wear out, and I call that words" (*T* 6, 104).

Within this ambivalence, however, certain options are clear. There is language and world; or there is silence and nothingness. Nihilistic self-erasure does at times seem to be exactly what "I" wants: "I am alone, I alone am, this time it's I must go" (*T* 3, 86). The desire may be to dismiss "their lies" so as to "be myself at last" (*UNN*, 225); but the self thus achieved strangely resembles a void: "Only I and this black void have ever been. . . . All is silent. . . . Nothing then but me—of which I know nothing" (*UNN*, 304). The result then is uncreation, apocalyptic negation, the "end of dream, of being past, passing and to be, end of lie. Is it possible, is that the possible thing at last, the extinction of this black nothing and its impossible shades, the end of the farce of making and the silencing of silence" (*T* 13, 139). The future and the past become nothing but lies. Language is no more than a "farce of making" that the narrator would have end. But the end of language here is not transcendence. It is utter annihilation of both word and world.

Speaking of *The Unnamable*, Beckett remarked that in it "there's complete disintegration. No 'I,' no 'have,' no 'being.' No nominative, no accusative, no verb. There's no way to go on."[83] The degree of disintegration is exactly the degree to which Beckett's nominative, accusative, and verb fail. In losing hold of these, the text does not gain a unity before and beyond these syntactic differentiations, an identity outside the modes of declaring it. The call for "no more denials . . . no more phrases" and the concession to be "dupes of time and tense" only "until it's done and the voices cease, it's only voices, only lies" (*T* 3, 85) lead ultimately not to the discovery of self beyond evasion, but to the evasion of self. The way of dispossession, of retraction, believing that "to grow less would help, ever less and less," in the end brings him to a silence not of plenum but of nought: "I'll be silence, I'll know I'm silence, no, in the silence you can't know, I'll never know anything" (*T* 8, 112). As "Text 8" concisely puts it, "Every day a little purer, a little deader" (*T* 8, 113).

In Beckett, the reduction toward essence issues in nothingness, as it does in mystical tradition. But Beckett displays how this nothing as pure essence finally implies the nothingness of all that it excludes: time, space, matter, world. This devaluation lurks, however, within the general structure of value asserted by traditional Western metaphysics, which negative theology radicalizes. "It has always spoken, it will always speak, of things that don't exist, or only exist elsewhere, if you like, if you must, if that may be called existing," "Text 13" remarks, but adds, "Unfortunately it is not a question of elsewhere, but of here" (138). Beckett's texts, more than they endorse this value structure, reflect and make visible its contradictions. "Yes, I have lost him and he has lost me, lost from view, lost from hearing that's what I wanted, is it possible, that I wanted that, wanted this?" "Text 11" asks. But it is a question Beckett's work poses to the whole structure of Western axiology.

In pursuing such paths of negation, of denial, of disintegration, Beckett arrives at nothing not as fullness, but as void; at silence not as plenum beyond language, but as linguistic failure; at unnaming not as ultimate name, but as a namelessness that represents nothing. In this he fulfills the negative model of mystical divestment only ironically, taking the sought-after nothingness at its literal word. But the nihilism that may then result is less a goal than a consequence of Beckett's project. Nihilism in Beckett recalls, I think, a Nietzschean nihilism. That is, it must be placed as a particular response to the failure of a particular structure of values:

Nihilism will have to be reached first when we have sought a "meaning" in all events that is not there. . . . Nihilism is reached, secondly, when one has posited a totality, a systematization, indeed any organization in all events and underneath all events. . . . But behold, there is no such universal! Nihilism has yet a third and last form. Given these two insights . . . an escape remains: to pass sentence on this whole world of becoming as a deception and to invent a world beyond it, a true world. But as soon as man finds out how that world is fabricated solely out of psychological needs, the last form of nihilism comes into being. It includes disbelief in any metaphysical world and forbids any belief in a true world. Briefly: the categories . . . which we used to project some value into the world—we pull out again, so the world looks valueless.[84]

As in Nietzsche, in Beckett the "meaning" posited as "totality," "systematization," a "universal" "is not there." Such metaphysical notions serve only in the end to empty this world and condemn it—"to pass sentence on this whole world of becoming as a deception and to invent a world beyond it" as "a true world." In Beckett, metaphysical notions of the self as essential, inward unity promise to be emblems of an ideal world above this world of space and time. But as in Nietzsche, Beckett's work assaults such metaphysical notions, the absence of which comes to look like absence simply. Yet Nietzsche first identifies nihilism not with the denial of metaphysical categories, but with their invention. Nihilism in this has two stages: first as the false investment of value in a "totality," a "universal" that leads to devaluation and reduction of meaning in this present world; and then as the recognition of its falsehood, withdrawing the categories "which we used to project some value into the world . . . so that the world looks valueless."

Beckett's work realizes not only the second element in Nietzschean nihilism—the denial of metaphysical values—but, even more so, the first. That is, Beckett's work shows how the traditional ideal of metaphysical truth and being is itself nihilistic. There is a rejection of metaphysical claim such as Nietzsche announces in the death of God, meaning, as Martin Heidegger comments, "that the supra-sensible world is without effective force."[85] One might say, however, that in Beckett God does not "die" so much as lose his job. A particular metaphysical conception of God has become obsolete, unviable, no longer functioning to endow life with meaning and purpose. It has ceased to be divine.

What Beckett shows is how accepting the traditional metaphysical ideal can mean devaluing this world, reducing it to nothing in relation to a Reality that remains not only beyond but fundamentally opposed to it. Beckett does this by adopting modes from the traditions of negative theology, as one of the most radical efforts to attain essence through the negation of all that is nonessence, all that is merely temporal, spatial, accidental. But in Beckett's work the negativity of negative mysticism is shown to be at the expense of the temporal-material world. As Marius Victorinus—whose translations of Plotinus Augustine read—comments, "Whereas negative theology speaks of the One as non-existent, in reality . . . it is the One that is the only true Existent and other things (including ourselves) are nothing in relation thereto."[86]

Negation is in Beckett a genuine impulse. But silence then announces linguistic self-annulment, and not fulfillment. In one sense, Beckett's work indeed seems no more than a linguistic antinomianism, a multiplication of language that asserts a wordless nothing to which Beckett gives no other name. Yet alongside such denunciations, there is in Beckett a no less profound distrust of negation, a dissatisfaction with finalities, an undoing of silence. If the narrator enjoins himself, "Better be silent, it's the only method, if you want to end," such ending is not goal but failure, an "end rent with stifled imprecations, burst with speechlessness" (*T* 2, 83). The cessation of words, "the words too, slow, slow, the subject dies before it comes to the verb, words are stopping too," is not positive achievement, but comic concession: "Better off then when life was babble? that's it, the bright side" (*T* 2, 82). And against it the self, accepting its selfhood as linguistic, can also declare, "To hell with silence, I'll say what I am, so as not to have been born for nothing" (*UNN*, 325–26).

Beckett's own language of self-negation finally fails to silence itself, and in so doing proves fecund. The movement into silence constantly impels the texts into further utterance. The evasions of figure prove self-evasive, the divestments of apophasis, self-canceling. Beckett's work, in denying self-denial and negating negativity, finally reemerges toward affirmation: first in the language it itself generates, and not only as concession but as positive realization. Its gestures toward reduction inevitably give way to reproductive and inventive energy. Beckett's texts arrive at a sense that silence not only cannot be accomplished, but that silence is not an accomplishment. This above all is affirmed at his moments of ending. The *Texts for Nothing*, even as they announce the end of language, speak on. *The Unnamable*, even as it seeks an "I in the silence where I am," retracts toward an "I" that goes on in language: "I don't know, in the silence you don't know, you must go on, I can't go on, I'll go on" (*UNN*, 414). Even the extreme negation of "Text 13" finally transforms into a generative power that cannot be denied. Its dream of "last images" brings forth out of the very substance of its words energies that make of its endings beginnings, its denials assertions: "And were the voice to cease quite at last, . . . it can't speak, it can't cease. . . . Born of the impossible voice the unmakable being, and a gleam of light, still all would be silent and empty and dark, as now, as soon now, when all will be ended, all said, it says, it murmurs" (*T* 13, 140). In an epitome of ambivalent language, the structure of the "Text" is contradictory. But in it, negation generates strangely positive movement. The voice that "can't speak" also "can't cease." And if the "impossible voice" gives birth to "unmakable being," then a possible voice murmuring on may yet make further worlds.

This is a defiant creation from nothing despite itself. What is more, it takes place in a language whose rhetorical accomplishment is not only stunning but self-insisting. The tropes and patterns, far from being transparent and self-effacing, obtrude into attention, demand analysis, and assert their own inventive power. Yet neither is Beckett's language an end in itself, self-reflexive in an autonomous linguistic world cut off from all representation. On the contrary, Beckett accepts language as a trope for the temporality, multiplicity, and exteriority with which it has been identified and for which it has been denigrated. The word remains the instrument and image of the created world. It is in this wider sense, as representing our world in all its immanence and actuality, that the positive force of language in Beckett is fully felt: as the medium of creativity, of imagination, an accessible, immanent, generative power. Beckett's use of negative tradition is finally ironic, presenting its paradoxically plethoric nothingness as in fact a void. His own negative modes, in contrast, convert nothingness into a fertile source of continuous imaginative effort. Figuration turned against itself ever turns back toward itself, so that in the end, what emerges is not the negation of figures but their affirmation, as inescapable in a positive necessity. What Beckett finally offers, then, is a defense of language as the medium in which, against and through all negation, we go on.

CHAPTER 5

Broken Wor(l)ds:
Aesthetics and History in Paul Celan

> All efforts to render politics aesthetic culminate
> in one thing: war.
> —Walter Benjamin

～

Broken Wor(l)ds

Paul Celan is an example. Critics of culture typically cite him as an extreme instance of an age in which art is hermetic, self-referential, and enclosed in its own language. Thus, Theodor Adorno calls Celan the foremost representative of a poetry intent on "the sealing of the artwork against empirical reality."[1] To George Steiner, he epitomizes the "deepening privacy," "hermeticism," and "autism" of a poetry in which "language is focused on language as in a circle of mirrors."[2] Michael Hamburger alludes to him as the most extreme of the postwar extremist artists (adding that "all art informed by an intense awareness is extremist in our time"), and commends him for a "reticence that leaves the unspeakable unspoken."[3] All agree that Celan's is a poetry in a closed circle, withdrawn into itself, whose obscurity so challenges interpretation as to border on silence as much as on utterance. In this, it seems to fulfill the tendencies foretold by José Ortega y Gasset of an art that presents "only the pure artistic elements"[4] and of the whole project announced by Mallarmé of making the world into a book—what Celan calls "thinking through the consequences of Mallarmé to their end" (*GW* 3: 194).

In his 1961 Meridian speech accepting the Georg Büchner Prize in literature, Celan places his work as part of a modern "calling-into-question of art" (*GW* 3: 193). His is an art that "balances itself on the edge of itself" in its "profound tendency towards silence" (*GW* 3: 197). But he does so in ways that no less reject an autonomous art. The linguistic circle drawn around Celan's work is, as it were, permeable at every point. It acts, to use Celan's own geographic image, as a meridian: "something—like language—immaterial yet earthly, terrestrial, something circular, crossing the two poles back into itself and thus—cheerfully—even crossing over the tropics / tropes" (*GW* 3: 202). If Celan's poems offer a language world, they do so only across wider territories—social, religious, and not least, historical.

How to read history within Celan's texts, the relation between history and lyric, remains, however, a central and pressing interpretive challenge. That Celan's language in some sense registers historical forces is impossible to avoid, given his biography. Born Paul Anschel in 1920 in Czernovitz, then a part of Rumania, Celan endured first the Soviets' occupation following the Hitler-Stalin pact in 1940, and then Hitler's. In 1941, the Soviet army withdrew, but Celan's family chose not to retreat with the Russians. Instead, along with other Jewish but German-speaking families, they identified with German culture and preferred to remain and welcome the advancing Nazi occupational force.[5] Falling into the hands of the Nazis, in the autumn of 1942 Celan's parents were shot after transport to Transnistria. Celan himself survived the war doing forced labor in Rumania.

Nevertheless, treatments of Celan's work tend to remain contained within boundaries that his poetic directly challenges. On the one hand, he has an acknowledged place in discussions of Holocaust literature. On the other, his texts are treated as autonomous structures in which extratextual concerns consistently disappear into aesthetic ones. They are then viewed, as James K. Lyon sums up, "from the vantage point of structure, linguistics, symbolism, philosophy, and occasionally ideology."[6] Accordingly, Celan's work has characteristically been approached through literary theory, as in Henriette Beese's *Nachdichtung als Erinnerung* and Winfried Menninghaus's *Paul Celan: Magie der Form*; through philosophical categories, as in Hans-Georg Gadamer's study *Wer bin ich*, Dietland Meinecke's *Wort und Name bei Paul Celan*, or Margret Schärer's *Negationen im Werke Paul Celans*; or through linguistics, as in Adelheid Rexheuser's *Sinnsuche und Zeichen-Setzung in der Lyrik der frühen Celan*. Alongside these theoretical-philosophical studies are those that approach Celan through the religious features and backgrounds of his work, such as Peter Mayer's *Paul Celan als Jüdischer Dichter*. And alongside these in turn are historical studies—Klaus Voswinckel's *Paul Celan: Verweigerte Poetisierung der Welt*, or Marlies Janz's *Vom Engagement absoluter Poesie* and Lielo Anne Pretzer's *Geschichts- und sozialkritische Dimensionen in Paul Celans Werk*, which situate Celan within his historical epoch but, strangely, no less than other studies see his art as an alternative world.[7]

Still to be achieved is a view of Celan's work in its integrity, where all these various concerns and impulses join together within his specific practices. In discussions of the Holocaust, the problem persists of establishing contacts between a language seemingly pure in its self-reflection and a surrounding social-historical world. There the poems selected for discussion, such as "Deathfugue" (Todesfuge) tend to be those explicitly descriptive of Holocaust events; and discussion tends to be determined by the broader issues of Holocaust studies rather than by Celan's particular poetic. Conversely, in studies of poetics, emphasis remains on the self-referential nature of Celan's art, its making of poetry into a theme, its approach to silence as this relates to the purity of its form. Again and again the poem is described as "a poem about poetry, about language and about progressive silence." We are reminded of how "many poetic texts in modernity are directed toward reflections about their own textuality, so as to be a poem about itself." Celan's language is described as "becoming in an unmediated way real, not as a system of conveying meaning from extralinguistic reality."[8] Peter Demetz explains Celan's progress from early texts to his later increasing abstractions as a relentless "search for the absolute essence of poetry," for "an ultimate language structure, unsullied and permanent (the Platonic idea of the poem)." Even attempts to discuss Celan's "debate with language" as a "debate with reality and the place of man within it" become discussions of how Celan's relation to the world primarily consists in a refusal to relate to it: "Language—and with it poetry—becomes in the face of discovered reality no longer the ability to express and make true statements. . . . The poem itself appears now as the attempt to undo language, so that poetry is no longer symbolic, but symbolist, no longer nature poetry, but 'pure poetry.'"[9]

Such formalist reification of the text, isolating textual structure and excising all interrelation with concrete sociopolitical situation, does particular violence to Celan's work. Against it stand Celan's own claims: to a poetry which he opposes to the "French," in that it "doesn't glorify, doesn't poeticize, but names and places, attempts to measure the realm of the given and of the possible" (GW 3: 167). As Gerhard Neumann observes, for Celan, in contrast with Mallarmé, "the isolation of language, its non-attainment of reality carries in itself the secret of an encounter with reality."[10] And while Beda Allemann sees Celan's as a poetry in which "language itself in an unmediated way comes to seem real and not a system of carriers of meaning meant to confront extralinguistic reality," he also acknowledges Celan's "motive of seeking reality."[11] This is a point to which Celan returns again and again. He tells us that he set out to write poetry in order "to orient myself, . . . to outline reality for myself." And he insists: "Certainly it is never language itself, language as absolute, but rather always in terms of the specific angle of inclination of the existence of the speaking I, for its contours and its orientation. Reality does not exist, reality is to be sought and won" (GW 3: 167).

This task of attaining reality begins in Celan's earliest work, often through direct historical reference—at least with regard to the vast numbers of the dead. These especially haunt his first, perhaps most immediately personal (and also revoked) volume of verse, Der Sand aus den Urnen (Sand out of urns): "When, sultry, the dead multiply. / Silent I sketch death" (wenn schwül sie das Sterben vermehren. / Schweigsam entwerf ich mir Tod; SU, GW 3: 16). Among these dead are his parents; and he receives, in another poem, a letter

from his mother concerning his father. She asks, "Child, oh a ker-
chief, to wrap myself with, when helmets flash . . . when snowy the
bones of your father dusts." (Kind, ach ein Tuch, mich zu hüllen
darein, wenn es blinket von Helmen . . . wenn schneeig stäubt das
Gebein deines Vaters; *SU, GW* 3: 20). This letter is brought to the
poet by "the autumn under the monastic habit" (der Herbst unter
mönchischer Kutte). Autumn, the season of his parents' deporta-
tion, is in Celan's work often penetrated by that violence, which in
turn spreads through and across landscape and volume: "Dande-
lion, so green is the Ukraine, / my blond mother came not home"
(Löwenzahn, so grün ist die Ukraine. / Meine blonde Mutter kam
nicht heim; *MG, GW* 1: 19), he writes in *Poppy and Memory*, a
volume caught between the need to forget as both an overwhelming
and an endlessly impossible task. In *From Threshold to Threshold*,
the pairs saved from Noah's flood instead are immersed in a wine
that never rests or erases: "In twos the dead swim, in twos, flooded
with wine" (Zu zweien schwimmen die Toten, zu zweien, umflossen
von Wein; *VS, GW* 1: 101), while the poet continues to lie "in the
shadow of erect corpses" (im Schatten aufgerichteter Leichen; *VS,
GW* 1: 89).

Obviously, this kind of direct reference is recognized as such,
and Celan's war background is always assumed. Yet historical questions are rarely integrated with questions of poetics. Even "Deathfugue," Celan's best-known memorial poem of strict forms and a
direct portrayal of concentration camp life, has been anthologized
for classroom use, accompanied by a note to instructors to direct
attention to the text "lest student discussion deviate from the work
of art to the persecution of the Jews."[12] When historical context is
admitted, it tends to become part of an ahistoricist linguistic argument. Thus, Janz, Voswinkel, and Pretzer, who attempt to discuss
Celan in socio-historical terms, do so in the context of Adorno's
aesthetic theory where the aesthetic object spurns marketability and
even utility. Here the refusal to communicate becomes resistance to
the "instrumental rationalization" of "alienated bourgeois capitalist society." Celan's thus becomes a "noninstrumental language"
in which the "darkness" of obscurity "counters the poem against

rapid consumerism"; and the impulse to "negation and destruction of language" brings it into resistance against the "culture industry" which would render poetry "harmless."[13] In the very effort to place Celan's language in social context, noncommunication and the self-reflexivity of language here remain central interpretive assumptions.

Despite the urgency of Celan's biography, it is difficult to contextualize him, to recognize the trace of events within texts that can appear hermetically sealed. This trace profoundly determines his silences—silences that certainly also bind him closely to inexpressibility as the failure of language before historical atrocity, as writers on the Holocaust emphasize and explore.[14] Yet history is inscribed not only in Celan's silences, but also in his language, and indeed on every level. In its individual words, its lyric structures, and its interlocking patterns, Celan's poetry acts as a field of historical record and historical investigation. That this leads to problems of religious and metaphysical claims only confirms his particular historical experience and context. Celan's work brings these several spheres—the aesthetic, the historical, and the metaphysical—into a particularly imperative relation. It is a peculiar task of his work to render their mutual confrontation. Within such encounter, Celan's own poetics takes place. His formal characteristics, his very language use, register forces that meet within the poems but are by no means contained by them.

Just how linguistic, historical, and religious modes interpenetrate in Celan can be seen in such a poem as "All Souls" (Allerseelen), one of several texts that serve almost as master or genre-poems, bringing together the various forces that meet and counteract in Celan's work:

> What have I
> done?
> Enseeded the night, as if
> others might exist, nightlier
> than this.
>
> Birdflight, stoneflight, a thousand
> inscribed paths. Glances,

robbed and plucked. The sea,
tasted, drunk away, dreaming away. One hour,
soul-eclipsed. The next, an autumn-light,
brought as offering to a blind
feeling, which came this way. Others, many,
without place and heavy out of themselves: sighted and
avoided.
Foundlings, stars,
black and full of speech: named
for a silenced oath.

And once (when? this too is forgotten):
felt the counter-hook
where the pulse dared a counteraction.

Was hab ich
getan?
Die Nacht besamt, als könnt es
noch andere geben, nächtiger als
diese.

Vogelflug, Steinflug, tausend
beschriebene Bahnen. Blicke,
geraubt und gepflückt. Das Meer,
gekostet, vertrunken, verträumt. Eine Stunde,
seelenverfinstert. Die nächste, ein Herbstlicht,
dargebracht einem blinden
Gefühl, das des Wegs kam. Andere, viele,
ortlos und schwer aus sich selbst: erblickt und
umgangen.
Findlinge, Sterne,
schwarz und voll Sprache: benannt
nach zerschwiegenem Schwur.

Und einmal (wann? auch dies ist vergessen):
den Widerhaken gefühlt,
wo der Puls den Gegenakt wagte.

(SG, GW 1: 183)

First, there is the declared act of poetic creation, "enseeding" the
night. The night, moreover—indeed the world and the very cosmos—is itself linguistic: "a thousand inscribed paths," "stars, black
and full of speech." Yet it is a linguistic realm whose fabric and

order have been fundamentally torn and betrayed: "named for a silenced oath." "Oath," however, points in two directions at once, to the religious realm also invoked in the poem's title, but no less (as is also true of the poem's title) to the concrete realm of human commitment and community.

Such multivalence of language is, however, by no means restricted to the particular content and specific centrality of the word "oath." It penetrates Celan's language at every moment, giving rise to word deformations, compounds, and neologisms that are among his most pronounced stylistic features: "birdflight, stoneflight"; "soul-eclipsed." Each and every word in Celan potentially fractures, pointing in many directions at once—including toward other words within his opus, without reference to which it is almost impossible to read him. "All Souls," for example, takes place in an "autumn-light," recalling autumn as a recurrent countersign for the season of his parents' death. In this way his words move into the surrounding word and world contexts.

Finally, within this poem emerge problems of location and of parameters, and intimately linked to these, problems of selfhood and of address. The poem boldly begins with an "I." Yet the borders of the I are insistently deformed and made permeable, indefinitely placed and impossible to locate. The I thus flows out into the night as insemination. "Glances," "a blind feeling" are announced but not ascribed to any person and have no markers establishing point of view. The sea is "tasted" but not by anyone specified, while "soul-eclipsed" describes not the person but the hour. At the last, the "pulse" is at once internal and external, within the I but also within the cosmic space into which the I has so penetrated as to lose self-definition. At the same time, and directly related to this disorientation of the self, is the difficulty of placing "others," who appear *ortlos*, without place, as *Findlinge*, foundlings cut off from the continuity of generations. Time in the poem has also lost identifiable place, as a single "hour" suspended without temporal interrelation.

And yet this self, in many ways so ill defined and indeed threatened in its integrity, stands ready and open toward "others" perhaps no less ill defined. The poem concludes as an unlocated pulse awaits or perhaps dares a "counteraction," some responsive moment, some responding gesture.

Contexts of the Self

A text such as "All Souls" points at once inward into the poet's interior life and outward toward public spaces. The latter movement is not restricted to direct historical reference only. The specific historical face of Celan's poems often remains riddling, enigmatic, effaced, but history does not enter into Celan's work only as particular events or memories. It is a constellation through which many different structures of Celan's world attain to form. This begins with the structures of the self, which, in Celan's work, are far from secure. Celan's world is a broken one, and this brokenness profoundly penetrates the self, itself a cross-territory of history, as in "Today and Tomorrow" (Heute und Morgen):

> So stand I, made of stone, into the
> distances to which I led you:
>
> Washed out
> by driftsand: the two
> caves on the lower brow-edge.
> Eyed darkness within.
>
> Pounded through
> by hammers heaved in silence:
> the place
> where the wing-eye grazed me.
>
> Behind it,
> secreted in the wall,
> the step
> on which the Remembered squats.
>
> Here,
> endowed by nights,
> a voice seeps,
> out of which you scoop the drink.

So steh ich, steinern, zur
Ferne, in die ich dich führte:

Von Flugsand
ausgewaschen die beiden
Höhlen am untern Stirnsaum.
Eräugtes
Dunkel darin.

Durchpocht
von schweigsam geschwungenen Hämmern
die Stelle,
wo mich das Flügelaug streifte.

Dahinter,
ausgespart in der Wand,
die Stufe,
drauf das Erinnerte hockt.

Hierher
sickert, von Nächten beschenkt,
eine Stimme,
aus der du den Trunk schöpfst.

(SG, GW 1: 158)

"So stand I." But the "I" that this poem seems so confidently to declare at once becomes split, divided between itself and a "you" half rhetorical, arrived at only across "distances." That this interior distance also composes a landscape—the "two caves" are eyes "on the lower brow-edge"—does little to give it clearer contour. The landscape-self remains a collection of parts without integrated shape, its own interior an inaccessible "darkness within," and its exposed parts subject to corrosive elements: "washed out by drift-sand." Nor does the self-consciousness with which the speaker observes himself restore a sense of unity. It only confirms a sense of disjunction, as the cave-eyes meet a "wing-eye" externalized and watching, but not reintegrated into any unifying perspective.

The distribution and dissolution of self represented here recurs throughout Celan's work. Different parts of the body are often isolated in grotesque or even violent fashion. He pursues himself into "the emptiness where entrails entwine" (Im Leeren wo sich die Kuttel rankt; *LZ, GW* 2: 277); to a place where "we are ladling nerve cells" (wir löffeln Nervenzellen; *FS, GW* 2: 181). There is a violence penetrating ever inward: "Behind skull-splinters (Hinter Schläfensplittern; *SP, GW* 2: 412); "The darkened splinter-echo, brainstreamward" (Das Gedunkelte Splitterecho, / hirnstrom- / hin; *SP, GW* 2: 414); "the spinal cord / clatters together" (miterklirrt / das Rückenmark"; *ZH, GW* 3: 75); "A bootfull of brain" (Einen Stiefelvoll Hirn; *ZH, GW* 3: 103). In this dismemberment, the eye has a special place. It recurs, disembodied, again and again from Celan's earliest to his last poems. His eyes are "Two sight-swellings, two scar-seams / here, too, across the face" (Zwei Sehwülste, / zwei Narbennähte, auch hier, quer durchs Gesicht; *ZH, GW* 3: 380). As in one of his famous poems, "Sprachgitter" ("Speechgrille" or "Language Grid"), eyes stare (through eyelashes?) as "between the staffs" (zwischen den Stäben), at once encaged and transfixing, visible but remote. As in "Today and Tomorrow," the eye's stare has spatial location: "The heaven, heartgray, must be near" (der Himmel, herzgrau, muss nah sein; *SG, GW* 1: 167). Celan's skies, at once interior ("heartgray") and above, are overcast in poem after poem by the gray smoke of historical bodies. "Auge der Zeit," "the eye of time" (*VS, GW* 1: 127), Celan calls it, in which "the dead sprout and bloom" (die Toten knospen und blühen). Or, as he writes in "An Eye, Open," another *Sprachgitter* poem, it is "the tear" that "brings you the images" (die Träne ... holt dir die Bilder; *SG, GW* 1: 187). Just so, the sequence of weeks is disturbed, unlinked, in "Today and Tomorrow" by an interior place behind which, "secreted in the wall, ... the Remembered squats." It is from this time-crevice that the poet's "voice seeps."

The question of Celanian temporal modes is of central interest to Hans-Georg Gadamer in his study of Celan's *Atemkristall* (later incorporated into *Atemwende*). In his analyses, at issue is the way in which consciousness takes place temporally, in momentary reductions, as in "Whitegray":

> Whitegray, ex-
> cavated steep
> feelings.

Inland, strewn-
here-and-about dune grass blows
sand pattern over
the smoke of the well-song.

An ear, disjointed, eavesdrops.

An eye, cut into stripes,
does justice to all.

Weissgrau aus-
geschachteten steilen
Gefühls.

Landeinwärts, hierher-
verwehter Strandhafer bläst
Sandmuster über
den Rauch von Brunnengesängen.

Ein Ohr, abgetrennt, lauscht.

Ein Aug, in Streifen geschnitten,
wird all dem gerecht.
                    (AW, GW 2: 19)

In Gadamer's reading, the disjointed eye and ear are expressions of the concentrated human effort to activate a poverty-stricken world. The well-song, to be heard at all, demands close attention, which comes only in bare, momentary flashes: "Only strained eavesdropping keeps this song audible, this self-affirmation of man in a sanded-over world, and only momentary flashes break through the strained glimpses of human order. The glaring atrocity of the closing metaphor of ear and eye lets the meagre poverty of the world be experienced, in which feeling hardly retains any effect."[15] Gadamer's analysis assumes phenomenological-existential categories of thought such as those developed by Martin Heidegger—Celan's relationship with whom remains puzzling and even troubling (in connection with Celan's visit to Todtnauberg, Heidegger's residence and the subject of another poem, Gadamer recounts Heidegger's praise of Celan's lore in natural history, his "Naturkenntnis").[16] For Gadamer, the "meagre poverty of the world" requires human encounter, intention, project to attain to meaning: "Meaning is

the 'upon-which' of a projection in terms of which something becomes intelligible as something." Or, in Heidegger's terms, in such
encounter man's "self-affirmation" takes place, his emergence by
word into existence: "Man is he who must affirm who he is. To
affirm means to declare. This affirmation makes plain the existence
of man." But such encounter takes place only within moments,
"Augenblicken," in which "the present is not only brought back
from distraction with the objects of one's closest concern, but it gets
held in the future and in having been. That present which is held in
authentic temporality, and which thus is authentic itself, we call the
'moment of vision.'"[17]

Acts of perception in "Whitegray" similarly reduce to "momentary flashes." Celan encounters the world through "an eye, cut into
stripes." There are only instants, disjoined, through a cut-apart
eye. In "Whitegray" this is a framing condition. Elsewhere, it is
the poet's focus, the poem's central and momentary object of
representation:

> Flashes of an eye, being hints
> No brightness sleeps.
> Un-dis-becoming, all places,
> gather yourself,
> stay.
>
> Augenblicke, wesen Winke,
> keine Helle schläft.
> Unentworden, allerorten,
> sammle dich,
> steh.
>
>   (FS, GW 2: 113)

The self must gather itself to stand steadily under the pressure of a
moment that disperses into an "all places," contracts into an "un-
dis-becoming." It is at no place in a temporal series. Systematizing
of temporal series or structures becomes suspect. As Celan writes
elsewhere, "The next millennium estranges itself" (Das Neben-
Jahrtausend fremdet sich ein; FS, GW 2: 130). Millennia, centuries,
seconds, seasons, birth, death, all become strangely truncated as

> Leap-centuries, leap
> seconds, leap-
> births, novembering, leap-
> deaths

> Schaltjahrhunderte, Schalt-
> sekunden, Schalt-
> geburten, novembernd, Schalt-
> tode
>
> (*LZ, GW* 2: 324)

They are not frames of reference against which experience can be measured, or into which experiences can be placed. Celan fails to establish from them or through them a latticework of coherence. The phenomenology of existential perception, of self-creation and world-creation from moment to moment, remains in Celan momentary only.

But Celan's is finally not a poetic of individual consciousness only. It shows consciousness as structured through history. In "Whitegray," for example, sand and eye form a bridge with "Today and Tomorrow." Sand here directly poses the problem of "pattern," of coordinates onto which experience can be placed. The "strewn-here-and-about dune grass" emphasizes how such patterns shift and blow, their instability. An ear, an eye appear in isolation and dismemberment. These are organs for directly perceiving the immediate world, and it is the immediate world that is here disjointed. One of its strata, however, is memory, surely among the things uncovered in the "excavated steep feelings." "Smoke of the well-song" may also signal the past world. In "Aspentree" (Espenbaum), a liturgy for his dead mother, Celan writes: "Raincloud, do you border on the well? / My silent mother weeps for all" (Regenwolke, säumst du an den Brunnen? / Meine leise Mutter weint für alle; *MG, GW* 1: 19). And the ear, like the eye, finds association in Celan's work with the temporally remote yet temporally frozen:

> Out of the transitory
> stand the steps,

> what has been trickled into the ear
> there the prehistoric culminates.

Aus der Vergängnis
stehen die Stufen,

Das ins Ohr Geträufelte
mündigt die Vorzeit darin.
(*SP, GW* 2: 387)

"Whitegray" thus implicitly alludes to the past, as present to
the poem's moment, and indeed as deforming even immediate
perception.

Celanian consciousness always remains historical, however Celan's work sustains and even proposes abstract phenomenologi-
cal interpretation. The space of Celan's poetry strangely blends
interior and exterior, private and public worlds. Indeed, it is a
peculiar trait of his poetics so to blur the line between these as
to make them indistinguishable. In regard to structures of the
self, there is a simultaneous movement of introjection and projection, often linked through event. This goes beyond the personal,
particular experiences of Antschel/Celan as an East European Jew
in Hitler's Europe, to general problems of culture and to the
way the self is integrally structured through socio-historical experience. In terms of Celan's poetic, this historicized self is tran-
scribed across a great range of verse practices, including not only
the constitution of the poems' speakers, but also their modes of
representation, of construction, and perhaps most importantly, of
address.

With regard to modes of representation, Celan's work has attracted the attention of such theorists as Theodor Adorno and Paul
de Man. Adorno in *Aesthetic Theory* identifies not only Celan but
also Beckett with a new anorganic representation. Adorno relates
this feature generally to the decline of nature as "an object of poetic
celebration" within the shifting historical circumstances that condition imagery itself: "Historical through and through," Adorno
comments, "the essence of imagery would be missed if one were
to try and replace historical imagery by an invariable one . . .
obliterat[ing] the concrete relations between people." Celan's self-
representation in terms of the anorganic is not a mere extension of
romantic self–world correspondences into the arena of technology

and mechanism, as though .the. self retained some stable identity that it expresses through new inventions. The representation of self in technological terms Adorno presents as itself transforming "constitutive modes of experience." In Celan, according to Adorno, it results in a move toward a "non-representational character," a hermetic withdrawal into anorganicism as abstraction, offering a "language of the lifeless as the only form of comfort in a world where death has lost all meaning."[18]

Adorno's argument for a retreat from representation keeps perhaps strange company with Paul de Man's reading of Celan. In his essay on "Lyric and Modernity," de Man sets out to complicate an evolutionary interpretation of the history of poetry as a "genetic process" of progressive "movement of lyric poetry away from representation." Instead, he insists on a continued representational element in the lyric, at least, as in Celan, as part of an "ambivalence of language that is representational and nonrepresentational at the same time." De Man, however, retains a representational element only finally to reject it: to underscore that "the understanding it reaches is necessarily in error," to show "the impossibility for a representational and an allegorical poetics to engage in a mutually clarifying dialectic."[19] Both thus see Celan as non-representational.

Celan's modes of representation instead, I would argue, work in a reverse direction. It is an autonomously hermetic and figural interpretation that is in error. Celan certainly marks the penetration of anorganic, technological modes into the most intimate personal spaces. The very world of the unconscious becomes a hurtling "Dream-orbit" (Traumantrieb) through spaces at once radically within and astronomically distant, with "planet-dust in the hollowed eye" (Planetenstaub in den gehöhlten Augen). Yet the space module that carries the self is a "poppy-capsule" (Mohnkapsel) of forgetfulness; and the spaces it travels through are "the swimming griefdomain," which "make note of" or "write down a further shadow" (die schwimmende Trauerdomäne vermerkt einen weiteren Schatten; LZ, GW 2: 303). That is, this inner figural space acts as a record for a grief and trauma that the "poppy-capsule," far from forgetting, translates and traverses. This transformed self as anorganic and technological force does not retreat from, but transcribes, a whole arena of socio-historical reference and process. The self, the subject, never exists in Celan in isolation. It takes its place only in terms of social modes also implicit in the technological sphere as social product, which in Celan are in turn directly linked to the whole arena of socio-historical, and indeed political, experience:

> The industrious
> natural resources, domestic,
>
> the heated syncope,
>
> the not-to-be-deciphered
> echo-year,
>
> the vitrified-through
> spider-altars in the all-
> overlooking flat building,
>
> the interval-sounds
> (still?)
> the shadow-palaver,
>
> the fears, ice-just,
> flight-clear,
>
> the baroque encloaked,
> speechswallowing showerroom,
> semantically illuminated
>
> the un-inscribed wall
> of a standing-cell
>
> here
>
> live yourself right through, without clock.
>
> Die Fleissigen
> Bodenschätze, häuslich,
>
> die geheizte Synkope,
>
> das nicht zu enträtselnde
> Halljahr,

die vollverglasten
Spinnen-Altare im alles-
überragenden Flachbau,

die Zwischenlaute
(noch immer?),
Schattenpalaver,

die Ängste, eisgerecht,
flugklar,

der barock ummantelte,
spracheschluckende Duschraum,
semantisch durchleuchtet,

die unbeschriebene Wand
einer Stehzelle:

hier

leb dich querdurch, ohne Uhr.

(*FS, GW* 2: 151)

This poem traces a movement from the exploitation of nature under the sign of the "domestic" to human destruction in a "speech-swallowing showerroom." This last image, with that of the "all-overlooking flat building," "the un-inscribed wall," the "standing cell" situates the poem within the experience of the death camp. But in this poem the death camp is specifically approached by way of an industrialization that in fact reflects structures fundamental to its operation and its relation to the surrounding culture. Industrialization is implicated not only in the machineries and technologies of the conduct of camp life, but as its very ethos. The concentrationary world stood in a number of complex relations with the productive capacity of the German war effort. It provided labor for industry—there is a letter, for instance, from a porcelain manufacturer, asking for government remuneration for losses incurred when the prison population operating his plant was wiped out in a typhoid epidemic.[20] Even more, the inmates were themselves referred to as *Stücke*, pieces, piece goods. The torture chamber could be referred to as the "business room," the deaths of prisoners registered by the set phrase "subtraction due to death."[21] The killing itself was called *fertig machen*, to make ready as in the final processing of a product, which of course faithfully registers the utilization of personal possessions and finally body parts of the industriously destroyed.[22]

The reduction of the person to material ultimately governed the entire conduct of camp life, from medical experimentation to the camp social organizations. This social aspect forms the basis of Bruno Bettelheim's interpretation of camp life, where he sees its entire structure as directed toward breaking down individual autonomy so as to destroy the very personhood of prisoners. Such an intention informed, in his analysis, every camp experience, from its first impact on the personality as one that "split [the] person . . . so that degrading experiences did not happen to 'me' as subject but to 'me' as object." The subsequent progressive deterioration of the individual Bettelheim traces as totally governing the camp regime: "Efforts to deprive the prisoners of even the smallest remnants of their autonomy were particularly vicious and all-pervasive . . . [and] brought about a commensurately severe personality disintegration, both in his inner life and in his relation to others."[23] Such psychological dissolution has a temporal correlative explored by Erich Kahler in *The Tower and the Abyss* in terms of the breakdown of the continuum of experience within camp life: "The individual does not know what he may experience; and what he has already experienced is no longer important for his person or his future. . . . Life becomes a chain of expected, avoided or materialized shocks, and thus the atomized experiences heighten the atomization of the individual."[24]

A radical instability in temporal continuum and experience such as Kahler describes suggests an interpretive framework for Celan's poems. Thus, "The Industrious Natural Resources" ends in negating the clock. Life transpires in the frozen moment of unmodified "fears," in the continued presence of a "speechswallowing showerroom," facing the wall of a "standing-cell" that is "uninscribed," unyielding to all semantic illumination. In the interminable "here" of an inescapable past, the fragmentation of time—and indeed of language—begins. Disintegration is registered as "syncope," a missed beat, as "shadow-palaver," babbled discourse; in "interval-sounds" mechanically repeated as redundant measure. Thomas Sparr sees these images as essentially "metapoetic" issues of literary construction and poetic temporality, into which historical references are themselves subsumed without any representational force.[25] Yet to make this poem an emblem of poetry, rather than a record in language of historical experience, seems to me a most peculiar twist. The language of the poem particularly asserts the historicity of language itself. Under the pressure of events, language takes shape only within a "not-to-be-deciphered echo-year," of time as a medium of resonance, but one severely disjointed and discontinuous. Or, in another possible reading, "Halljahr" may play on "Jobeljahr," Jubilee, here, however, only as an indecipherable interruption.

The severe discontinuities within concentration camps may be one source and model for Celan's own severe discontinuities. In this sense, such reference remains highly specific to Celan's particular experience and to the particular features of the concentration camp. But, according to Hannah Arendt, the camps represent the central institution of a totalitarian regime. Arendt carries Bettelheim's analyses of individual psychopathology into the sociopolitical realm. The assault on individual autonomy so as to suppress "the infinite plurality and differentiation of human beings" by reducing each person to "a bundle of reactions" she sees as the realization of the "guiding social ideal of total domination in general."[26] And there are still further contexts. Celan began a correspondence with Erich Kahler after reading his *The Tower and the Abyss*.[27] There Kahler argues that the camps represent in intensified form general social conditions which made them possible and of which they are only the most extreme and negative expression. Atomization, the "breakdown of the human form," the "disintegration of the individual," are all features of modern, mechanized society. As technology advances, "the human power over the world escapes the control of man and threatens him." And Kahler claims that the fragmentation of the life of the individual into isolated experiences and contradictory responses "is potentially present everywhere in modern civilization."[28]

"The Industrious Mineral Wealth" may then also suggest a continuity between life within and life without the camp, not only
within a totalitarian regime but generally, and not only as part of
ordinary economic institutions—Arendt is careful to distinguish
the economy of camp life from a normal economics of production,
because productivity is neither its central organizing principle nor
its central goal—but as their political transposition.[29] The camps
themselves, in Kahler's analysis, were governed by "the mechanized
processes of modern industry and technology and the exploitation
of matter which they imply."[30] While in no way mitigating the singular horror and special status of the death camp, Celan's work
suggests how its reification of person, its reduction of the human to
material, is a pathology that implicates the society beyond it which
supported it. Similarly the poem "Chymical" (Chymisch) follows
the alchemical transformation, as it were, of the "sister-shape"
(Schwestergestalt) into chemical ashes and smoke (SG, GW 1:
227). A language of industrial process merges into death-camp
tropes:

> The excavated heart,
> in which they install feeling.
>
> Grand-homeland ready-made
> part.
>
> Milk-Sister
> Shovel.
>
> Das Ausgeschachtete Herz,
> darin sie Gefühl installieren.
>
> Grossheimat Fertig-
> teile.
>
> Milchschwester
> Schaufel.
>
> (FS, GW 2: 150)

The heart's interior space becomes the (linguistic) site of mecha-
nisms of excavation and installation, of marketing and prefabri-
cated parts, ominously concluding with milk-sister–shovel—war

words established through interweaving usages in Celan beginning
with "Deathfugue." Figural and literal acquire in such texts a relation neither antithetical nor dialectical, but something closer to
riddle:

> The colliding temples,
> naked, where masks are rented out:
>
> behind the world
> the unbid hope throws out
> the trailing rope.
>
> In the oceanic wounded-edges lands
> the breathing number.
>
> Die kollidierenden Schläfen,
> nackt, im Maskenverleih:
>
> hinter der Welt
> wirft die ungebetene Hoffnung
> die Schlepptrosse aus.
>
> An den meerigen Wundrändern landet
> die atmende Zahl.
>
> (FS, GW 2: 152)

Extremes of stark, juxtaposed formal units here turn toward neither abstract aesthetic essences nor self-referring allegorical figures.
It is in fact the challenge of the text to propose its iconicity as
a burden on the reader, on whom responsibility falls to construe
its reduction. For the poem finally presents, in a surreality which,
however, reality itself approximated, a lesson in reduction: depor-
tation (colliding heads; rented masks; trailing ropes; the destruction of hope; wounded-edges) as the reduction of human beings to
numbers.

Deadly Abstraction

This riddle, or problem, of the consequences of formal abstraction becomes in Celan much more than an aesthetic question. Or
rather, Celan's work charts how aesthetic questions such as formal
abstraction in fact spill over into the realm not only of culture but
of politics. In the copy of *Poppy and Memory* Celan sent to Erich

Kahler, he inscribed a passage from Kahler's work: "The general, the eternal, the timeless does not endure, except as it emerges out of here and today and actually so, authenticated as its own and our being, and . . . what is not power within us, has no power over us."[31] What attracts Celan to Kahler here is the attack Kahler launches against categorical claims to the "general, eternal, timeless." Such categories only have force and value to the degree that they are acted upon and concretized in reality, in the "here and today and actually so, authenticated as its own and our being." But Kahler's *The Tower and the Abyss* traces the increasing distance between the values supposedly held by Western culture as against the actual conduct of modern Western life. Kahler defines a value as "a fundamental significance which man attaches to matters of his life and through which he orients himself in his conduct." But the modern reduction of men to function has caused behavior to splinter; beliefs are not applied in the context of performed actions. Beliefs thus lose their relevance and force. Unless they are "embedded in life," they are no longer valid and cannot be sustained even as beliefs. They retain their value only as they are incarnated in actual social institutions and realized in human behavior.[32]

Kahler here addresses, in terms of a humanist, axiological critique, questions of culture also central to Marxist critical theory. Walter Benjamin, for example, had analyzed fascism as a late capitalist effort to "organize the newly created proletarian masses without affecting the property structure which the masses strive to eliminate." Writing before the war on the relation between technological innovation, aesthetic representation, and politics, Benjamin foretells the reduction of the human to material, and forewarns that "the increase in technical devices . . . will press for an unnatural utilization [in] imperialistic war . . . which collects in the form of human material the claims to which society has denied its natural material."[33] Adorno, writing after the war, focuses above all on the failure of "culture" to resist such perversion: "Auschwitz," he writes, "demonstrated irrefutably that culture had failed . . . That this could happen in the midst of the traditions of philosophy, of art, and of the enlightening sciences says more than that these traditions and their spirit lacked the power to take hold of men and work a change in them. There is untruth in those fields themselves, in the autarky that is emphatically claimed for them."[34]

Adorno's analysis laments, in accord with the commitment of the Frankfurt School, the "autarky" or split of culture from so-called "material existence as a lesser aspect of man's condition."[35] As he argues in *Negative Dialectics*, danger erupts through the disjunction between the ideal and the real, requiring a redefined relation between them: "We cannot say any more that the immutable is truth, and that the mobile, the transitory is appearance. The mutual indifference of temporality and eternal ideas is no longer tenable."[36] Adorno may, as Martin Jay argues, nevertheless still grant to culture and the realm of ideas a priority, seeing the fault in the failure of ideas sufficiently to determine social and economic reality.[37] But Adorno's argument that cultural accomplishment never takes place independently of historical and socioeconomic realities, never exists in an autonomous world of spirit to be experienced as an inner, private achievement, has strong resonance for Celan's work. Above all his suspicion of ideology as form—where "form and order is in complicity with blind domination"—is also Celanian: "Whoever glorifies order and form as such, must see in the petrified divorce [from material conditions of life] an archetype of the Eternal" as "fatal fragmentation."[38]

In Celan's representations as they raise cultural questions, it is not merely culture's autonomy and failure to penetrate material realms that is problematic. It is rather the too thorough domination of reality by a predetermined ideal that is deadly. At issue is not so much cultural "autarky," but what might be called ideological hegemony: not the failure of the cultural institution to dominate material conditions, but its absolute domination of them, the limitless appropriation of material reality to a specific cultural ideal and ideology. Jean Amery describes the SS state as "an idea becoming reality."[39] Chaim Aron Kaplan similarly writes in his Warsaw Ghetto diaries that the Germans are "a people of the Book," adding that "where plunder is based on an ideology, on a world outlook which in essence is spiritual, it cannot be equaled in strength and durability."[40] National Socialism did not assume the mutual indifference of temporal reality and a prior, determining ideology. Rather, it insisted on their total integration, the imposition of ideological absolutes within the social and political sphere. Within the Frankfurt School's own analysis of Nazism, National Socialism imposes "technical rationality as the guiding principle of the society," reducing the legal system into the political machine and, in the realm of economics itself, establishing a "deliberate and generally successful policy of [economic control]." It therefore represents a kind of triumph of reason, where "rationality is the whole apparatus of law and law enforcing made exclusively serviceable to those who rule."[41]

Celan's writing warns against assigning to abstract construction an ideally unlimited power. "Deathfugue," with its dance of death, its fugal juxtaposition of the "Golden-haired Margaret" to whom the camp commander writes and the "Ashen-haired Shulamith" whom he destroys—that is, with its reduction, musical patterning, severe formalization—ultimately projects a pattern of abstraction as both impelling and suspect. It does so in ways that Celan's poetry explores again and again:

> Landscape with urn-beings.
> Conversations
> from smoke-mouth to smoke-mouth.
>
> They eat:
> the mad-brand-name-truffle, a piece
> of unburied poetry,
> found tongue and tooth.
>
> A tear rolls back into its eye.
>
> The left, orphaned
> half of the pilgrim's
> shell (they bestowed it on you,
> then they tied you up),
> eavesdropping, shines out into the room:
>
> the clinker-playing against death
> can begin.

Landschaft mit Urnenwesen.
Gespräche
von Rauchmund zu Rauchmund.

Sie essen
die Tollhäusler-Trüffel, ein Stück
unvergrabner Poesie,
fand Zung und Zahn.

Eine Träne rollt in ihr Auge zurück.

Die linke, verwaiste
Hälfte der Pilger-
muschel—sie schenkten sie dir,
dann banden sie dich—
leuchtet lauschend den Raum aus:

das Klinkerspiel gegen den Tod
kann beginnen.

(AW, GW 2: 59)

Like "Deathfugue," although less overtly, this macabre poem portrays the concentrationary world, and in terms consistent with those of the fugal poem. Thus it introduces obliquely in its last image a concern with music which "Deathfugue" announces in its title. "Das Klinkerspiel," a neologism, combines the image of bricks tightly wedged against each other (ovens of crematoria that produce "urn-beings"?) with an image of (random) sounds playing: *klingeln* (to ring), *klimpernspiel* (tinkling), *klingendem Spiele* (fife and drum). Particularly the last, the military band, evokes associations with "Deathfugue," where the camp guard "commands us to play for the dance" and where camp life is itself constituted of fugally juxtaposed motifs. This is, however, not mere abstraction or metaphor. Every camp had its orchestra composed of prisoners, whose duty was to play at executions as well as during regular morning and evening roll-calls. The music had moreover an integral function within camp regimen, one with the full force of terror: a failure to march to the correct tempo was punishable, and could even be fatal. "The voice of the Lager," Primo Levi calls the music. "The perceptible expression of its geometrical madness, of the resolution of others to annihilate us as men in order to kill us more slowly afterwards."[42] A geometrical madness: Levi's description echoes another sequence in the poem—"They eat: the mad-brand-name-truffle, a piece of unburied poetry, found tongue and tooth." Poetry too is mad—and yet also grotesquely familiar, like a name-brand (häusler) product. Procured in a bestial manner, unearthed from the soil, tongue and tooth, it stands as a border crossing between the savage and the civilized, the mark no longer of their distinction, but of their continuity and mutual reflection.

The image of music is pivotal here. Thomas Mann, adopting it in *Dr. Faustus* as a symbol for German culture, remarks: "The relation of the German to the world is abstract and mystical, i.e., musical." There is then a danger that German inwardness, "Innerlichkeit," will force such a "musical culture" onto the "non-metaphysical and 'human' realm of social and political reality."[43] Music is a sphere of necessary laws without reference to an accidental world external to it. The vision of pure relations to which the musical mind has access can "refuse to relate outward, to take reality for arbiter."[44]

A poem such as "Landscape with Urn-Beings" begins to probe such ideological territories, with their aesthetic corollaries. The musical imagery, especially when mediated through its more overt presence in "Deathfugue," inevitably asserts not only the specific historical site of music in death camps but the further ones of music within a tradition of German culture, its long symbolic association with philosophical idealism educed by Thomas Mann in *Dr. Faustus*. Thomas Mann's Devil accordingly invites Leverkuhn "to break through time itself," to enter an absolute world beyond time, beyond the conditions of the mutable world of his own humanity, and thus "dare to be barbaric—twice barbaric indeed, because of coming after the humane." Particularly the modes of representing music within ideological contexts are important to other long Celan poems based in musical motifs, such as "Voices" and "Stretto." In "Landscape," music takes its place, as does poetry, in a structure, a landscape, out of which the living human has been reduced, bleached, indeed reversed: "A tear rolls back in the eye." Humane response itself is excluded, defeated, as is any framework for its significant articulation:

> The left, orphaned
> half of the pilgrim's
> shell (they bestowed it on you,
> then they tied you up),
> eavesdropping, shines out into the room:

A pilgrimage begins in longing but points toward fulfillment. Its arc moves from sorrow to joy in reaching what will justify sorrow, in the established pattern of theodicy. Here there is only an orphaned left half (a play on *Häftlinge*, the prisoner of the camp?) of a pilgrim shell (elsewhere Celan writes of a "deathshell" [Totenmuschel]; *FS, GW* 2: 147), which fails to achieve completion. Granted the first half of the pilgrim shell, the pilgrim fails to receive the second half. It is a half-theodicy: longing, search, need, sorrow, but no fulfillment, justification, peace, reconciliation. The poem is an interrupted arc, a search without finding, a suffering without redemption. Theodicy itself is emptied, a half-shell, incomplete.

Nevertheless, Celan concludes: "The clinker-playing against death can begin." Against death: the very instrumentation that signals deathliness also, here, opposes it. One recalls Celan's specific controversy with Adorno, who, apparently in response to "Death-fugue," had declared, "To write poetry after Auschwitz is barbaric. And this corrodes even the knowledge of why it has become impossible to write poetry today."[45] To this Celan retorted: in poetry "we know at last where to seek the barbarians."[46] (Later, Adorno retracted: "It may have been wrong," he concedes in *Negative Dialectics*, "to say that after Auschwitz you could no longer write poems. . . . But it is not wrong to raise the less cultural question whether after Auschwitz you can go on living." To this Celan had less to reply; he committed suicide in April 1970.)[47] What exactly can art accomplish, in rendering into formal beauty events that defy representation? Is Celan's severe formalization an escape, even a transfiguration? Or is it a form of resistance and exposure?

In a poem such as "Landscape with Urn-Beings," the orders of abstraction are exposed as potentially lethal. Celan's radical forms are self-exposing. And they never claim to achieve determinate coherence, but rather show abstraction as resistant to interpretation, as in itself empty of human experience. This is a diffidence Celan generally urges. It extends to a refusal of comprehensive formulas, a suspicion of any accomplished translation from realm to realm, or representation of realm by realm. It radically suspects metaphor itself. Already in the early essay "Edgar Jené and the Dream of Dream," he had mocked metaphoricity: "Old identity-tradesman [Identitätskrämer]! what have you seen and recognized, brave doctor of tautology?" (GW 3: 155). Later events gave this personal skepticism frightful application, in war-events that defy and indeed forbid representative claim. Jean Amery, speaking in *At the Mind's Limit*, warns against metaphoric transfigurations of the concentrationary world: "One comparison would stand for another and we would be hoaxed into a hopeless merry-go-round of figurative speech."[48] The experience defies and fractures analogy; and, in Celan's work, few attempts at direct description are made.

Instead, Celan's work points always toward, and resides along, a border of representation that insists on its own limits. Retaining this precarious position between representation and its impossibility is fundamental and central to his entire project—one way his art "balances on itself." This is the case even, or especially, where abstraction takes on representational force. The image of hell is a case in point. The smoke-mouths of urn-beings recall infernal realms, such as those where Dante's damned also spoke in flame. But this analogy, too, has severe limits: one hell represents the other, yet also does not. Dante's hell had an established place within the economy of divine justice, making it, in orthodox Christian theology, an indispensable part of the great structure of redemption finalized in heaven. Here the structure of theodicy is contested. Indeed, the very appeal to another world as reference for this one emerges as terrifying. The image of the war's world as infernal is in fact an established topos for its representation. Carl Jung, for example, even before the war, had warned of an awakening of "chthonic daemons" in which "the forces of the unconscious have broken into the premises of what seemed to be a tolerably ordered world"; and George Steiner has described the camps as "Hell made immanent . . . the transference of Hell from below the earth to its surface" in "the deliberate enactment of a long, precise imagining."[49] What Celan brings to awareness is the demonic nature not of hell only, but of all absolute imaginings. In this regard, there is little to choose between hell and utopia. Thus W. H. Auden calls Hitler a utopian: "Even Hitler would have defined his New Jerusalem as a world where there are no Jews, not where they were being gassed by the million day after day in ovens, but he was Utopian, so the ovens had to come in."[50]

The image of utopia, like that of hell, suggests a pathology of the metaphysical: not the collapse of metaphysical belief, but its aggressive displacement onto the physical world—the incursion into physical, temporal, conditional reality of a metaphysic. This is an inversion of religious systems that try to sanction the physical world in the metaphysical, the temporal in the absolute. Instead, the absolute is instituted as the suppression of the mutable, accidental, conditional world. In this pathology, absolutist structures are not defeated: they conquer.

The world of Dachau was in this sense an abstract world of pure formal relations. Its order followed inexorably from principles accepted absolutely. For those principles, all individuality, idiosyncracy, and accidental human attributes were to be eradicated. But purity of form, when applied to the nonmetaphysical and human realm, renders it inhuman. It invites, then, imagery drawn from another world. Arendt, for example, writes of the camps: "Seen from the outside, they and the things that happen in them can be described only in images drawn from a life after death, that is, a life removed from earthly purposes . . . a world which is complete with all sensual data of reality but lacks that structure of consequence and responsibility without which reality remains for us a mass of incomprehensible data."[51]

The images of hell and utopia raise questions about absolute states, imagined as ultimate ends commanding limitless means. In Hannah Arendt's analysis, such pursuit of the idea breeds a "contempt for reality and factuality . . . for the sake of complete consistency." And this entails the elimination of "spontaneity itself as an expression of human behavior" and "transforming the human personality into a mere thing."[52] From this point of view, the camps do not represent a breakdown of structure or even of rationality. They instead displace the spontaneous, unpredictable resistance to system in the nonabsolute, conditional, and unfinalized human world in the name of something absolute, totally finalized, and unconditioned. But this, indeed, is what the Nazis, in their dream of a millennial Reich, set out to accomplish, with the camps the fullest realization of their ideal order, the order of the ideal.

The result is a strange alienation between what is traditionally meant by culture as humanistic attainment and a reality of human degradation. But there is also a strange confusion between the two—an application, in Walter Benjamin's terms, of the principles of the formal orders of aesthetic achievement to the sociopolitical world: "Fascism is the introduction of aesthetics into political life."[53] Auden makes a similar point when he remarks that "a society which was really like a good poem, embodying the aesthetic virtues of beauty, order, economy, and subordination of detail to the whole, would be a nightmare of horror."[54]

The absolute and the aesthetic are, as autonomous values, demonic. Ideal worlds are, it turns out, terrifying models for the material, conditional world we inhabit. This terror is something Celan's work invites us to contemplate:

> Cello-entree
> from behind the hurt:
>
> the powers, stacked
> toward anti-heavens,
> steamroll the inexplicable in front of
> runway and entrance . . .
>
> Cello-Einsatz
> von hinter dem Schmerz:
>
> die Gewalten, nach Gegen-
> himmeln gestaffelt,

wälzen Undeutbares vor
Einflugschneise und Einfahrt . . .
(*AW, GW* 2: 76)

Music, the soul of German longing and aesthetic perfection, becomes here a kind of scarring (or worse: does "Einsatz," the formal notation for a musical entrance, play on the Nazi Kommando "Einsatzgruppe"? The very language seems poisoned). The higher realms become fearful, reversed powers. Abstraction here remains stark, yet Celan employs it toward its own exposure, as something resisting the coherence of experience. It is Celan's peculiar mode—neither "nonrepresentational" nor simply representational, but an image of representational limit, respecting what this poem cites as "the inexplicable."

Language Histories

The very language seems poisoned. Celan is far from alone in being haunted by this suspicion. Thomas Mann had denounced "books that could be printed from 1933 to 1945 in Germany [as] less than worthless . . . an odor of blood and shame sticks to them."[55] Karl Kraus declared in the face of rising National Socialist propaganda, "The word went to sleep when that world awoke."[56] Celan himself joined Gruppe 47, a postwar group of German writers who shared an "intense concern with the German language, grievously deformed by the National Socialists" and through which publication of *Poppy and Memory* was made possible.[57] Such history penetrates Celan's every German word. Its tensions become the opening topic of his speech accepting the Bremen prize for literature, not least through its Heideggerean pun on "thinking" and "thanking" (*denken/danken*): "Thinking and thanking are in our language words of the very same origin. He who follows their sense finds himself in the realm of meaning of: 'to think of,' 'to be mindful of,' 'memory,' 'devotion.' Allow me to thank you from out of this realm" (*gedenken, eingedenk sein, Andenken, Andacht; GW* 3: 185). The ironies multiply: thanking a German audience by reminding them who he and they are; referring in the process to Heidegger's "What is Called Thinking?" with all the disturbance of

Heidegger's own Nazi involvement and his own "return" to a purer, poeticized German; and finally, implicitly declaring that for Celan, not only "thanking" but any German word is a call to remember. This sense of language as historical field is one Celan asserts at the outset of his career, in his 1948 essay on the surrealist painter Edgar Jené. There he contests the idea of language as preserved from, beyond, or impervious to the mark of history:

> Man not only languished in the chains of external reality but was also gagged and could not speak—and when I refer to speech I refer to the entire sphere of human communication and expression—because his words (gestures and motions) groaned under the burden of a thousand years of false and distorted sincerity—what was less sincere than the assertion that words somehow or other had basically remained unchanged! (EJ, GW 3: 157)

A "friend" in the essay argues for an essential language that retains its pristine innocence and purity against all temporal contamination. He tries to conjure, through the magic of naming, a "world purified of the dross of centuries and old lies," to attain a "state of timelessness, eternity" in which return to a primeval beginning is attainment of an ideal end. Against such a vision of linguistic absolutes, Celan asserts a radical vision of historicity. He insists on "the basic realization that something which has happened is more than simply an addition to a prior condition, more than an attribute of reality which may be more or less easily abstracted from it; it is rather something which changes the very essence of this reality, a powerful forerunner of constant transformation" (GW 3: 156).

Celan's poetic practice is deeply penetrated by this sense of history in language, which bears the record of its uses: a sense of both the historicity of language itself and its historical roles. This begins with his writing at once within and outside German. Celan's idiom is based in German, but by no means follows its normative syntactic patterns or even lexical base. The words open toward German usage, but do not conform to it. They evoke, indeed address, a German context of usage, but as this context intersects with the specific and particular idiom within each poem and within the inter-context of Celan's own writing. It is a peculiar and extreme feature of Celan's work that words acquire their meaning, that their significance can only be located, through the complex evolution of their appearance within his work. Words insistently call up their other appearances, each assertion an invocation, in a continual event of refinement, alteration, and opening toward ever-transforming meaning:

> With changing key
> you unlock the house in which
> drifts the snow of the silenced.
> Depending on the blood, which pours
> from your eye or mouth or ear,
> your key changes.
>
> Your key changes, the word changes,
> that is allowed to drive with the flakes.
> Depending on the wind that presses you forward,
> the snow crowds around the word.

> Mit wechselndem Schlüssel
> schliesst du das Haus auf, darin
> der Schnee des Verschwiegenen treibt.
> Je nach dem Blut, das dir quillt
> aus Aug oder Mund oder Ohr,
> wechselt dein Schlüssel.
>
> Wechselt dein Schlüssel, wechselt das Wort,
> das treiben darf mit den Flocken.
> Je nach dem Wind, der dich fortstösst,
> ballt um das Wort sich der Schnee.

> (*VS, GW* 1: 112)

Recalling the poem "Whitegray," here too a grotesque fragmentation of body disjoins eye, mouth, and ear. But here the determining context is that of language structure itself, as linked to the very notion and definition of selfhood and of home. Self, home, and language (and music? "key" is also "clef") reflect and represent each other within the poem's patterns of figuration. They are mutually constituting, or rather, mutually vulnerable in their multiple exposure to the "snow" that, wind-driven, at once invades home, buffets

self, and gathers around language, both giving it shape and engulf-
ing it.

This relation to "Whitegray" is not external or posterior.
"Whitegray" thematizes the fragmentation of temporal moment
and spatial part, the isolation of perceptual apprehension when
these are not integrated into a continuum. Among such pieces, the
poet is left suspended in the kind of moment that "Whitegray" as
text represents. But fragmentation enters into Celan's whole poetic
practice, governing the interrelation among his multiple utterances.
The constituent parts of the poem are never without connection to
their other appearances both within Celan's own corpus and beyond it. Each word in Celan is indeed a changing key, never complete within its own context, never finally established, always open
toward further and prior appearances: the word as a history, with
future and past.

Such linguistic interreflection is fundamental to Celan, where it
has, however, a double intention. On the one hand, it acts as a
fragmenting, centrifugal, endangering force, a radical questioning
of the possibility of coherence. It is in this sense quite distinct in
effect from a search for Heideggerean "purity," or for language as
an originary historical ground. On the other hand, as in "With
Changing Key," there is not only fragmentation, but also a resistance to it. Words—changeful, spurting blood, set against the
weight and wind of driftsnow—are nevertheless forming. Self/
house/language is offered as a figural reflection and representation,
although, and this is no less imperative, never as a finalized enclosure, never as an autonomous, self-complete structure.

Distrust of language, then, balances against an imperative call
to responsibility for it. Both impulses take shape in Celan through
his linguistic distortions, breakage and distribution of words, referential shatterings, and syntactic refusals. These stylistic features
are Celan's formal answer to such a charge as Hermann Burger
makes when he speaks of Celan's as "the flight into paradoxical
stammering [as] the final consequence of a poet, who despite the
violent deformation of language in the years after Hitler's seizure of
power . . . still employs it to bear witness to his soul."[58] Celan's

predicament is, however, not simple dissolution. It is use of a deformed language in full cognizance of its deformation, but perhaps toward a reformation both respectful and hopeful.

In this enterprise, Celan by no means evades the past. To the contrary, he registers its linguistic invasion. Thus, there are particular words that irrevocably carry for him a meaning derived from war: *ashes, smoke, shovel; sister, mother, almond eyes; autumn*— the means, season, and objects of death. The very word *word*, because it is a German word, carries a contagion: "A word, you know: a corpse." (Ein Wort, du weisst: Eine Leiche; *VS, GW* 1: 125). But the history of this distortion is also, for Celan, the history of his own linguistic fatality. For German is his mother tongue: "Do you still allow, mother, alas, as once at home, / the soft, the German, the painful rhyme?" (Und duldest du, Mutter, wie einst, ach daheim / den leisen, den deutschen, den schmerzlichen Reim; *SU, GW* 3: 25).[59] If Celan is to try to recover the past at all, what other past, what other language, is there for him to salvage?

> Whichever stone you lift up—
> you expose
> those who need the protection of stones:
> naked,
> they now renew the entwining.
>
> Whichever tree you fell—
> you construct
> the bedstead on which
> the souls pile up once more,
> as if this eon
> too did not
> quake.
>
> Whichever word you speak—
> you thank
> the decomposed.
>
> Welchen der Steine du hebst—
> du entblösst,
> die des Schutzes der Steine bedürfen:
> nackt,
> erneuern sie nun die Verflechtung.

Welchen der bäume du fällst—
du zimmerst
die Bettstatt, darauf
die Seelen sich abermals stauen,
als schütterte nicht
auch dieser
Äon.

Welches der Worte du sprichst—
du dankst
dem Verderben.

(*VS*, *GW* 1: 129)

Every act of construction uncovers an alarming substructure. It threatens to expose what has remained hidden, too painful to confront, but nevertheless persisting through all subsequent experience. The raising of stones is a disturbance. Even if the purpose is new building, it removes a prior shelter, which, however unstable, still had its function. And the new construction is never free. The trees felled thus become reinhabited by the unquiet souls, a further place of their abode. To build is in this sense to be doomed to repetition. Yet it still threatens a betrayal of the past, a pretense that "this eon" is not shaken by past ones. As to language, every word is marked with death.

To build is then to build out of debris, in precarious, oxymoronic relation to the base. Stone and tree are entangled in destruction, and the words of art are drawn from contaminated sources. All available material has been left over from wreckage, its use threatening justifications that themselves imply betrayals. The poet therefore remains uncertain, not knowing whether speech is a testimony to, or a revision and betrayal of, the events that found it.

Or silence. Celan offers many tropes for language's processes. Often these involve the notion of construction evoked here, that is, of building some kind of "bedstead," or, more often, simply a home. The longing for home, for a return to lost places—the "Homecoming" of one poem's title (*SG*, *GW* 1: 156)—is poignant throughout Celan's writing. This is a return that his poetry pursues and represents not only in its language, but as itself linguistic, as

a search for lost words, and for the power to speak them. It is a
threatened power. Within the idiom that establishes linguistic effect
and meaning in his poetry, words such as *home* and *word* align
with others: *snow* and *crystal* and *silence*. The "Homecoming" is
a track through a "snowfall, denser and denser" by a "self that slid
into dumbness." The retracing of a past also linguistic, without
which no poetry can be uttered, becomes equally a risk of its utter loss.

> "Underneath"
>
> Led home into forgetting,
> the guest-conversation of our
> slow eyes.
>
> Led home, syllable by syllable, divided
> among the day-blind dice, which
> the playing hand grips, large,
> in the awakening.
>
> And the too much of my speaking:
> heaped up around the small
> crystal in the garb of your silence.
>
> "Unten"
>
> Heimgeführt ins Vergessen
> das Gast-Gespräch unsrer
> langsamen Augen.
>
> Heimgeführt Silbe um Silbe, verteilt
> auf die tagblinden Würfel, nach denen
> die spielende Hand Greift, gross,
> im Erwachen.
>
> Und das Zuviel meiner Rede:
> angelagert dem kleinen
> Kristall in der Tracht deines Schweigens.
>   (*SG, GW* 1: 157)

To go home is to go home to forgetting; to the never-quite-belong-
ing of the guest; to a place of radical contingency, as of "day-blind
dice" in a "playing hand." Yet this is the path of return, "syllable
by syllable." The two impulses meet here, the "awakening" as well

as the "forgetting," the "too much" of speech, as well as the "crystal" of silence.

What empowers this linguistic way, which is, however, always at risk? Celan's own poetics offer some hint. Individual words appear in Celan always as pointing toward other appearances, other usages, both within and beyond their places within his poems. Far from refusing referential language, as Harald Weinrich, for example, claims of the word *snow*, in order to construct a "Metalanguage" of "language about language," these repeated word-chains link texts to each other but also beyond. This is a measure of their possible contamination (and even "crystal" may recall Kristallnacht);[60] but it is in Celan the only means of articulation.

Celan's poetic, that is, is one of address: from word to word, within the full contingency of events and utterances, and also on the whole level of utterance. Celan radically calls on the reader to reconstruct his words. This address is directly inscribed within the verse as an integral formal element in Celan's insistent invocation of, or toward, a "you." As he calls it in "Underneath," his is always a "guest-conversation." To be a guest is to be at once familiar and strange, to be given place but not to belong. It is a vulnerable relation, yet exactly because of this, one invested with respect and even privilege. In Celan, the images of the guest and of conversation reflect each other. Every participant in discourse is a guest; every guest commands a place at once distant and yet mediated through relation. The linguistic structure becomes, in this way, an intercourse, an exchange, in some sense always social, and also always vulnerable. Even "silence" is here distributed, socialized, between "my speaking" and "you." Silence, too, takes place in Celan within a texture of relation in the effort to construct a home or a poem, in the arc of address—even if this effort is defeated.

Interrupted Discourse

The address that informs even Celan's single words through their scattered contexts also directs his entire utterance, and in the most pronounced ways. Every individual word points to its other appearances within his work, and beyond it, to other literary and sociopolitical uses. But the most characteristic and unmistakable penetration of address into his work is his use of direct appeal to a "you" as his fundamental formal structure. It is in terms of such address, or dialogue, that Celan himself describes his poetic enterprise. In his Bremen speech, for example, the poem is presented through the figure of conversation, even if precariously as a message in a bottle:

> The poem can, as a manifestation of language and consequently in its essence dialogic, the poem can be a message in a bottle, sent in the—certainly not always hopeful—belief that somewhere and sometime it could be washed on land, on heartland perhaps. Poems are on the way also in this manner, they move towards something. Towards what? Towards something that stands open, something that can be occupied, towards a responsive "you" perhaps, toward a responsive reality. (GW 3: 186)

In Celan's poetics of address, words are "on the way," are moving "toward." Each word is thoroughly dialogized, in ways like those Mikhail Bakhtin proposes. In particular, Celan's poetics recall Bakhtin's notion of the "microdialogue" as "dialogic relationships . . . inside the utterance, even inside the individual word," so that in the word different "voices . . . hear each other constantly, call back and forth to each other, and are reflected in one another."[61] The Celanian word is never closed, never finalized; it always opens toward past and further uses, within his own texts and within historical usages. His words evoke and invoke, call up and answer to, moments of utterance, which therefore always face each other, intend each other. And they do so, above all, through direct address to a "you" that structures not only the verse form, but also the speaker, and not least, the audience of the poem—a possible "responsive you," a partly constructed "responsive reality."

The extent to which Celan's poetic utterance takes place in relation to a public space, a public world of language-use both as history and as dialogue is most simply evident in his use of multilingual, multinational counters or place names that also imply political events: "Frihed," the Danish word for freedom, is invoked when the "free-starred Above" (frei-sternige Oben) is glimpsed through "bullet-holes" (Einschuss-stellen; AW, GW 2: 77). The "Ausgärten" of Vienna contains a "dead merry-go-round" (*SG, GW* 1: 194). "Cologne" cathedrals are the place of the "Exiled and Lost" (Verbannt und Verloren; *SG, GW* 1: 177). "In Prague," "half of death . . . lay ash-image-true around us" (Der halbe Tod . . . lag aschenbildwahr um uns her; *AW, GW* 2: 63). The French Resistance is conjured in memories of lying "deep in the Macchia" (Wir lagen schon tief in der Macchia; *LZ, GW* 2: 239). And the "Moldau" is where "explosives smile at you" (Sprengstoffe lächlen dir zu; *SP, GW* 2: 406).

Celan himself had grown up in the multiethnic, multi-ideological territory of Czernowitz, subject to violent confrontations of competing bids for hegemony. In his poems, there is the sense of the word as passing across many tongues, in ways that suggest community but also threaten it. Words are both shared and exclusive. They are, as in "Give the Word," "passwords," used in order to be told "pass, pass, pass" (*AW, GW* 2: 93), or they are barriers to passing. "Schibboleth" (*VS, GW* 1: 131), as Derrida has shown, plays on both possibilities.[62] As the mark of different pronunciation, it represents difference itself. This is a boundary that must be respected, and the poem culminates, like the later poem "All in One," in the Republican challenge to the fascists: "no pasarán."

This constitution of Celan's verse as social discourse offers the greatest promise for recognizing its integration of textual and historical impulses. Far from working within a symbolist tradition of "language negating information and communication to escape the wear and tear of public life," Celan's is, as Marlies Janz puts it, an "engaged poetry," or, in Lielo Anne Pretzer's terms, a poetry with a "historical-social-critical dimension."[63] Janz in fact devotes her study of Celan to exploring the "relation between aesthetic autonomy and social address" such that "self-reflection of the poem is identical with the reflection of its social content." Pretzer similarly seeks to show how in Celan history and language are a "dialectical unity," in which "abstract linguistic-reflection . . . reflects the social content of the poetry."[64]

Yet these studies remain on the one hand thematic, and on the other enclosed within notions of self-reflexive linguistic orders.

That is, they continue to see Celan's art as directed "against conventional language" and as a "deconstruction of conventional reality."[65] The poetry remains a mode of retreat, an "absolute poetry symbolizing the negation of external control," albeit now with a political intention: to suggest "an aesthetic freedom comparable to political freedom"; to question "bourgeois norms of reason, morality, religion and aesthetics" a questioning which, however, finally involves a "descent into dumbness," although one that "itself has a political aspect."[66] Political action, then, mostly takes the form of protest by withdrawal into a world of art. Moreover, this reading of Celan through Marxist-based categories points, I believe, in directions other than his own with regard to the poems' subjects or speakers. Thus Pretzer speaks also of the "deconstruction" of the "traditional . . . bourgeois subject" as the "for-itself of the autonomous subject."[67] But while Celan's speakers depart from, and critique, traditional representations of the subject, Celan cannot be easily identified with a specific socioeconomic critique based in class consciousness. Nor do his representations accord with a collective subjectivity hypostasized into class and instrumental to some materially driven objective historical force.

The public space of Celan's language does, however, have important implications for the place and notion of the subject. In Celan, the subject, as we saw above, is always inscribed within a context. It takes shape in its relation to a world of which it is part. This taking-shape as taking-part occurs above all in Celan through the structure of dialogue, in which the subject is itself dialogized. It is never autonomous in foundation, nor merely inward in location. Rather, it comes into being in the act of address, as does the subject of its address, even when the speaker seems to be addressing himself. "The poem becomes," Celan states in his Meridian speech, "a poem of one who—as before—perceives, who faces that which appears, who questions this appearance and addresses it. It becomes dialogue—it is often a despairing dialogue. Only in the space of this dialogue does that which is addressed take form and gather around the I who is addressing and naming it" (GW 3: 198).

The I addressing, the you addressed, emerge only in relation to each other, a relation of dialogue. That is, the subject is always socially constituted, never existing independently either in origin or as end. This socially constituted self Celan distinguishes, however, from a Marxist one, in his reply to the question, "Is a Revolution Inevitable?" There he proposes a revolution that is "social and at the same time anti-authoritarian," beginning "here and now with the individual" (GW 3: 179). Social but individual: Celan represents the self as an individual who is both affirmed and yet placed in terms of specific conditions and in relation to other speakers.

And yet, in the very site of this sense of the self as a social, speaking being, Celan also entwines the image of the suppression, indeed erasure, of the speaking self. The Nazi regime, in its linguistic as in its other programs, denies the possibility of opposition, of multiple viewpoints, rhetorics, or expressions. There is in a sense no interlocutor, no other, no one to address within Nazi social and linguistic totality. And this, of course, had special application to the Jew, who was not only denied the right to speak, but utterly excluded from the totalized community, even denied the name of human. If, as Jean Amery says, exiled Germans could still identify with their native culture and language, the German Jew was, in contrast, violently ejected from the culture, and even from the hope of its redemption. And if, as George Steiner claims, the Jewish speaker's relation to German is always distinct from a native one, with German always a "language which had sprung from historical realities and habits of vision alien to his own," then National Socialism resolved this "alien" relation by destroying it.[68]

Celan writes facing exclusion from community as the space of communication. He writes having to create and keep open dialogical space, against a terrible pressure for its closure. Both impulses situate the obscurity and silence for which Celan's work is known and which he himself insists upon: "The poem today shows, in a way that has only indirectly to do with the not to be undervalued difficulty of the choice of words, of the more rapid slant of syntax, or of the more awake sense for the ellipse; the poem shows, this is unmistakable, a strong inclination towards silence" (GW 3: 197).

The inclination to silence invoked here is not only a technical matter. It is not a failure to represent reality (or even failure as "imitative" of a reality itself incoherent). Nor is it a retreat from "speech as mimesis of the world" so that poetry finally "points to itself and the inadequacy of its own language."[69] Celan's is not a poetry of failed representation but of interrupted discourse. The words fracture, the syntax slants, the ellipses penetrate in recognition of the founding of language in exchange, interchange, address offered and received, and also in response to the foundering of language when such interchange becomes ruptured.

There are many, many Celan texts which refuse the power of language to render a coherent image of reality. But woven through them, as the fragile thread sustaining representational claim, is the need to direct one's speech toward another, to address it to someone who will receive it—alongside the possible disappointment of this need:

> It is gathered, what we saw;
> at the parting of you and of me:
> The sea, that threw nights for us on land,
> the sand, that flew through them with us,
> the rust-red heather up there,
> in this the world happened to us.

> Versammelt ist, was wir sahen,
> zum Abschied von dir und von mir:
> das Meer, das uns Nächte an Land warf,
> der Sand, der sie mit uns durchflogen,
> das rostrote Heidekraut droben,
> darin die Welt uns geschah.
>
> (VS, GW 1: 99)

This is how the world happens: gathered, parted; sea-flung, sand-blown. It is a flux of dispersion. Yet it is channeled through "the parting of you and of me," a personal (dis)orientation. Celan's texts at times seem lost in inorganic spaces. Especially in later poems, the cosmos swirls as overwhelming, impersonal arena that threatens to lose all binding principle, as everything explodes into whirling, humming meteors. Even then, however, the entropic force acts through, and in terms of, an "us" at once addressed and inaccessible:

> What threw us
> together, scares apart
>
> a world-stone, aphelion, hums.

> Was uns
> Zusammenwarf,
>
> ein Weltstein, sonnenfern,
> summt.
>
> (*LS, GW* 2: 246)

Dispersed cosmos is a field of disrupted address, which severely fractures utterance. Yet address offers the only promise for reconstitution. "Night" (Nacht) is thus composed as inorganic scene, threaded through by voice and response:

> Pebbles and rubble. And a shard-tone, thin,
> as the hour's encouragement.

> Eye exchanges, final, untimely:
> image-steady,
> made wooden
> the retina—:
> the sign of eternity.

> Thinkable:
> up there, in the world-grid,
> starlike,
> the red of two mouths.

> Audible (before tomorrow?): a stone
> that takes the other as goal.

> Kies und Geröll. Und ein Scherbenton, dünn,
> als Zuspruch der Stunde.

> Augentausch, endlich, zur Unzeit:
> bildbeständig,
> verholzt
> die Netzhaut—:
> das Ewigkeitszeichen:

> Denkbar:
> droben, im Weltgestänge,
> sterngleich,
> das Rot zweier Münder.
>
> Hörbar (vor Morgen?): ein Stein,
> der den andern zum Ziel nahm.
>   (*SG, GW* 1: 170)

Pebbles and rubble, disparate and resistant. Yet through them, against them, sounds a "tone": itself a shard, a fragment, but a first sign of "encouragement." It takes shape within Celan's pervasive figure of eyes, here in an attempted exchange of glances; and as placed within a fuller portrait that includes "two mouths." These point toward a discourse that may yet make things "thinkable," may find their place in a world where connections do begin to emerge as a grid, "Weltgestänge." The poem stands open, listening for something "audible," directing itself toward an "other" as its goal.

The poem can occur, then, only as a trajectory of speech, directed toward a possible auditor. But Celan writes in the face of the erasure and suppression of the audience that makes discourse possible. His poems make visible these counterpressures and commitments, not only in poetic imagery, or syntax, or structural design, but within the speaking voice as it constitutes itself in its directed utterance. The poems in this sense do not simply register the poet's failure in the face of a "world emptied of significance."[70] They are not simply defeated representation or failed language, but rather interrupted discourse, an image of language when dissevered from audience and community:

> Your eyes in the arm,
> the
> burnt-apart
> they cradle you
> further, in the flying
> heartshadow, you.
>
> Where?
>
> Assign the place, assigns the word.

Extinguish. Lack.

Ash-bright, ash-right,
swallowed.

Measured, unmeasured, displaced, deworded—

dewo

Ash-swallowed, your eyes
in the arm
ever.

Deine Augen im Arm,
die
auseinandergebrannten,
dich weiterwiegen, im fliegen-
den Herzschatten, dich.

Wo?

Mach den Ort aus, machs Wort aus.
Lösch. Miss.

Aschen-Helle, Aschen-Elle—ge-
schluckt.

Vermessen, entmessen, verortet, entwortet.

entwo

Aschen-Schluckauf, deine Augen
im Arm,
immer.

(FS, GW 2: 123)

This poem has been described as an "eigenwilligen Sprachspiele," a willful language game.[71] But it is neither arbitrary nor linguistically autonomous. The imagery of burning and of ashes evokes the war-cremated. The "flying heartshadow" bespeaks the shadow of history cast over all Celanian language. The "eyes in the arm" are Celan's familiar eyes of time frozen into space, through which the self is distributed, without integration, as is the self's language. Discontinuities, unintegrated events, dislocation become events in a linguistic/spatial field. "Ash-bright" becomes "Ash-right"—in German, from "Aschen-Helle" to "Aschen-*Elle*": a yardstick, a unit of measure. But the unit mismeasures, and the very words for measurement undergo displacement and deformation: "vermessen, entmessen," measure, unmeasure. Words for placement are themselves displaced, and break down, including words for word-placement. Thus, space and language transmute into each other and finally disintegrate: "verortet, entwortet, entwo," displaced, deworded, dewo. This last fragment reiterates the poem's larger question, wo?—where?—projecting a self without direction, left among pieces of time, space, language.

And yet the poem is designed through a structure of address, in which the self is not the sole circumstance, nor an independent term of discourse—even if, as here, the address may also be self-directed. Yet exactly who else may be included within this address is another problem the poem poses. And it shows how mere self-address becomes a mode of self-fragmentation, while personal coherence depends on finding an interlocutor outside oneself. Public and private realms prove to be continuous, not least in discourse, which must traverse some public space, mediating the difference between the you and the I, and serving mutually to constitute them. But the Nazis suppressed the you. Celan's language is the record of that primary violence.

Silence becomes Celan's inscription of this rupture in the exchange that alone enables discourse. But silence has also in Celan another force, points in quite other directions. Celan also insists on the place of silence as an indelible mark within utterance, a boundary against claim, a curtailment of what may otherwise strive for too complete enclosure. It is, in this sense, a historical space for attempting to regain orientation, but also the limit of this attempt. In his Bremen speech, Celan makes this a biographical point:

Attainable, near and preserved, in the midst of all losses, remained only one thing: language. It, language, remained preserved, yes, in spite of everything. But it had to go through its own answerlessness, its dreadful silence, go through the thousand darknesses of deadly speech. It went through it and gave no words for what had happened; but it went through these events. Went through and was allowed to come to light again, "enriched" by it all. In those years and in the years that followed I have tried to write poems in this language: in order to speak, to orientate myself, to find out where I was and where I was going, to outline reality for myself. (GW 3: 186)

Passing through a death-bringing speech, Celan answers death back in its own language. Language offers a possible link between present and past, a possible framework in which to place his experience. This power of language to frame experience is vital. But its impulse to order is not for Celan absolute, uncircumspect, or unitary. Poetry requires no less an "obscurity," a reticence against explanation, "for the sake of an encounter—from a great distance or sense of strangeness." And quoting Pascal, he warns, "Ne nous reprochez pas le manque de clarté car nous en faisons profession"—do not reproach us for the lack of clarity which we have made our profession (GW 3: 195).

Broken Silence

Language too has its borders and its boundaries, its gaps, its obscurities. Celan in his own language insists on strangeness, without which there can be no encounter, but only engulfment. Against a language of/as appropriation, Celan offers a language of/as address: "Only in the space of this dialogue does that which is addressed take form and gather around the I who is addressing and naming it. But the one who has been addressed and who, by virtue of having been named, has, as it were, become a thou, also brings its otherness along into the present, into this present" (GW 3: 198–99). To address the other is to call forth both the other and the self, who both come to be within the space of discourse. But this always remains a space of difference, as a guard against intrusion and appropriation. The other always "brings its otherness" into "this present," which is always bound by, and partial because of, its specific time and place. Celan in his language, then, is not striving toward purity, closure, finalized form. Instead, he sees language as an opening, realized only through "this present" of particular events, always respectful of a resistant "otherness" and therefore also partial. Yet this partiality offers the only chance for the poem to point to what Celan goes on to call "openness, emptiness, freedom." Only "proceeding from the attention devoted to things and actual creatures" do we reach "the vicinity of something open and free" (*GW* 3: 199–200).

Such a commitment does not, however, translate into one specific formal mode. As John Brenkman rightly warns in discussing what he calls a socially critical hermeneutics, "We cannot presuppose that the unifying dimension of the work is—necessarily and categorically—the manifestation of a resistance to oppressive social conditions, any more than we can presuppose the opposite, that its unifying dimension is the mark of subjugation to 'ideological closure.' Such judgments have to be made contextually and through specific interpretations."[72] Neither aesthetic unity as such nor irreducible multiplicity within a work need entail a specific ideological stance. To the extent that Celan's aesthetic may be theorized in terms of stances at all, it seems to point not toward one or another ideology, but away from ideology altogether, where ideology is taken in Hannah Arendt's sense. In her analysis of totalitarianism, she argues that "all ideologies contain totalitarian elements" in their "claim to total explanation," making the logic of all events "the consequence of the 'idea' itself." Once ideological "claims to total validity are taken seriously they become the nuclei of logical systems in which . . . everything follows comprehensibly and even compulsorily once the first premise is accepted."[73] Arendt here uses the term *ideology* in ways decidedly different than does, say, Adorno, who defines it as "socially necessary false consciousness," and especially the "ideology of culture as [bourgeois] class privilege."[74] Arendt reserves the term *ideology* for the imposition onto reality of an idea claiming absolute validity beyond historicity, even if in the name of history itself. This seems finally more helpful toward discussion of Celan. Such usage is perhaps surprisingly confirmed by Julia Kristeva, who in "Psychoanalysis and the Polis" sees as a most "intrinsic reason" for the totalitarian phenomena of fascism and Stalinism "the simple desire to give a meaning, to explain, to provide an answer, to interpret."[75] She, in turn, recalls Bakhtin, who speaks of utopianism as a "faith in the omnipotence of conviction," and quotes Dostoevsky's notebook response to the claim "that to be moral one need only act according to conviction" with the response: "On the contrary, it is immoral to act according to one's convictions."[76]

Celan is in this sense anti-ideological exactly in his insistence on, in Arendt's phrase, the "outside factor," on the different and the other as a space kept open, to be respected and even guarded. "The poem must keep its possibilities open," he once remarked. "A given form makes the poem opaque, closed."[77] His reply at the Librairie Flinker points in similar directions. There he repudiates the "musicality" of language unless "placed in a region where it no longer has anything in common with that 'melodious sound' which more or less undisturbed sounded side by side with the greatest horror." Instead, he proposes a language of "precision," one that "doesn't transfigure, doesn't poeticize, it names and places, it attempts to measure the range of the given and the possible" (GW 3: 167).

Celan's sense of the danger of systemic explanatory orders emerges perhaps most urgently in his trope of "utopia," which he associates in the Meridian speech with "toposresearch" (Toposforschung) and "topoi" (GW 3: 199). Utopia here evokes impulses at once aesthetic, ideological, and religious. As to traditional theological structures and metaphysical claims, Celan remains profoundly suspicious of them. Religious dogma can take on the role and repressive force of ideological politics. Ideology, conversely, can posit its convictions with all the authority traditionally reserved for religious claims. In short, religion and ideology may be continuous and overlapping. Both act then through what I am calling incursions of the metaphysical into the physical: a displacement of the absolute into the sphere of conditional, mutable life. But this is to destroy the conditions that make life human. As Otto Pöggeler observes:

Does not the absolute of utopia have a double meaning? . . . Is there no danger that the utopia of yesterday can be the dictatorship of today? . . .

that the absolute . . . annihilates the human? and this not only in politics, but also in art, in which the last and highest achievement, is the "absolute-ness" that the poem would lay hands on? . . . Perhaps there is a hidden confluence between art and politics, a nearness between the apparently separate . . . is it not possible that politics and art today in different realms are driven by the same impulse: the will, to force man over into the absolute and to be therefore utopia?[78]

Such an aesthetic of the absolute is not pursued by Celan. His is not, as another critic would claim, a "reduction of language as a descent out of the visible world into an . . . inner utopia."[79] Instead, Celan raises questions regarding the whole valuation of ideal realms as the source and reference for truth accepted in Western culture from its beginnings. Always the absolute, the unconditioned, the realm of idea has been valued not only as the highest, most utopian, most true world, but as the source for all value and truth in the phenomenal world as its more or less poor material reflection. The pursuit of the idea, its instrumentation, has always been seen as the path toward redemption of the temporal, conditional sphere. It is the dream of overcoming all that prevents this finite world from fully realizing absolute value, absolute truth. Yet, as Celan makes us feel, the ideal ought not be claimed without limit. This may in fact logically distinguish ideology from a proper religious mode: ideology would be the refusal of all limiting boundary; religion, despite its historical collapses into ideology, would properly insist on the boundaries of the human. One would claim absolute hege-mony: the other would absolutely limit human hegemony.

In Celan, the word "eternity" is characteristically invoked with suspicion (as in the poem "Night," for example, where it seems to betray the finite eyes, making them seem "untimely" within an absolute) and therefore as false measure: a beyond time that negates time. To accept the stance and measure of eternity is to dis-place and subject actual experience to a realm which is not only alien to it, but which, as an imposed standard, must distort the experience in its temporality and multiplicity. Yet even in "Night" the image also remains ambivalent: "the retina, made wooden—: the sign of eternity." Is this sign a negative one, as perhaps hinted by the ligni-

fication of the eye? Or does it promise some stability, the validation
of memory itself?

For Celan is no less painfully aware of the rift in the world made
by the utter repudiation of any absolute. This is as great a danger as its displaced appropriation—and may indeed be a force behind such displacement. Celan is acutely aware of the vertigo described by Nietzsche, and which Heidegger sums up: "When God
dies as the metaphysical ground and the goal of all reality . . . then
man no longer knows where he is or where he is going."[80] Celan's is a powerful poetic of just such disorientation. In one poem,
"The Higherworld Lost" (Die Hochwelt verloren), life becomes a
"madjourney" (die Wahnfart; FS, GW 2: 199). The heavens as
a "god-removed star-heap blue" (gottentratene Sternhaufen-Blau)
opens into a "midsun, between two bright shots, abyss" (Mit-
sonne, zwischen zwei Hellschüssen Abgrund; ZH, GW 3: 101).
The horizon becomes a "star-nonsense" (Sternunfug) when gaped
at by "believing-unbelieving souls" (gläubig-ungläubigen Seelen;
ZH, GW 3: 111). Facing such chaos, Celan also resists it:

> The sky-heated
> fire-rip through the world.
>
> The Who's-there?—calls
> in its midst:
>
> through you here
> it was mirrored on the shield
> of the Eternal Bedbug,
> sniffed around by False and Disturbed,
>
> dragging the endless loop, nonetheless,
> that remains navigable for the un-
> toward answer.
>
> Der mit Himmeln geheitzte
> Feuerriss durch die Welt.
>
> Die Wer da?—Rufe
> in seinem Innern:
>
> durch dich hier hindurch
> auf den Schild

> der Ewigen Wanze gespiegelt,
> umschnüffelt von Falsch und Verstört,
>
> die unendliche Schleife ziehend, trotzdem,
> die schiffbar bleibt für die un-
> getreidelte Antwort.
>
> (*AW, GW* 2: 101)

The heavens, rather than representing a source of order, now themselves are torn apart as by fire, tearing the world in turn. Instead of binding, the heavens scatter, a failed shield (in "Who Rules?" [Wer herrscht?], too, the absent ruler is indicted as a "grave-shield of one of the thought-shadows" [der Grabschild eines der Denkschatten; *FS, GW* 2: 116]). Its eternity is mocked in the figure of a "bedbug" (can this recall the "vermin" of Nazi extermination propaganda?) both subject to, and causing, falsehood and disturbance. In this empty space a question opens toward an answer that is not forthcoming. Yet the question, "Who's-there," remains turned toward the absence it also records, while its call continues to define the space through which it reaches. Indeed, the question's answer, even as absent, is still the object that makes navigation possible. It retains a force of orientation, reaffirms the validity of the question and the possibility of, in some terms, an answer.

This double force of the absolute is inscribed in Celan's figure of utopia. In pointing toward the absolute as the ground of an order without which experience dissolves, utopia remains vital. As a reproach that seeks to efface and suppress the conditional, it is terrifying. But Celan is careful to locate his "U-topie" within his texts: in their "attention dedicated to things and creatures . . . into the region of utopia" (*GW* 3: 200). It takes shape there as a carefully orchestrated distribution of silence and language—a silence that is broken by language, a language that is broken by silence. The texts resist and question the sources and spheres, claims and limits, justifications and dangers of totalized coherence. They also register and fear the absolute failure of order, and in this assert a need for order. Celan's poems, early and late, are thus deeply marked both by the threat of incoherence and chaos when orders are too thoroughly resisted, and by the need to press back against the pressure of order. This too realizes Celan's image of his verse as "balanced on the edge of itself," balanced between the intention of order and the resistance to it.

The claims of both coherence and resistance to it penetrate Celan's very language, which becomes, in this sense, a subject of his verse. His effort is to define and place a principle of order without betraying the heterogeneity, mutability, and contingency of historical and human experience. Language becomes the arena of this task:

> Wing-night, come from afar and now
> for ever stretched over chalk and lime.
> Pebbles, rolling abysswards.
> Snow. And still more of the white.
>
> Invisible
> what seemed brown,
> thought-colored and wild
> overgrown with words.
>
> Lime, yes, and chalk.
> And pebbles.
> Snow. And still more of the white.
>
> You, yourself:
> bedded in the
> alien eye that oversees
> all this.
>
> Flügelnacht, weither gekommen und nun
> für immer gespannt
> über Kreide und Kalk.
> Kiesel, abgrundhin rollend.
> Schnee. Und mehr noch des Weissen.
>
> Unsichtbar,
> was braun schien,
> gedankenfarben und wild
> überwuchert von Worten.
>
> Kalk ist und Kreide.
> Und Kiesel.
> Schnee. Und mehr noch des Weissen.

Du, du selbst:
in das Fremde
Auge gebettet, das dies
überblickt.

(VS, GW 1: 128)

Chalk, lime, pebble, snow, white: the first stanza. Lime, chalk, pebble, snow, white: the third stanza. Listed elements, one by one, a composite without composition. As darkness comes, spanning the scene, it hides and makes invisible, rather than uniting or composing. Celan presents a piecemeal world, which from some point of view might come whole. This point of view, however, is inaccessible. A unifying eye that would draw the pieces together into a picture and provide an organizing vantage point is posited, but it remains out of reach, strange, alien.

This eye recalls Celan's many others, as, for example, the eye of "Streak" (Schliere), which is said "to preserve a sign borne through the dark, / revived by the sand (or ice?) of / an alien time for a more alien forever" (SG, GW 1: 159). Here, too, the eye enters the scene of history, of a "Wing-night, come from afar and now." It evokes an attempt to mediate and organize the pure flux of time and space without which experience veers into chaos. Yet exactly how to be itself in flight, and yet a stable viewpoint, remains a problem posed without resolution: the eye, remaining "alien," is invoked only to be declared absent.

Does Celan's use here of the "alien" have the force of an almost gnostic despair of meaning as inaccessible? Hans Jonas identifies the "alien" as a central topos of gnostic writings, where, from Mandean literature to Marcion, the divine is designated as "the alien life," "the alien God," or simply "the alien" in its nonmanifestation within the phenomenal world. It asserts in such contexts a rift between physis and metaphysis so absolute that although a Deity is assumed, he is entirely transmundane. The world does not reveal him. Its operations in fact deny him: "In its theological aspect this doctrine states that the Divine is alien to the world and has neither part nor concern in the physical universe; that the true god, strictly transmundane, is not revealed or even indicated by the world."

There is, that is, so severe a disjunction between a divine realm and earthly conditions that they become essentially antithetical. A metaphysical realm is so extremely asserted as to deny reality to the material realm. For all its absolute priority, the metaphysical has no relation, indeed no role, within the phenomenal, temporal realm. Of this disjunction, Jonas remarks, "A transcendence withdrawn from any normative relation to the world is equal to a transcendence which has lost its effective force. In other words, for all purposes of man's relation to the reality that surrounds him this hidden God is a nihilistic conception: no nomos emanates from him, no law for nature and thus none for human action as a part of the natural order."[01]

This image of the alien bespeaks a complete break between absolute and phenomenal realms, making the former inaccessible and the latter meaningless. And yet, in Celan's poem, the "alien eye" also provides a resting place: for the "you, yourself," which is proposed here with all the force of address. The address redirects toward the linguistic imagery this poem also proposes: of a scene "thought-colored and wild, overgrown with words." Thought and language, principles that should make sense of the sensed, only run wild, an overgrowth of multiplicity without ordering force. But language also takes shape as the poem, a directed discourse to a "you" who in this sense is given place and a home.

The poem is thus not a single image, either of order or of disorder, but of their mutual pressure and of their distinct claims—and dangers. If, here, the absence of the organizing "eye" threatens, it is an absence that also has, in Celan, positive function. Like the silence that disturbs finalized utterance, absence has a beneficial as well as a threatening aspect. For it can serve as a counterforce against total possession, as a limit on complete systemization, even as self-limitation against complete self-appropriation. Absence, like silence, acts to acknowledge and hold open the space of difference that is also the space of integrity. A negative movement, it rescues movement from the final negativity of totalization. In Celan, it is the very edge of the balance. It requires a language that holds itself back from direct assertion, from overclaiming; a language that, in this, can even point in a redemptive direction, although one less utopian than messianic:

> Word-deposit, volcanic,
> overroared by ocean.
>
> Above,
> the flowing mob
> of anticreatures: it
> flagged down—image and after-image
> cruise idly timewards.
>
> Until you whirl out the word-
> moon from which
> the miracle ebb occurs
> and the heart-
> shaped crater
> conceives/witnesses naked for the beginnings,
> the births
> of kings.
>
> Wortaufschüttung, vulkanisch,
> meerüberrauscht.
>
> Oben
> der flutende Mob
> der Gegengeschöpfe: er
> flaggte—Abbild und Nachbild
> kreuzen eitel zeithin.
>
> Bis du den Wortmond hinaus-
> schleuderst, von dem her
> das Wunder Ebbe geschieht
> und der herz-
> förmige Krater
> nackt für die Anfänge zeugt,
> die Königs-
> geburten.
>
> (AW, GW 2: 29)

This frequently discussed poem represents at once many of Celan's most characteristic and determining features. Enacting an explosion of linguistic power, it radically asserts a linguistic reality, with words in cosmic configuration: a word-volcano erupts, fueling a word-flood which, in the tidal imagery that controls the poem, fills the air, and surges as an ebb and flow in the gravitational field of the "word-moon."

This assertion of linguistic world is recognized by Peter Horst Neumann, who adopts its opening image of "word-deposit" as an emblem for Celan's general stylistic tendency to compound word formations from disparate word parts. He sees this as a "symbolist poetics" that opposes poetic to normal speech, stripping the former of its mediating powers of communication, "corresponding to no reality and instead creating its own poetic reality, which remains restricted within the measured space of the poetic language."[82] Hans-Georg Gadamer also reads the poem in linguistic terms, distinguishing in the poem superficially driven speech from the hidden ground of language through which the authenticity of true being is made visible. Thus, the opening section of the poem represents inauthenticity. The "anticreatures" are mere "image and after-image" of true words, a "mob" without "name or future or homeland" subordinated to time that drives it "without direction or goal," "without inner duration." But the second section registers the radical language-turn to authenticity. The miraculous rebirth of kingship is a "metaphor" for language, whose rule is recognized as the ground for further linguistic authenticity in the guise of new poems: "Every true poem touches on this hidden depth of language-ground and its creative figures."[83]

Both Neumann and Gadamer oppose the language of poetry to the "normal" speech of communication. As Gadamer states, the "poem speaks of the experience of words as a volcanic explosion, which takes off against the everyday impulse of language" so that "the whole desert of conventional language runs out like brackish water." In this, their readings accord with attempts to interpret the poem in more directly historical terms such as those proposed by Pretzer and Janz. They see Celan's language here as "non-instrumental" in counterthrust against oppressive social and political conditions and the place of language within them. But where Gadamer sees the image of the "birth of kings" as a redemptive force, Pretzer and Janz consider such a positive reading a betrayal of the actual historical situation, which remains unredeemed, and of the political action which alone can redeem it. The image of the "birth of kings," according to Pretzer, "provides a glimpse beyond" actual conditions. But the power of the poem to achieve any such "beyond" is severely curtailed. Under current conditions of alienation, a feigned "restored world" can do no more than "unmask the illness" of current social reality. In itself it must fail to provide any positive image of "the hope for a better world."[84]

Pretzer and Janz each reject a redemptive force, especially in a religious sense. Religion merely displaces political protest onto a plane of unreality that ultimately only affirms the status quo— "a justification for those in power to perpetrate the inhumane." To them, the redemption Celan cites is "not religious," but rather "articulates a need for redemption and not an absurd belief in redemption."[85] But while Celan does criticize religious structures that would promise reward and resolve suffering by transferring redemption to another world, he retains a powerful religious impulse. It is one, however, that searches for a significance that is earth-centered, historical, immanent. It would assert temporal life as the site of values, but grounded in some absolute that guarantees their stability and supports their realization. In this language becomes, as Gadamer suggests, a redemptive force. But it does so as a linguistic figure for a redemption mediated through history—one that, as in Benjamin's messianism, is at once historical and religious.

This redemptive movement is traced in "Word-Deposit." Declaring a dynamic linguistic world, a world in all the motion of change and alteration represented by erupting volcanoes forming new layers of world-soil, Celan in the poem posits two stances: the aimless flood-mob of "anticreatures" who, as Gadamer writes, cruise idly in a time without direction or purpose; and opposed to this, the miracle of the word-moon, thrust into a new orbit that testifies to a messianic rebirth. This rebirth, however, remains temporal. It does not signal a removal from earth to heaven. On the contrary, the poem's imagery radically insists on a continued earth-centered perspective. The miracle of the word-moon is experienced as an ebb of waters no longer tidally flooding, but rather moving within the redefined gravitational pull of the renewed heavenly body, and thus gaining direction and orientation. This ebb remains temporal and terrestrial. The word-moon is a messianic and not an apocalyptic sign. It testifies not to the end of earthly life but to its renewal in positive relation to a heavenly power above it, one felt within its process and flow as the responsive tie between moon and water, heaven and earth.

"Word-Deposit" remains a poem describing the poetic process. The word-movements of poetic creativity construct the ebb and flow of the world of the poem. On this level of poetics, the poem similarly reflects two possibilities: the creation of a detached counterworld of "anticreatures," and a call to the "you" to participate in an open process of creation that changes the course of time's tides. This "you" addresses both poet and reader, in challenge and invitation: to decipher, to weigh, to piece together, or to fail to do so. In this, "Word-Deposit" gathers together many impulses central throughout Celan's work. It recalls his image of the meridian, of language as "immaterial but earthly," and thereby connecting, orienting, "circular, turning across the two poles." The meridian is both worldly and of words, creating in its compass a linguistic world in which "tropics" are also "tropes." Finally, it is "something which binds and which, like the poem, leads to an encounter" (GW 3: 202). The world/word circle it traces promises a renewed space in which the "immaterial" and the earthly, the world above and the world below, move forward in mutual affirmation.

But this promise, here sketched and envisioned, often remains in Celan painfully elusive. It is countered by a no less powerful sense of disjunction between the hope of redemption and the realities of earth, the axiological failure to inform experience with value and the chaos that results. Thus Heaven, in one poem, is felt "pustule on pustule," while earth scatters, "shadow on shadow" (VS, GW 1: 133). Nor can aesthetic order alone relieve or redeem the conflagration of time. Celan's poetry provides an image for both the urge to coherence and its distrust, the desire for redemption and its

continued failure. The poems court, in this, an active obscurity.
They insist both on silence and on the breaking of silence, where to
be "unreadable" is both risk and invitation:

> Unreadable this
> world. Everything doubles.
>
> The strong clocks affirm
> the split-hour,
> hoarse.
>
> You, clamped
> in your deepest,
> climb out of yourself
> for ever.
>
> Unlesbarkeit dieser
> Welt. Alles doppelt.
>
> Die starken Uhren
> geben der Spaltstunde recht,
> heiser.
>
> Du, in dein Tiefstes geklemmt,
> entsteigst dir
> für immer.
>
> (*SP, GW* 2: 338)

The image of doubling here points toward any number of dualisms
that, in Celan, lead to the illegibility this poem announces: between
fact and meaning, action and value, time and redemption. The
double conjures ideal worlds such as those postulated by Platonist
metaphysics, which, as Aristotle first complained, may pose more
problems than they resolve. For, as he remarks, it is unclear "what
on the earth the Ideas contribute to sensible things." While the Platonists "fancy we are stating the substance of perceptible things,"
they in fact "assert the existence of a second class of substances,
while our account of the way in which they are the substances of
perceptible things is empty talk."[86] The Ideas, instead of serving as
ontological ground for perceptible things, seem only to duplicate
them as a second set of objects whose correspondence to the first
remains both logically and axiologically problematic.

In this poem, the world as double loses sense. Time splits apart, with "strong clocks" hoarse in their attempt to fix and affirm the "split-hour." Yet, against this, the poem continues to take form as address. That the "you" remains poised between an inaccessible indifference and an orienting appeal is the poem's particular art. For "you" may remain sequestered in itself, resisting address and response. Its ascent may be an ever increasing detachment from a world it leaves behind in disarray. Or, the poem may be a call, bidding the "you" to act as a positive double, as it climbs forth out of hidden depths, into the time and language of possible relation and positive orientation.

That these several readings cannot be resolved is part of the poem's own illegibility. But to be unreadable here is also a positive pressure. It is to refuse the closure of linguistic resolution, which would betray all that remains—especially in terms of history—inexpressible because inexplicable. Its silences are a potent, unconverting testimony. But it also responds to, and against, engulfment in events beyond interpretation. That is, it marks a double resistance: against overwhelming silence, against appropriating speech.

"But, the poem speaks!" Celan exclaims in the Meridian speech. "It is mindful of its dates but—it speaks." It does so, however, only in that "it always speaks on its own behalf, for its most particular concerns," speaks for someone "from the angle of inclination of his own existence, of his creatureliness" (GW 3: 197). The recalcitrance of the date, of history, of individual experience and memory: these situate any discourse, and must always be acknowledged. Yet the poem does not speak only to or of itself, but toward a you. It travels the "ways of a voice toward a perceptive you" (GW 3: 201) to take place in a "mystery of meeting" (Geheimnis der Begegnung; GW 3: 198). The figure of Celan's poetry is above all one respecting this mystery. It faces in full awe, and even terror, the possible blankness of no response, no auditor. It is therefore perhaps even more a call than an address. Celan makes visible in his texts the fundamental shape of language as a trajectory across distances, between speakers. His then are poems, as he states in the Bremen speech, "on the way . . . towards something that stands open, . . . towards a responsive you, perhaps, towards a responsive reality." He offers his texts as "the efforts of one who . . . exposed to the open in the most awful manner, goes with his existence to language, reality-wounded and reality-seeking" (GW 3: 186).

CHAPTER 6

The Letters of Creation:
Paul Celan and the Kabbalah

In thirty-two wonderful Paths of Wisdom did . . .
the King of ages, the merciful and gracious One,
the Dweller in eternity, most high and holy,
engrave his Name by the three Sepharim—
Numbers, Letters, and Sounds.

—Sefer Yetzirah

᠊ᢈ᠊

Mystical Negation

Blasphemy is not a modern phenomenon, but it is a modern profession. It exerts repeated pressure on Eliot's prose; it is a haunting presence in Beckett's art; and in Celan's poetry, it becomes a deeply inscribed and potent force. There it permeates not only the religious but also the linguistic dimension of his work. Language remains in many senses Celan's central engagement. But language involves for Celan a historical and religious venture as well as a poetic one. *No One's Rose*, Celan's third volume, is often cited as a turning point of Celan's awakened interest in his Judaic background, while his late Jerusalem poems are seen as a final recognition of, if also a resistance to, that background. However, I would argue that a religious impulse persists in Celan's work from the earliest through the last volumes. It does so not only through overt reference, but through the linguistic interest that stands at the heart of his poetry. That is, ultimately Celan's whole language-centered poetic cannot be separated from the Jewish contexts he also invokes.[1]

Above all, Celan's linguistic concern cannot be separated from the context of Jewish mysticism, in which language has a central, even defining place. Celan's interest in mystical sources has of course been recognized almost from the outset, and has attracted repeated, if sporadic, attention. His at first hesitant and then insistent use of modes of negation for designating the Godhead; the "you" of dialogue that pervades his poetry; the presence and pressure of silence in and upon his work: all have rightly been identified with mystical practice and mystical paradox. Indeed, in exploring such Judaic and mystical motifs, critics have pursued the hint provided by Celan himself. In his Bremen speech he says, "The landscape out of which I come to you—by what detours! but is there then such a thing as a detour?—is probably unknown to most of you. It is the landscape, in which a not inconsiderable part of the Hasidic stories were at home, which Martin Buber has retold us in German"(GW 3: 185). Celan's own detours had led him through a childhood Hebrew education for which he seems not to have evinced enthusiasm, preferring instead a Gymnasium curriculum, and finally the study of Romance languages and literatures. Only later did he turn back toward Judaic study, with special attention to the writings of Martin Buber on Hasidism and of Gershom Scholem on Kabbalah (which is why their work so often seems like commentaries on his), after the Second World War had divested him of home, family, and community.[2]

A mystical context for Celan's writing first attracted attention through his use of terms of negation in ways peculiarly marked. This is the case in the poem "A Day and One More" (Ein Tag und noch einer), for example, which introduces Celan's characteristic use of the "niemand," no one:

> Foehn-like you. The silence
> flew before us, a second,
> distinct life.
>
> I won, I lost, we believed
> in dark wonders, the branch
> quickly written onto the sky, carried us, grew
> through the stretched white into moon-orbit, a tomorrow
> sprang up into yesterday, we brought

the scattered candlestick, I flung
everything into no one's hand.

Föhniges Du, Die Stille
flog uns voraus, ein zweites,
deutliches Leben.

Ich gewann, ich verlor, wir glaubten
an düstere Wunder, der Ast,
rasch an den Himmel geschrieben, trug uns, wuchs
durchs ziehende Weiss in die Mondbahn, ein Morgen
sprang ins Gestern hinauf, wir holten,
zerstoben, den Leuchter, ich stürzte
alles in niemandes Hand.

(*SG, GW* 1: 179)

The conclusion of this *Speechgrille* poem appeals to "no one" for
the first time in Celan's work in what has come to be recognized as
its mystical usage in his writings ("niemand" makes one earlier
appearance, in "Count the Almonds" [Zähle die Mandeln; *MG,
GW* 1: 78]). There it seems an ordinary pronoun, though such common usage need not contradict its more specialized meanings, as
will be seen. Declaring the belief even in "dark wonders" to be past,
and left only with the disrupted religious object, the "scattered
candlestick," the poet flings "everything into no one's hand." The
wreckage of his faith he thus seems to discard. Instead of giving
everything into the hand of God, he gives it into the hand of no one.

But, as Peter Paul Schwarz was the first to remark, Celan's "no
one" belongs to a particular context and has multiple meanings. As
a negation in place of God, it seems outright blasphemy. Nevertheless, it can be as well a mystical designation for the Godhead, in
which case it is not blasphemous, or not simply so: "The blasphemous character of this expression becomes doubtful, if one recalls
that the observant Jew out of piety does not pronounce the name
of God, but rather circumvents it. Indeed, this circumventing the
name of God with No One . . . is practiced in Jewish mysticism as
the paradoxical equivalent for the divine Being, which, as above the
reality in transcendence, is absolutely inexpressible." In light of the
Jewish practice of not directly naming God, and of the mystical

practice of designating him by negation, Celan's use of negation thus stands "in a peculiar twilight between blasphemy and piety."[3] This recognition by Schwarz of a Judaic and mystical significance in Celan's work has been subsequently pursued. Thus, in *Celan und die Mystiker*, Joachim Schulze explores the mystical context for Celan's *niemand*—a context that, he argues, resolves the question of blasphemy into mystical paradox—and identifies many other mystical and kabbalistic motifs in Celan's work.[4] Peter Horst Neumann similarly cites the taboo against speaking God's name as background for the use of *niemand*, and explains it in terms of attempting to name what is beyond naming: "The absolute, insofar as man can experience it and can mediate it by language, is itself a paradox. . . . Therefore Celan's writing is directed, in that this paradox is raised into its characteristic stylistic figure, to represent this absolute. Where the name of God cannot risk being expressed, it can still be indicated through the indefinite pronoun *no one*."[5]

In a poem such as "A Day and One More," with its "wonders" and "scattered candlestick," the mysterious "silence" of its first stanza and the mystical "no one" of its end, some religious dimension is clearly indicated. Yet identifying these motifs as Judaic, Hasidic, or kabbalistic does not finally explicate the poem, nor does it unravel the complexity of Celan's relation to Jewish material. Indeed, the identification of Celan's mystical interest has in some ways obscured as much as illuminated his work. Problems arise especially when Celan's mysticism is conflated with mystical notions that touch upon the systems out of which he worked, but remain distinct from them. There is, for example, a tendency to speak of a mystical union in Celan; of the dissolution of the individual and the temporal into an eternal, absolute realm beyond this world; and correspondingly, of the dissolution of language into some ineffable totality beyond utterance. These in turn become the terms for explicating not only Celan's use of mystical paradox with its accompanying terms of negation, but also his pervasive use of the "you" of address, and the role of silence in his work.

Thus, Peter Paul Schwarz identifies the "you" of Celan's early poetry with the transcendent dead, and sees in Celan's dialogues, as well as in his motif of silence (closely linked to negation), the attempt to surpass time and language in a "mystical communication with the thou of the dead." "This union," he continues, "realizes itself outside of actual temporal process." It seeks an "Überzeit," a Supratemporality, that reconciles the "contradictions between I and Thou, living and dead, through a mystical union in love."[6] Neumann, following the suggestions of Schwarz, similarly extends mystical paradox not only to the meaning of "no one" but also to Celan's "thou" and to silence in Celan, which he sees as a function of the ineffable nature of Celan's experience. Thus Celan is said to be attempting to achieve "an absolute language" (die Sprache des Absoluten), leading him to the mystical "paradox . . . in which he expresses the inexpressible," and which is "finally the paradox of the mystical mediation of experience in language."[7] Hermann Burger, too, in *Auf der Suche nach der verlorenen Sprache*, begins by remarking that "Celan's poetry is rooted in the mystical tradition of Hasidism." But he then continues: "Celan's is a quest for a language which has been nourished outside of the time of his terrible experiences" and which therefore takes a "utopian direction."[8] This, no less than Neumann's absolute speech, presents Celan's work as an attempt to enter the supratemporal and the supramundane. And Joachim Schulze places Celan's mysticism in the tradition of Meister Eckhart, Angelus Silesius, Jakob Boehme, and Pascal, a tradition in which "man surrenders himself completely, and divests himself of his ego" so that "the soul dies away in God." With this, Schulze concludes, citing Eckhart, "it completely separates itself from this world and travels to the place it has earned . . . in Thee, o eternal God, who must be its life because of this dying through love."[9]

But the status of negation, of dialogue, of silence, and ultimately of language in Celan must be approached in terms not of mysticism in general, but of Jewish mysticism with its distinctive features. All mysticisms share certain common terms, and certain Jewish mystics record experiences like those familiar to Christian ones. Nevertheless, Judaic mysticism remains defined within the specific context of Judaic structures and assumptions. These differ in fundamental ways from the structures and assumptions governing Christian mysticism, and serve to distinguish Judaic from Christian mystical phenomena even when they share topoi, terms, and a common philosophical basis in Neoplatonist, Aristotelian, and gnostic mystical developments. Despite apparent and also actual similarities between Judaic and Christian mysticism, in which negation and silence, for example, have a no less central importance, the emphasis, valence, resonance, and basic meaning of these terms within Judaic and Christian structures remain distinct—with important consequences for their meaning and function within Celan's poetry.

This distinction can be seen perhaps most dramatically in Jewish mysticism's peculiar and passionate commitment to language and textuality—the Letter in all its aspects and senses. Within both rabbinic and mystical tradition, language is not only a central but, I would claim, *the* commanding image and figure. It conditions all other terms, such as negation and silence, that are shared with other religious and mystical systems. This commitment to the Letter profoundly reveals the attitudes, values, and orientations implicit within the entire Judaic religious structure. It gives rise to a mysticism that in general strives neither to enter into absolute and eternal realms, merging with atemporal transcendence, nor to transcend language and displace it with the ineffable.

Instead, the temporal world of particular sites and moments, of concrete and diverse materiality, defines the sphere of activity—even, to a startling degree, of mystical activity. This priority of the temporal is announced in the title of "A Day and One More," while the force of the concrete, the discrete, the material, is registered through the initial apostrophe to the wind: "Foehn-like you, the silence / flew before us, a second, / distinct life." In addressing the foehn, a wind that blows on the north side of the Alps, Celan emphasizes the particular name of a concrete phenomenon. As "you," Celan further recalls the wind as *ruach* of divine action, often translated as spirit, but which in the Hebrew language and context never loses its sense as the physical force of air or breath in motion. In biblical usage, the term evokes divine inspiration, as of Moses, Joshua, the Judges, and the prophets. Martin Buber, in *The Pro-*

phetic Faith, underscores how in each case ruach comes at a particular moment, into a particular situation. The prophetic experience constitutes "a relationship which embodies itself in a concrete event, which continues to operate concretely."[10] In Celan's poem, it comes as a flying "silence," recalling, among any number of biblical prototypes, the prophet Elijah. The ruach of the Lord, it is written, carries Elijah he knows not where (1 Kings 18: 12). Elijah is then swept to Mount Sinai, where he receives a revelation: "And behold the Lord passed by, and a great strong wind rent the mountains, and brake in pieces the rocks before the Lord; but the Lord was not in the wind; and after the wind . . . a fire, but the Lord was not in the fire; and after the fire a voice of slender silence (*kol demmama dakah*; 1 Kings 19: 11–12).[11] Elijah hears the voice as this silence.

Celan, in his own time and place, names the ruach as "foehn-like." He sees its stillness flying before him, promising for him, as for Elijah, "ein zweites, deutliches Leben," a second, distinct—and, with a play on another meaning of *deutliches*, perhaps articulate—life. This silence, like the wind, takes place neither in the atemporal nor in the metaphysical; it flies palpably in the poet's world and meets him there. It is exactly as temporal and placed that this "silence" is encountered. Moreover, within the poem, this trope of silence is placed within a further trope of language, in the image of "the branch, quickly written onto the sky." The sky becomes a sheet of paper, the branch a specimen of writing. The world itself is become a linguistic structure, with the branch-as-writing an object in the cosmos, pulled into a "moon-orbit." The branch also suggests the image of a "Tree"—both a general trope for Torah and a central kabbalistic image of divine configuration. It serves as an instance of linguistic imagery as it functions in Celan, bringing together poetic, religious, and mystical material. But whether the biblical text is called the Tree of Life, or whether its letters take shape as the branches of mystical divine names, the temporality of language is by no means erased. Rather, it is explicitly asserted: "A tomorrow / sprang up into yesterday."

Yet such temporality is not without risk, not without disruptive danger. The "no one" to which it conducts this poem, if not simply negative, is highly equivocal. Within the trajectory of linguistic venture, a failure of recovery, a triumph of the forces of sheer dispersion, is not only possible, but threatening. In Martin Buber's terms, the divine as word does not involve "transposition of something originally beyond time into historical time" but rather "embodies itself in the concrete event, which continues to operate concretely."[12] But it also exposes itself to the challenge of historical event, to possible temporal dispersal and defeat. Even this danger, however, reasserts the temporal nature and measure of a divinity conceived in linguistic tropology; so that, in the poem, even so otherworldly a topos as "no one" acquires a this-worldly emphasis. And the silence at the poem's center is inscribed within a linguistic world, valued through and by temporal experience.

Linguistic Return

Language is fundamentally temporal and historical in Celan, and this has many implications for his work. On the one hand, and against most mystical impulses, it directs Celan's work away from an effort to overcome the distinction between an eternal world and the world of time, or to establish itself in the former. On the other, it opens the realm of divinity to direct incursion by historical trauma. If the divine, especially figured in linguistic terms, ventures into time, then it becomes measured by, and exposed to, the dispersions of time, its exiles and terrors:

> We are near, Lord,
> near and graspable.
>
> Grasped already, Lord,
> clawed into one another, as
> though the body of each of us
> was your body, Lord.
>
> Pray, Lord,
> pray to us,
> we are near.
>
> Nah sind wir, Herr,
> nahe und greifbar.

Gegriffen schon, Herr,
ineinander verkrallt, als wär
der Leib eines jeden von uns
dein Leib, Herr.

Bete, Herr,
bete zu uns,
wir sind nah.
(SG, GW 1: 163)

Membership in the body of the Lord is a membership in the violent body of history, of the masses of war-dead. Celan plays, at the poem's opening, on the words of Hölderlin's "Patmos": "Near, and hard to hold is God" (Nah ist, Und schwer zu fassen der Gott). Now, it is we whom the Lord must attempt to grasp. Not man, but God, must renew the terms of exchange between heaven and earth.

Blasphemy here is at once historical, religious, and linguistic crisis. Every word in Celan retains the markings of history. This is especially true for the words of his tradition, and not only in his relation to it, but in the status the tradition itself accords to language and writing. The Hasidic "landscape" Celan recalls in his Bremen speech was a "landscape where men and books lived." As Martin Buber attests, in the typical Hasidic story "the words used to describe experiences were more than mere words; they transmitted what had happened, and with such actuality that the words in themselves became events." [13] Gershom Scholem similarly observes that "in the place of the theoretical disquisition, or at least side by side with it, you get the hassidic tale. . . . To tell a story of the deeds of the saints has become a new religious value, and there is something of the celebration of a religious rite in it." [14]

Celan's is literally an inheritance of language; his tie to his tradition is profoundly linguistic, as is the tradition itself in many senses. Accordingly, when he presents the destruction of this Hasidic landscape by war as a destruction of words, this too is literal. "Voices: wind-suitable, heart-near, blaze-buried" (Die Stimmen: windgerecht, herznah, brandbestattet; SG, GW 1: 169), he writes. "All the names, all the burned-away-together names. So much ash to be blessed" (Alle die Namen, alle die mit-verbrannten Namen. Soviel

zu segnende Asche; *NR, GW* 1: 227). The war-destroyed are destroyed names. Their world is become word-particles, scattered and
distributed through an abyss of historical space. The "deaths and
all born out of them," he writes, "the race-chain still hangs in the
Aether"; and they do so as "face-writings, into which the whirling
wordsand has pierced—small eternity syllables" (Die Tode und
alles / aus ihnen Geborene . . . die Geschlechterkett . . . die hier
noch hängt, im Äther. . . . Aller Gesichter Schrift, in die sich schwir-
render Wortsand gebohrt—Kleinewiges, / Silben; *NR, GW* 1: 274).

Fragmented language is now all that is left to Celan from his
childhood world. It is therefore in the shape of words that his past
most haunts him. Each evening is an "evening of words" (Abend
der Worte) in which "the scar of time is opened and floods the land
with blood" (die Narbe der Zeit tut sich auf und setzt das Land
unter Blut; *VS, GW* 1: 117). His nights are a darkness that "tracks
you down in words" that are also tears, "the salt from your lashes"
(spürt dich im Wort auf, im Wunsch, im Gedanken . . . das Salz aus
den Wimpern; *MG, GW* 1: 63).

History as linguistic world is both haunting and scattered.
Words are all that is left of the past. To salvage these words is to
reassert the world to which they belonged, although always in the
face of loss. As in "A Day and One More," the future is disturbed,
but also made possible, by the past: "a tomorrow sprang up into
yesterday." For Celan, turning back and toward his heritage is an
act of linguistic return, retracing a word-path, as in the poem "The
Sluice" (Die Schleuse):

> Over all this your
> grief: no
> second heaven.
>
> . . . . . .
>
> To a mouth,
> for which it was a thousand-word,
> lost—
> I lost a word
> that was left for me:
> sister.

To
many-godded-ness
I lost a word that sought me:
Kaddish.

Through
the sluice I had to
rescue in the saltflood the word back
and out of and over:
Yiskor.

Über aller dieser deiner
Trauer: kein
Zweiter Himmel.

. . . . . .

An einen Mund,
dem es ein Tausendwort war,
verlor—
verlor ich ein Wort, das mir verblieben war:
Schwester.

An
die Vielgötterei
verlor ich ein Wort, das mich suchte:
Kaddisch.

Durch
die Schleuse musst ich,
das Wort in die Salzflut zurück-
und hinaus- und hinüberzuretten:
Jiskor.

(NR, GW 1: 222)

The poet names the sluice of language through which he reaches
toward the word that reaches toward him. The flood of tears is its
medium, and no ascent to a higher heaven is either redemptive or
possible. Instead, he must go across the voided line of "answerlessness," as he calls it in his Bremen speech: the "frightful dumbness"
of "the thousand darknesses of deathbringing speech . . . with no
words for it," but which become nevertheless the words "preserved," in which "I have tried to write poems" (GW 3: 186). Just
so here, the lost word is shattered ("a thousand-word") as is the

very word of God ("many-godded-ness"). Yet these words also remain and seek him. The poet recovers and is recovered by them, as they grow ever more personal, ever more inflected through traditional modes and discourses: sister, Celan's general word for the many dead; *Kaddish*, a communal prayer consecrating the dead; and *Yiskor*, the memorial prayer reserved for near relatives.

The saltflood that drowns with grief thus also conducts the poet back to his lost words and rescues them for his present. It has often been asserted that *No One's Rose*, in which "The Sluice" appears, represents a return to Jewish themes after Celan "had abandoned his Jewish voice" in his earlier poetry.[15] But the interest in language that is already overwhelming in the earlier volumes is inseparable from Celan's Judaic concern as a tradition of the letter. Conversely, what might appear as a purely linguistic interest, even in the more overtly Jewish *No One's Rose*, may have a no less specifically Judaic force:

> A boomerang, on breathways,
> so it wanders, the wing-
> mighty, the
> true. On
> star-
> orbits, kissed by world-
> splinters, scarred by time-
> grains, by timedust, co-or-
> phaned with you,
> Lapilli, endwarfed,
> enminimized, an-
> nihilated,
> spent and discarded,
> itself the rhyme,—
> so it comes
> flying, so it comes
> again and home,
> its heartbeat, for a thousandyear long
> held in like the
> only pointer in the orb,
> that a soul,
> that its soul
> inscribes,

that a soul
numbers.

Ein Wurfholz, auf Atemwegen,
so wanderts, das Flügel-
mächtige, das
Wahre. Auf
Sternen-
bahnen, von Welten-
splittern geküsst, von Zeit-
körnern genarbt, von Zeitstaub, mit-
verwaisend mit euch,
Lapilli, ver-
zwergt, verwinzigt, ver-
nichtet,
verbracht und verworfen,
sich selber der Reim—
so kommt es
geflogen, so kommts
wieder und heim,
seinen Herzschlag, ein Tausendjahr lang
innezuhalten als
einziger Zeiger im Rund,
das eine Seele,
das seine
Seele
beschrieb,
das eine
Seele
beziffert.

                              (*NR, GW* 1: 258)

    This poem has been called a mirror-image of poems in poems, and the path it describes is certainly a linguistic one.[16] The "boomerang" is itself a word, a "rhyme," traveling on breath-ways. But it is not only a word of poetry. It is a historical word that travels through time and events—"scarred by timegrains, by timedust," marked with the ash of destruction. And it is a word, like the words of "The Sluice," that returns to its origins: "So it comes again and home." In all these aspects—as poetic, as historical, as originary— the word is in motion. Celan emphasizes above all its temporality, its existence within time—and does so exactly in tracing its path homeward. The origin toward which Celan's word moves already implies language to be time-bound and time-involved, even when language is more than human, as Celan here suggests it to be. This word is "wing-mighty," "the true." That Celan chooses the adjectival form *wahre*, true, rather than the nominative substantial *Wahrheit*, truth, need not subvert its suprahuman status. The true is not simply transcendent. It is conditioned by time, unfolded within a history that remains the arena of any venture, divine or human. Just how, or whether, these two ventures may be aligned is, however, deeply problematic for Celan, even as it is poetically pressing. Celan's work is profoundly informed by the fate of the divine word in its career through the world, by the possibility of its conjunction with human language—or their mutual betrayal.

The notion of the divine as deeply implicated in time and history is by no means restricted to esoteric speculation, although it is in many ways radicalized in Judaic mystical discourse. Buber asserts it as a grammatical fact in the biblical Name of God, which is not an announcement of supratemporal being, but rather a pledge to historical involvement: not "I Am," but "I will be there."[17] The Hebrew is in fact inflected in the imperfect tense, rather than in the perfect tense of completed action. This Name is not cited in Celan's text; but another, no less temporally mediated Name may be invoked. Klaus Voswinkel identifies the "boomerang" as an image of the Shekhinah, which he describes, citing Buber, as "the indwelling presence of God . . . that wanders through the world, suffering with the destiny of the Jews and above all, in the hour of redemption, becoming united again with God." Because it suffers and wanders as Israel does, Celan addresses the Shekhinah when he writes "co-orphaned with you"—although Voswinkel considers its redemptive promise "no longer in Celan a living possibility."[18]

In "A Boomerang," it is especially as name, as word, that the Shekhinah appears, "on breath-ways." As "the wing-mighty, the true" it is "kissed" in its flight; but it also wanders and suffers through time, "scarred by timegrains, by timedust, co-orphaned with you." Experiencing time's disruptions and exiles, it becomes "world-splinters." Its path is thus in one sense a path of history as dissolution. Yet this same path may have another shape, offsetting disintegration, and no less tied to the notion of the Shekhinah. "When they were exiled in Egypt," the Talmud says, "the Shekhinah followed them. . . . In Babylon, the Shekhinah was with them. And when in the future Israel will be redeemed, the Shekhinah will then be with them, as it is written, 'The Lord thy God will turn thy captivity' (Deut. 30: 3), i.e., God will return with thy captivity."[19] Celan's poem also retraces this hope of redemption in the path of return that the poem's "word" and the poem itself traces. This is a path backwards as the word "comes again and home," but at the same time it is a movement toward completion. Thus the word is "kissed" by world-splinters; and the "heartbeat" is held (like a breath) "a thousandyear long," measured in the periodicity of millennial dream and direction. It is a "pointer in the orb," the hand of a world-clock facing toward restoration.

But: the "pointer in the orb" is "einziger," single, without a partner. And it is stopped. The closing suggestion of millennial hope only follows profound rupture. This is first felt in the poem's own language, which is fragmented to an extreme, both in syntax and in highly neologistic word forms. The "wing-mighty" word is "co-orphaned," "endwarfed," "enminimized." In this, Celan creates new terms and deforms old ones on the model of a word that may be for him no less originary: *vernichtet*, annihilated. At the center of the poem's verbal trajectory stands not the integrity of the word in history, but its implosion. History as expressed program of annihilation scatters its word into "Lapilli," fragments of stone. The "wing-mighty" word as substantive projectile shatters in its flight through a disrupted neologistic word/world.

Yet facing the word that at once hurls homewards and is stopped—and "innehalten" may also mean to pause, as for breath, in speaking—is a "soul" that writes and numbers. These may be the numbers of a halted millennial counting; but the numbers may also be, as in Hebrew, letters. The soul at the end is engaged in a linguistic act, as an act of accounting, and also, perhaps, as its own possible creative writing. The shape of the poem finally depends upon language as a radically temporal venture. In this it subverts any finality of form or closure in poetic language, which also leaves open the question it almost desperately poses. The linguistic venture may go forward as a positive unfolding; or the word may be neither recollected nor re-collected, but instead pulverized and discarded. Spent in its journey through time, it may have lost its redemptive power, may indeed leave little to be redeemed. But whether the poem traces a positive direction through time, or a dispersion under the pressure of time and history as annihilation, both the hope of millennial promise or its failure in dissolution take place in a reality that is radically linguistic and temporal.

Language Worlds

In "A Boomerang," the "wing-mighty" travels as word into the world, "itself the rhyme." But the world through which it moves is also made of language, "breathways" that are "star-orbits." Language becomes, in the poem's trajectory, more and more substantive. Here it is not only a question of a tradition of words passed on, or of a return to traditional words. This is not only language as spoken, or remembered, by men. It has become a reified substance that constitutes the world. The poem crosses into the kabbalistic language-world, in which both God and creation are letters: the textus or weaving of divine Names.

This reification of language is one of the earliest and most pervasive impulses of Kabbalah. Already in rabbinic literature, God is described as creating the world through the letters of the Torah alphabet. In one talmudic legend, two thousand years before the heaven and the earth, Torah was created, "written with black fire on white fire." God, when he resolved to create the world, first "took counsel with Torah."[20] The Sayings of the Fathers, a basic and familiar text, likewise declares (6, 10), citing Prov. 8: 22: "The Lord possessed the Torah as the beginning of his way, before his works, from of old." Claims such as these were incorporated into Christian thought with reference to Christ as Logos, the Word in person; but in Judaic tradition, they always refer to word as text, as Torah, as divine creative instrument. In mystical lore, this trope of the Word acquires special importance and ever more powerful force: "All creation—and this is an important point for most Kabbalists—is, from the point of view of God, nothing but an expression of His hidden self that begins and ends by giving itself a name, the holy name of God, the perpetual act of creation. All that lives is an expression of God's language."[21]

The kabbalistic doctrine of divine language as the substance of reality finds its early mystical expression in the *Sefer Yetzirah*, where letters and their numerical equivalents are presented as the primary cosmogonical instruments and patterns. There the "world-process is essentially a linguistic one, based on the unlimited combinations of letters."[22] The act of creation is, in this figural system, a process of writing, and the created world an inscription. In such terms, the biblical verse "And the earth was void and without form" is explicated in the *Zohar*:

This describes the original state—as it were the dregs of ink clinging to the point of the pen—in which there was no subsistence, until the world was graven with forty-two letters, all of which are the ornamentation of the Holy Name. When they are joined, letters ascend and descend and form crowns for themselves in all four quarters of the world, so that the world is established through them, and they through it.[23]

Creation is also a mode of revelation, not only as inspired matter, but radically as language. As Scholem explains, "The process of creation is not different from the process that finds its expression in divine words and in the documents of Revelation, in which the divine language is thought to have been reflected."[24] But if divine expression is linguistic process, so is the process within divinity itself, as elaborated through the divine attributes as the Sefirot. The Sefirot, the ten attributes of God, find many figural expressions. They are said to be rays of light, a tree's branches, limbs of the body, garments. But among the most central of these image systems is the Sefirot as language, the ten Names of God: "The world of the Sefirot is the hidden world of language, the world of divine names. The Sefirot are the creative names which God called into the world, the names which He gave to himself. . . . The process of life in God can be construed as the unfolding of the elements of speech."[25]

Out of such language mysticism poem after poem in Celan is constructed. Such long, ambitious poem-projects as "Voices" (Stimmen) and "Stretto" (Engfuhrung), both earlier than *No One's Rose*, already fully register linguistic reification as the fabric of Celan's world—the first tracing voices through water, night, and rubble; the second, a tracking through grass "written-apart." Throughout his later work, Celan's cosmos takes shape as letters, writing, language: the "radiant wind of your language" in his famous "Genicht," no-poem (*AW, GW* 2: 31); the "singable remainder" that breaks through the "sickle-script" at the "snow-place" (*AW, GW* 2: 236); the Prague landscape as suffused by "bone-Hebrew" (*AW, GW* 2: 63).[26] As in the Kabbalah, creation itself becomes a text, a weaving, of letters, which also compose the divine Names.

But if God creates the world through the letters that also spell his own name, he remains, in another sense, beyond the linguistic creation, in himself. The idea of the imageless and formless God familiar to all Judaism, who is never fully disclosed yet who expresses himself in word and deed, becomes radicalized in the Kabbalah, transformed into its language of mystical negation. The Godhead comes to be denoted as the *En Sof*, the without-end, the mystical Nothing. In this the Kabbalah elaborates and develops notions implicit in other Judaic forms. Thus Buber calls the very ethos of Hasidism its sense of "God in all concreteness as speaker, the creation as speech: God's call into nothing and the answer of things through their coming into existence, the speech of creation enduring in the life of all creation, the life of the creature as dialogue, the world as word."[27] The Nothing that God called into being acquires in Kabbalah dramatic delineation and position. Writes Scholem: "Only to us does it present no attributes because it is beyond the reach of intellectual knowledge. . . . It signifies the Divine itself in its most impenetrable guise. And, in fact, creation out of nothing means to many mystics just creation out of God. Creation out of nothing thus becomes a symbol of emanation."[28]

About this hidden, absolute "Divine itself" nothing can be known or said. But from it, in a complex and richly imaged system, come the emanations by which the world was created and through which God manifests himself. In this sense God is called Nothing; but negation becomes a center out of which creation emerges—a process suggested in a *Lightforce* (Lichtzwang) poem:

> Palevoiced, torn
> out of the depths:
> no word, no thing
> and of both the only name,
>
> fall-fair in you,
> flight-fair in you,
>
> wounded winnings
> of a world.
>
> Fahlstimmig, aus
> der Tiefe geschunden:
> kein Wort, kein Ding,
> und beider einziger Name,
>
> fallgerecht in dir,
> fluggerecht in dir,
>
> wunder Gewinn
> einer Welt
>
> (GW 2: 307)

The Nothing, here, is cited as "depths" of "no word, no thing." But this is also their "only name." Nothing can be predicated of this nothing, evoking the divine as an "other," to use Emmanuel Levinas's term, who is not an "intelligible essence," "not under a category. . . . He has only a reference to himself; he has no quiddity." [29] Buber similarly refers to a divine "other" not as a "quintessence" but as an "absoluteness." "God is not spirit," he writes. "But what we call spirit and what we call nature hail equally from the God who is beyond and equally unconditioned by both." The Kabbalah names this transcendence the Without-Name, the mystical Nothing, not, as Scholem writes, as a "subject" but as the "origin of Being, the Beginning of which the first word of the Bible speaks." [30]

How this Nothing became something is the process that the Kabbalah explores and that "Palevoiced" evokes. Celan, commencing from the "no word, no thing," proceeds to "wounded winnings of a world." The Godhead, remaining beyond, is neither known nor seen. But the winnings of a world proceed from and refer back to him: "fall-fair in you, flight-fair in you." The movement remains linguistic: beginning as "only name," its activity is verbal: "pale-voiced." But it is double: descent and ascent, falling and flying, creative but also violent: "torn" from the depths, it wins a world that is, however, also wounded. The name unfolds in creation, and is finally experienced as the world itself. But the "winning" is a difficult one.

Here we must recall the historical destructions deeply impressed through Celanian language, but also the disturbances envisioned in kabbalistic creation myths. In some sense the fall of the universe from harmony is seen as linguistic disruption. There is a break in the configurations of the divine Names as these manifest God and divine action in the created world. In that creation has been disrupted, the divine letters too are scattered. God himself is dispersed. The Lurianic Kabbalah develops this Zoharic notion of the disrupted Sefirotic harmony into cosmic trauma, "the Breaking of the Vessels." In this myth, the creative movement begins in a retraction or withdrawal of the divine into itself—an act of separation (*Tzimzum*) allowing an originary space for creation. Into this space the divine then sends forth its Name-manifestations—an act of creation and revelation at once, in which "God's ineffable Name is differentiated and finitized in the Torah as divine self-revelation." But these are unable to contain God's power, and shatter and disperse through a disordered creation, interrupting "the stream of life from sphere to sphere," bringing "separation and isolation into the world."[31]

This divine exile is especially associated with the figure of the Shekhinah. The Shekhinah, signifying the presence or "dwelling" of God in the world, emerges in Talmudic and Midrashic literature as a divine Name, designating God especially as he is present to Israel in her Exile. "Come and see," the Talmud invites (T.B. Megillah 29a), "how beloved are the Israelites before God; for wherever they went into exile, the Shekhinah followed them."[32] Both Jehudah Halevi and Maimonides closely linked the Shekhinah to the prophetic experience.[33] But the Shekhinah's traditional sense as naming God in his closeness with the historical destiny of Israel is then adopted and radicalized in the Kabbalah. The *Zohar* incorporates it into the structure of the Sefirot: the tenth Sefirah becomes identified as the Shekhinah—the "ten stages of the inner world, through which God descends from the inmost recesses down to His revelation in the Shekhinah." The Shekhinah is thus the "last attribute through which the Creator acts in the lower world."[34]

With the Lurianic Kabbalah, the cosmic trauma felt within the very Godhead comes to be expressed as the exile of the Shekhinah itself. "Only after the restoration of the original harmony in the act of redemption, when everything shall again occupy the place it originally had in the divine scheme of things," will the exile of the Shekhinah end, and will it regain its place in a restored world. This redemption is characteristically also envisioned within a linguistic figure: the very letters of the divine name, dispersed since the creation, will be reunited, so that God and his Name will again be One.[35]

Mystical Language, Mystical Silence

It is precisely with regard to history that the whole tendency, and power, of the figure of language emerges, both in Celan and in the Kabbalah. Within mystical discourse it is typically silence, not language, that is granted highest figural status. Silence represents the transcendence of time and external and material form, a union with the eternal from which language, as embodiment rather than spirit, as temporal rather than immutable, must be excluded. Language, conversely, becomes the figure for time, materiality, exteriority, multiplicity, and differentiation. This distribution of representative status we have seen, for example, in Pseudo-Dionysius, in his repeated insistence on the ineffable throughout the *Mystical Theology* as the very goal of devotion: "Speech ascends from the particular to the universal, and going up is withdrawn as it rises, and after the whole ascent it becomes inwardly silence, entirely united with the ineffable" (*MT* 3). This ultimacy of silence in turn takes its place within a metaphysic that rigorously insists that the divine is immutable and indeed impassible. The theological attribute of *apathia* precludes divine subjection to or even contact with change or suffering of any kind. "The essence of God," writes Augustine in *On the Trinity*, "by which he is, has nothing changeable" (*TR* 15.11). Thomas Aquinas concurs: "God is altogether immutable . . . eternity lacks succession, being simultaneously whole" (I: Q.3 art. 7). Silence, then, marks the vision of, or participation in, the divine immutable eternity. As the sign of what stands beyond linguistic division and succession, it is also the sign of what stands beyond temporal division and succession.

This figural status of language and of silence is in some sense retained within Judaic culture. Language remains the figure for temporality, differentiation, materiality; silence, for the absolute as beyond expression or representation. But the tropes take on fundamentally different roles within the commitments and conceptions peculiar to Judaism. Passibility, the responsiveness of God to temporal events, is both asserted and assumed in Judaic interpretations of Scripture. The Church Fathers felt driven to defend God against such anthropomorphisms as emotion, against any suggestion that God ever changed his mind, and even against the use of the verb "become" when predicated of God.[36] But the responsiveness of the Judaic God implied in the language of the Hebrew Scriptures is adopted in rabbinic discussion and understanding. Exactly how to formulate it did pose a philosophical problem, especially for Maimonides, for example, in his passion for harmonizing Greek ontology with rabbinic Judaism. Maimonides' own formulation finally distinguishes between a divine-in-itself about which nothing can be predicated, and divine actions which take place in the temporal world. This represents his effort to formulate in philosophical terms the persistent assumption in Jewish exegetical and liturgical practice that God responds to earthly events, that he rejoices with Israel and mourns for her. Within the rabbinic discourse of midrash, a double aspect of divinity as "absolute transcendence" and "transcendent relationality" is implied in commentaries such as those on the Presence of God in the Sanctuary (*mishcan*, an etymological source for *Shekhinah*): "Said the Holy One blessed be He, 'I do not think as you think . . . but I shall descend and contract (*ve'azamzem*) My presence within the cubits of the sanctuary.'" This midrashic tradition then developed into a kabbalistic theme of divine contraction, reciprocity, and even dependence on Israel.[37]

In more familiar theological terms, Jaroslav Pelikan notes in his history of Christian tradition that in Judaism "the immutability of God was seen as the trustworthiness of his covenanted relation to his people in the concrete history of his judgment and mercy, rather than as a primary ontological category. But in the development of the Christian doctrine of God, immutability assumed the status of an axiomatic proposition."[38]

Gershom Scholem considers the interaction between divinity and temporality to be one of the fundamental impulses of the Kabbalah; David Novak, Moshe Idel, and Steven Katz all underscore a sense of "reciprocity" between human and divine realms as a feature distinguishing Judaic from other Neoplatonist mysticisms.[39] But reciprocity is not restricted to mystical writings. A midrashic commentary on *Lamentations*, for example, tells how, at the destruction of the Temple, "the Holy One, blessed be He, summoned the ministering angels and said to them, 'If a human king had a son who died, what is it customary for him to do?' They replied, 'He sits and weeps.' He said to them, 'I will do like-wise,' as it is written, 'And in that day did the Lord, the God of Hosts, call to weeping, to lamentation, and to baldness.'"[40] Nicholas of Lyra singled out exactly this midrash for rebuke as the "false and puerile tale" of God lamenting the destruction of his temple.[41] But he only confirms the position of the Church, as summarized by Apollinaris: "Anyone who introduces passion into the divine power is atheistic and blasphemous."[42]

Within the Judaic structure, an ineffable Godhead remains central—indeed, the very center: beyond description, beyond knowledge. But it is the reference point for all description and experience, while the proper sphere of activity, even of religious life, remains situated within description, text, language. Language and silence thus acquire a distinctive figural role and valence. Silence no longer represents participation in an impassible, immutable world from which language is excluded and seen as a loss of spirituality, inwardness, truth, and being. Although silence still designates the divine-in-itself as beyond speech and transcending all predication, language rather than silence is the realm of religious devotion and relation. Buber thus cites the ecstasy of a rabbi over the introductory phrases "And God said," or "And God spoke."[43] The ultimate goal here is not withdrawal from the world of time and matter, with transcendence of language into silence its highest expression. Gershom Scholem, when he raises the question of the mystical attempt to "express the inexpressible in words," similarly underscores that in the Kabbalah, as distinct from other mysticisms, a concern with the ineffable is offset by a "metaphysically positive attitude towards language as God's own instrument." Instead of silent transcendence, the Kabbalists accept a "superabundantly positive delineation of language as the mystery revealed of all things that exist," and as "the medium in which the spiritual life of man is accomplished and consummated."[44]

It is in light of this positive figural valence granted to language that Celan's texts, especially his mystical ones, must be read. Dietland Meineke, for example, cites the poem "Your Being-Beyond" (Dein Hinübersein) as kabbalistic in its reference to the Lurianic "Breaking of the Vessels." He sees this as a sign of a divine withdrawal from time and history, which the poet would emulate.[45] Its linguistic figuration points, however, in an almost opposite direction:

> Your
> Being-Beyond this night.
> With words I fetched you back, there you are,
> all is true and a waiting
> for the true.
>
> The bean-plant climbs
> in front of our window: think
> who is growing up beside us and
> watches it.

God, so we read, is
a part and a second, scattered:
in the death
of all those mown down
he grows himself together.

There
our glance leads us,
with this half
we keep up relations.

Dein
Hinübersein heute Nacht.
Mit Worten holt ich dich wieder, da bist du,
alles ist wahr und ein Warten
auf Wahres.

Es klettert die Bohne vor
unserm Fenster: denk
wer neben uns aufwächst und
ihr zusieht.

Gott, das lasen wir, ist
ein Teil und ein zweiter, zerstreuter:
im Tod
all der Gemähten
wächst er sich zu.

Dorthin
führt uns der Blick,
mit dieser
Hälfte
haben wir Umgang.

(NR, GW 1: 218)

As so often in Celan, the text takes place as dialogue, addressing a "you" who remains unspecified. Especially at the outset, it here could invoke any being-beyond: a beloved, the dead, or God. But whoever is addressed, language is declared the primary power reaching toward the beyond to fetch back from it. This second direction must be underscored. For in the poem, it is language-as-world that remains the sphere of activity, the domain of relationship. There is no effort to enter into the beyond as such, no dissolving into it. Instead, the stance of the poem is insistently situated within the linguistic, temporal world. The poem is placed in time— "this night"—and calls the "being-beyond" to a temporal appearance: "There you are." Even truth is situated in the immediate world and given a temporal mode. As in "A Boomerang," the substantive *Wahrheit* is avoided and instead given an adjectival form, which is both declared and yet declared to be in process: "all is true and a waiting for the true" (auf Wahres).

This temporal mode is further asserted in the second stanza, in the image of the growing plant. The figure, like God in the next stanza, suggests the kabbalistic Sefirot in their several aspects. Manifesting the Godhead in emanations, the Sefirot are sometimes figured as Tree, a traditional topos for the Torah as well as Tree of Life. Here the poem bids us "think who is growing up beside us and watches it." This "who" strangely multiplies, defying containment, as does the poet, who has become plural, encompassing into his speech reader and perhaps interlocutor. At once both "beside us" and watching with us, the "who" enters into temporal stance, just as in the guise of a growing plant it enters into temporal process.

Such divine temporality is, in the third stanza, given its most dramatic—and explosive—expression: "God, so we read, is a part and a second, scattered." The radical nature of this subjection of God to temporal categories emerges in the dangerous negativity of Celan's third stanza. There Celan expressly situates the scattering of God as historical event: "In the death / of all those mown down / he grows himself together." Celan here sounds the blasphemous note of some of his most powerful verses. It recalls, for example, the poem "Late and Deep" (Spät und tief), where God is painfully indicted by his image in history: "They shout: You blaspheme! . . . You grind in the mills of death the white meal of Promise" (Sie rufen: Ihr lästert! . . . Ihr mahlt in den Mühlen des Todes das weisse Mehl der Verheissung; *MG, GW* 1: 35). Here, Celan introduces one of the Kabbalah's most radical figures: the temporalization even of transcendence. The whole structure of Sefirotic activity implicitly introduces into divinity itself a temporal aspect. There is a dispersion of God, both within the divine world of Names and attributes, and in the created world marked by the cosmic trauma of the Fall. In Luria, this primeval catastrophe extends beyond any sin of man to implicate the very fabric of both creation and Creator. As such it represents not only a profound penetration of God into history, but also of history into God. God himself, in one Lurianic topos, is said to be exiled from himself, wandering in history until the time of final restoration or Tikkun, when the scattered sparks of his divinity will once more be gathered, and the exile of God will end.[46] In "Your Being-Beyond," the being-beyond is also a being-here. He "grows himself together" as a positive motion through time, perhaps to restoration; but he also does so as a "mowing down" in death, deformed through historical destruction. This is the ambivalence of the poem's close:

> There
> our looking leads us,
> with this half
> we keep up relations.

The Being-Beyond remains the direction in which the poet points himself, returning the gaze of the watching "who" of the second stanza. Across whatever distance and disruption, relation is then affirmed and sustained. But exactly with what, or where, remains unclear. "With this half": is this the Godhead accessible in time, entering into the temporal mode of growth, but also into division and deformation? And if so, which is more pronounced: divine nearness or divine disruption?

Here (as in many Celanian blasphemous utterances) religious forms and topoi, instead of praising God, attack and accuse him; yet even as they do, God remains the object of address, both as recipient and as mode of orientation. This double intention of attack and address rends the text itself into parts, scattered in an ambiguous utterance. Celan's own language is implicated in the risk of process that may or may not remain oriented. In this it is like the language in which Celan both reads and addresses the Godhead, and also the language which fetches back and attempts, perhaps unsuccessfully, recuperation. But both success and failure take place through a language deeply inscribed as historical and temporal life.

This is no effort to achieve a mystical "expression of the inexpressible"[47] as either absolute language or linguistic transcendence, no effort to transcend time and displace it by an eternal realm. The poem rather proposes language as the realm in which divinity itself becomes accessible within historical modes. In one sense, the Being-Beyond remains beyond, a reference point that makes the true possible. In another sense, it is approached in terms of immediate events, experienced as "a waiting for the true" not closed and immutable, but rather a concrete unfolding within temporal conditions. The Shekhinah as scattered asserts not a withdrawal of God from but an entrance of God into history, asserts the divine as taking part in the temporal process, even through all the traumas history offers.

"Rise Up Jerusalem"

The language imagery of a text such as "Your Being-Beyond" strongly insists that experience and activity be located in time, not only for the human, but also for the divine, with language the peculiar realm of their intercourse. Just this kind of language imagery, moreover, defines what is distinctive in the Kabbalah, as against other religious and mystical traditions. Negativity in the Kabbalah, as elsewhere, in one sense precludes temporal experience. But it does so exactly to open an intercourse, which then takes place within the conditions of time and space. The relationship between divine and human remains fundamentally a relationship in language, which represents here as elsewhere the worldly conditions of time, multiplicity, materiality—the conditions that continue to situate the human speaker. But this linguistic relationship is not secondary to a silence that would claim to exceed it as the true, ultimate relation. Although the Godhead itself remains ineffable, this silence is a sign of its final distinction from all created conditions, and not a realm into which the creature himself or herself strives to enter, transcending language into a silence beyond all linguistic distinction. The creature, instead, retains a distinctive individuality, established within the dimensions and differentiations of the created world: a world-as-language, from which the creature addresses the divinity beyond in linguistic modes.

This, at least, is the structure described by Scholem and Buber, in whose work Celan bases his own language mysticism—writers who insist that even within mystical circles union with divinity is not the normative goal. "If the term [mysticism] is restricted to the profound yearning for direct human communion with God through annihilation of individuality," writes Scholem, "then only a few manifestations of Kabbalah can be designated as such, because few Kabbalists sought this goal." Elsewhere he reiterates:

It is only in extremely rare cases that ecstasy signifies actual union with God, in which the human individuality abandons itself to the rapture of complete submersion in the divine stream. Even in the ecstatic frame of mind, the Jewish mystic almost invariably retains a sense of the distance between the Creator and his creature. . . . Many writers deliberately place [their notion of communion] above any form of ecstasy which seeks the extinction of the world and the self in the union with God.[48]

Steven Katz similarly argues that in Jewish mysticism "one does not have mystical experiences of God in which one loses one's identity in ecstatic moments of unity, . . . the Jewish mystic rarely, if ever, has such experiences."[49] Other writers on the tradition concur. Thus, Martin Buber writes of Hasidism: "We unify God when living and dying we profess his unity; we do not unite ourselves with Him. The God in whom we believe, to whom we are pledged, does not unite with human substance on earth."[50] But the precept is ancient. Thus, one commentary on the verse "And the Lord came down upon Mount Sinai" (Exod. 19: 20) warns: "One might think that the Glory actually descended from heaven and was transferred to Mount Sinai, but . . . neither Moses nor Elijah ever went up to heaven, nor did the Glory ever come down to earth."[51] The separation between divine and human remains absolute, yet across its difference the word of Torah links them together.

Moshe Idel has recently raised questions regarding the role of union in Jewish mystical experience. He emphasizes the continuity, or at least influence, of Neoplatonist, Aristotelian, hermetic, and also gnostic mysticisms within the historical development of Judaic mysticism. Yet Idel also concedes a normative and "nomian" mysticism, which continued to focus on "the nature of the ten Sefirot and the mystical meaning of the commandments," as well as on mystical interpretations of texts. That is, the kabbalists always remain devoted to the letter—whether law or text. In this the Kabbalah remains "part of the classical rabbinic conception of the commandments," a "strictly nomian system" continuous with exoteric observance and exegesis. And the degree to which the letter remains the center of Jewish mystical activity is striking, as Idel shows in his recent essay, "Reification of Language in Jewish Mysticism," where he goes on to contrast "the positive attitude of Jewish mysticism toward language and the negative conception of language in Christian mysticism." [52]

Celan's own knowledge of Kabbalistic sources was in any case mediated by sources such as Scholem provided, or based in the ordinary Judaism of his childhood. It is, moreover, the linguistic center of the tradition that finds expression in Celan—as a site where, as David Novak emphasizes, the "Kabbalah presented itself as a deeper manifestation of Rabbinic Judaism, not as an innovation that might challenge it." [53] Especially in the Kabbalah's language mysticism, communication with the divine is mediated through discourse-structures, text, and the letter. Relation to the divine, then, never fully subsumes language into silence as the mode of participation. Language remains instead the sphere of encounter.

This distinction may be more clearly seen through Celan's references to Meister Eckhart. Werner Weber reports that Celan told him he had based his poem "You Be like You" (Du sei wie du) in a sermon by Meister Eckhart on Isaiah 60: 1, *Surge illuminare*, or "Rise up Jerusalem." There, Eckhart declares, "the highest flows into the lowest, . . . God dethrones (*enthöht*, "unhighs") himself, not absolute but rather much more inward, and this unhighing as interiorizing . . . in turn makes us high, raises us up. What was above becomes inward, . . . a mindedness in which a secret, hidden

Knowing is meant."⁵⁴ Weber sees this as Celan's meaning in "Du sei wie du" as well, and reads "Jerusalem" in the poem as Eckhart's "sign" of the "light of the inward God." Even John Felstiner, in his impressive translation and discussion of this exceedingly difficult text, accepts a continuity between Eckhart's language and Celan's renderings of it, from "Isaiah's pre-Christian Hebrew to Saint Jerome's fourth century Latin to Meister Eckhart's medieval German and then into Paul Celan's lyric voice, the messianic word underway and translated through time":⁵⁵

> You be like you, ever.
>
> *Ryse vp Ierosalem and*
> *rowse thyselfe*
>
> The very one who slashed the bond unto you,
>
> *and becum*
> *yllumyned*
>
> knotted it new, in myndignesse,
>
> spills of mire I swallowed, inside the tower,
>
> speech, dark-selvedge,
>
> kumi
> ori.
>
> Du Sei Wie Du, immer.
>
> *Stant vp Jeherosalem inde*
> *erheyff dich*
>
> Auch wer das Band zerschnitt zu dir hin,
>
> *inde wirt*
> *erluchtet*
>
> knüpfte es neu, in der Gehugnis,
>
> Schlammbrocken schluckt ich, im Turm,
>
> Sprache, Finster-Lisene,
>
> kumi
> ori.
>
> (LZ, GW 2: 327)

As Felstiner's translation shows, Eckhart's text is woven into Celan's not only in direct quotation, but throughout Celan's archaized language. Yet there are also departures. Written for a childhood friend from Czernowitz during Celan's visit to Jerusalem in 1969, the poem concludes with the Hebrew de-translation of the *Surge illuminare* Eckhart cites in Jerome's Latin and then translates into Middle High German (*inde wirt erluchtet*). *Kumi ori*, arise, shine, proclaims the redemption of Jerusalem and the return of her exiles in the original language that has, in Israel, been no less resurrected.

This linguistic return, however, does not mark continuity with its Latin and Germanic renderings. These, rather, are part of the break the poem asserts in the "slashed bond," now to be newly knotted. For Jerusalem is not only the inward place that Eckhart intends, either in Jewish tradition, or for those who now reinhabit her and would recognize this Hebrew (something no German audience can now do, as Felstiner points out). Redemption is not only an inward, spiritual event, but must also be—this is insisted on—an exterior, historical one. Such exteriority in turn situates Celan's linguistic imagery in the poem. From historical "spills of mire" he turns to "speech, dark-selvedge" (Felstiner's translation of *Finster-Lisene*): a "column that buttresses" the corner of a building, also a "woven edge that keeps fabric from unraveling." Language as buttress and border: it is this that both reweaves the broken knot and retains the sense of breakage. As both it is Celan's appropriate avenue toward renewal, toward reawakened light. Its call to rise is appropriately addressed by the poet to the "you" of the opening—a you not interiorized, not inward, but other and beyond, and accordingly approached through speech as the mode of reknotting the slashed bond.

Meister Eckhart, instead, repeatedly emphasizes that God "is united with the soul and it with him and it shines and glistens with him as a single One and as a pure clear light in the heart of the Father." This union is, moreover, inexpressible: what "no one can really grasp in words," what "is free from all names and stripped of all forms, completely and utterly free."[56] While Eckhart's radical identification with God finally led to his condemnation for heresy, this did not prevent his work from being widely read; and he himself claimed to be merely following Augustine, whom he cites: "The soul is completely united with God in image and likeness, if it touches upon him in right knowledge." Moreover, Eckhart's stance toward language remains characteristic, as another citation from Augustine confirms: "The eternal word remains in itself, . . . it is equally in God, and it is nothing but a single moment, . . . a true eternity."[57] The ultimate relation to divinity would be union; and the ultimate representation of union would be its status beyond representation, its unrepresentability in language, its silence. Language, caught within the temporal realm that Eckhart wishes to transcend, can never represent this transcendence. At most, it can serve as a (negative) trope for what is beyond language, for an ultimacy which excludes it and indeed compared with which it remains fallen.

Divine Address

The language mysticism that frames Celan's work assumes a rather different stance toward language, world, and transcendence. The image of world as reified divine utterance stresses and extends what Scholem calls the "correspondence between creation and revelation."[58] Linking the world to the divine word, it makes creation a manifestation of God himself, no less woven than the letters of his name. This both implicates the divine in the very structure of the world and its events, and situates the human relation to him:

> I can see you still: an echo
> palpable with feel-
> words, at the parting-
> ridge.
>
> Your face shies gently,
> when all at once
> it becomes, lamplike, bright
> in me, at the place
> where one says the most painful never.

Ich kann dich noch sehn: ein Echo,
ertastbar mit Fühl-
wörtern, am Abschieds-
grat.

Dein Gesicht scheut leise,
wenn es auf einmal
lampenhaft hell wird
in mir, an der Stelle,
wo man am schmerzlichsten Nie sagt.

(LZ, GW 2: 275)

The you here, as elsewhere, need not be divine. In Celan, the person addressed varies, and is of less structural significance than the fact of address and the situation of dialogue as such. But the situation of dialogue is founded upon assumptions regarding the relative positions of the two interlocutors. The ultimate model for this stance, the basic pattern of this relation, is an address in which the auditor is divine—in a sense, one aspect of his divinity is this ultimacy as model and founding pattern. "The extended lines of relations meet in the eternal Thou," writes Martin Buber. "Every particular Thou is a glimpse through to the eternal Thou." [59] In this poem, a delicate, nonexclusive ambiguity is sustained between any specific you and the you as divine.

Yet divinity is suggested, especially in the image of the face which "shies gently." This tentative gesture may seem implausible for the divine, but it registers the sense of the divine such as Buber describes, as both irrevocably separate and accessible. Just so, here the "face" retreats, but gently, and therefore also in invitation. In the same way, it can "still" be seen, but as across a distance, "at the parting-ridge." There is, in the Celan poem, at once distance and proximity; just so, writes Buber, "God is wholly raised above man, he is beyond the grasp of man, and yet he is present in an immediate relationship with these human beings who are absolutely incommensurable with him, and he faces them." And elsewhere Buber writes: "Although God is definitely distinct from the world he is not in any way withdrawn from it," adding, in an image with resonance for this poem, that "God is both distinct and radiating." [60]

In the poem, too, it is at the parting-ridge, when the face "shies gently," that "all at once it becomes lamplike, bright in me." The poet has experienced an illumination, has had a vision: "I can see you still." But, as Buber also remarks, "God gives His light as word." As Moses Cordovero said: "Through ten utterances, that is, Sefirot, was the world created . . . and He combined within them the effusion of revelation of his splendor." Light and language, that is, mark a dual trope in which, as Scholem summarizes, "the process which the Kabbalists described as the emanation of divine energy and divine light, was also characterized as the unfolding of divine language."[61] Thus, the poet sees "an echo," senses with "feel-words."

This language imagery impels the poem and frames the stances within it. Language, above all, represents what Buber calls a "double stance" of "distance and relation": "Man alone speaks, for only he can address the other just as the other being standing at a distance over against him; but in addressing it, he enters into relationship." It is dialogue as a "face-to-face" with God which is not "interpenetration," in which God is both "self-revealing and self-concealing," remaining "unseen in all his appearances."[62] Emmanuel Levinas, in *Totality and Infinity*, makes this thematics of language his central concern. For him, language is not only a medium of relation, but is itself both foundation and structure: the "face-to-face founds language" and also finds realization in it. Asserting both radical autonomy and strong connection, both separation and distinction, language becomes in Levinas the very structure not only of religious but of all ethical relation: "The relationship of language implies transcendence, radical separation, the strangeness of the interlocutors, the revelation of the other to me."[63] It reveals the one to the other, but not through what he calls disclosure. Revelation is "the manifestation of a face over and beyond form," a form never in itself visible or determined. It is discourse rather than disclosure or even representation of its speaker, acting as an expression that "precisely maintains the other to whom it is addressed, whom it calls upon or invokes." The face in this is not image, but discourse; does not show itself, but instead "announces" itself: "The face speaks. The manifestation of the face is already discourse . . . a presence more direct than visible manifestation, and at the same time a remote presence—that of the other." [64]

But the interplay within this disjunctive proximity is not, at least for Celan, particularly stable. And for him there is greater danger of too great disjunction than of too overwhelming presence. Even illumination here takes "place" in what is also a space of negativity: "where one says the most painful never." This "never" registers the poet's sense of such an experience as unexpected, indeed of its presumed impossibility, which has been surprised by its coming to pass. Yet, as negative assertion, it inscribes a sense of denial and doubt. It is a linguistic gesture as a never-saying, one which even as it speaks seems to call dialogue into question. Certainly for Celan, discourse with a "you," especially a divine one, is much less certain than it is for Buber. [65] At the same time, however, "never" here acquires the additional force established within the uses of negation throughout Celan's work. The light and sound (light as sound) that flare from it inevitably evoke the whole sphere of the no one, the nothing, *niemand* and *nichts*, which Celan repeatedly addresses and which is, in the Kabbalah, the center of all revelation. The "never" is painful in accordance with Celan's own uncertain relation to God. Yet, as with other negative designations of the Godhead, this "never" may not be necessarily, or only, denial. It may, then, mark the nothing that, beyond creation and language, is nevertheless their source. Or it may be nothing more than the negative declaration of impossibility, of a silence from which nothing indeed comes forth.

In this latter case, however, silence will not be ultimate expression, a beyond-language as fullness and attainment subsuming all difference. It will not fulfill the inexpressibility topos. Rather, silence will be a failure of language. It will be language made dumb in the face of a meaning ultimately inaccessible, an event too terrible to declare or formulate, a despair of any significant order. Silence will not, that is, paradoxically assert penetration into a divine or ideal realm beyond utterance. It will instead mark the final unavailability of any reference point for orienting language and experience.

Silence points here in two almost opposing directions. Nor does
Celan resolve this conflict. His work is painful exactly as it refuses
to declare a positive silence or a negative one, repeatedly posing the
question of choice without certainly offering a decision. And yet, in
either case the figural valence of silence and language achieves in
his work almost a reversal of its accepted status within traditional
Western metaphysics. Silence may still designate the ultimate and
absolute source of being, but exactly as what remains beyond being,
never to be penetrated, always respected as exterior and other. Or
it may designate the failure of all relation to any such ultimate
source. But positive relation, positive experience, remains linguistic,
and language an exterior relation that continues to represent, both
as medium and as trope, the material, differentiated, temporal
world. This is the proper realm of human activity, even of religious
activity facing an absolute beyond it.

In Celan, rather than being excluded from the relation to the
divine, language is the medium through which such relation takes
place. This is exactly because language is external and temporal;
for man, too, is distinct from God and is a temporal being—conditions that he cannot overcome and does not seek to. Language
respects and represents that absolute distinctness, while equally
asserting a relation across and in terms of it. Meister Eckhart
concludes: "The man who wishes to come to the highest goal,
who wishes to be forever in God's presence, forever truly near to
him, . . . must lift himself above all earthly things."⁶⁶ But, as one of
Buber's Hasidic tales insists: "I do not want the rungs of the spirit
without the garment of flesh."⁶⁷ For Buber, exactly because the divine remains unconditionally beyond, human relation with it takes
place within the world of time and space. "There can be no knowledge of God separated from the knowledge of men," Buber asserts.
"That he reveals himself and that he conceals himself belong indi-
visibly together; but for his concealment his revelation would not
be real and temporal." Such temporal revelation is above all described and implied by linguistic tropes and terms: God appears
"in all concreteness as speaker." He does so by announcing himself
not as "being (esse)," as divinity who "exists absolutely and eter-

nally," but as "being present (adesse)," a God who "wants to remain with his people, to go with them, to lead them."[68] Levinas pursues a similar direction when he writes, "It is on the earth, among men, that the adventure of the spirit unfolds."[69] Or, in Scholem's imagery of the Kabbalah, revelation as language expresses the divine nature precisely as it "pertained to creation and insofar as it was able to manifest itself through creation."[70] God addresses the world through the two texts of revelation and creation; and from within that language humankind turns and responds to him.

The Letters of Creation

The world as divine language is an ultimate image for significance and even a sacramental meaning within material creation. As it faces, reflects, and answers to God, life within the world of space and time takes on order and value. This, according to Gershom Scholem in "The Name of God and the Linguistic Theory of the Kabbalah," constitutes the very "paradigm of a mystical theory of language." Its most pivotal and radical marker is the status of the Letter within it. There is an "indissoluble link between the idea of the revealed truth and the notion of language," so that "the word of God makes itself heard through the medium of human language." This asserts a "superabundantly positive delineation of language, as the mystery revealed of all things that exist." And this positive value extends to creation itself, which is also revelation, and is therefore also linguistic. Language as revelation here is meant not in an abstract sense, but quite specifically as "acoustic and perceptible (in a sensual context)."[71] The radical link—indeed identity—between revelation and creation such that "language and being are both born of one name" posits the reification of language as worldly, material creation. The image for this materiality is, perhaps above all, writing. "The creative force which resides in words and names . . . referred back to the fundamental elements in which, for the mystic, the image of sound and the written image coincide reciprocally." Quoting from the earlier *Ursprung und Anfänge der Kabbala*, to which Celan had access, Scholem expands:

For the Kabbalists, of course, linguistic mysticism is at the same time a mysticism of writing. . . . Writing for the philologist is no more than a secondary and extremely unmanageable image of real and effective speech; but for the Kabbalist it is the real centre of the mysteries of speech. The phonographic principle of a natural translation from speech into writing and, vice versa, from writing into speech operates in the Kabbala under the conception that the holy letters of the alphabet are themselves those linea-ments and signs, which the modern phonetician would be looking for on his record. The creative world of God is legitimately and distinctly marked precisely in these holy lines.[72]

The radical identification of creation with language leads the Kab-balists to thematize writing, exactly in order to represent the mate-rial world as "marked," in Scholem's phrase, by divine Name and relation. Letters come to be seen as "hidden, secret signs of the divine in all spheres and stages which the process of the creation passes through. The Hebrew word 'oth means not only letter but also . . . sign, and more specifically mark (or signature)." The ori-ginary creative energy is even described radically as "writing—the hidden signature of God," a textus of letters within the Godhead that "precedes the act of speaking. . . . Speech comes into being with sound evolution of writing, and not vice versa." The Godhead itself remains in some sense beyond this lettristic activity: either with a name that remains unknown, or as "nameless," while "all names are condensations of the energy which radiates forth from him."[73]

The Kabbalah here as elsewhere develops into powerful figural expression the lettrism that has always been central to Judaic cul-ture. This lettrism includes not only the dedication to the "letter" of religious observance, as the indissoluble site of all spiritual inten-tion and devotion, but also the commitment to the actual letters of the sacred text as vehicles for potentially infinite meanings. Exegesis extends, in the tradition associated with Rabbi Akiva, to every mark, every space, every notation, every spelling convention. Jo-seph Dan reviews and explicates this lettrism as the basis of mid-rashic exegesis of the Bible in general—a practice which, as he em-phasizes, forbids translation into languages other than Hebrew. The

Jewish interpreter would use "a total text, hermeneutically discussing not only the meaning of terms and words, but also their sound, the shape of the letters, the vocalization points and their shapes and sounds, . . . the numerical value of the letters, words, and whole verses, the possible changes of letters . . . and the countless ways other than ideonic content and meaning by which the scriptures transmit a semiotic message." [74]

Kabbalistic exegesis continues to weave itself around biblical texts, as the basis for both religious practices and mystical interpretations. In either case, the letter remains central, as the material body without which meaning cannot be elaborated. Indeed, meaning itself is less a spiritualization of the letter than the elaboration, contextualization, and configuration of its material body into significant orders. Its high status finds expression in positive figures of the body itself, which is adopted as "a powerful symbol of the sefirotic realm." Both body and text are the "starting points for contemplation, material to be penetrated without obliterating its basic structure," whose significance is shared throughout the religious community. [75]

Celan's poetic profoundly echoes the reified letters of Kabbalah, in which language materialized as world asserts that the world must be experienced as ordered, sacramental, divine utterance. The trope of the "letters of creation" projects world as the "mark" left by God and "creation therefore as linguistic movement." [76] This marking involves both positive production and defensive sustenance. Language constitutes the basic fabric out of which all the world's variety is woven: "The letters of the divine language are what lie at the basis of all creation by way of their combination." It also marks boundaries for containing forces of dispersion, as "seals which prevent creation from breaking asunder." The substance of this linguistic activity remains the divine names—"all created things are endowed with reality as they participate in divine names." And this is what asserts "the secret laws and harmonious order which pervade and govern all existence." [77] At stake, then, in both Kabbalah and Celan, is ultimately the significance and coherence of the world, its positive order:

Things were created in a specific order, since creation was intentional, not accidental. This order, which determines all the processes of creation and of generation and decay, is known as Sefirot, "the active power of each existing thing numerically defineable." Since all created things come into being through the agency of the Sefirot, the latter contain the root of all change, although they all emanate from one principle, Ein-Sof, "outside of which there is nothing."[78]

For Celan, this lettristic creation represents the radical venture of historical life. At stake is the possibility of the world as negotiable, inhabitable, constructive. A significant world is one bound together by and as language, a world that language articulates, thing by thing. Articulate order is implicit in the trope of lettristic world that governs poem after poem in Celan:

> What STITCHES
> this voice? On what
> does this voice
> stitch,
> here, beyond?
>
> The abysses are
> sworn onto the white, out from them
> arose
> the snow-needle,
>
> swallow it,
>
> you order the world,
> that counts
> as many as nine names
> named kneeling
>
> Tumuli, Tumuli,
> you
> hill your way, living,
> come
> in the kiss
>
> a fin-beat
> steady,
> lights the bays,
> you drop

anchor, your shadow
casts you into the bush,

advent,
descent,

a beetle recognizes you,
you are forth-
coming,
caterpillars
enweb you,

the great
globe
allows you a passage

soon
the leaf knits its vein to yours,
sparks
must pass through,
one panting breath long,

a tree is your right, a day
it deciphers the number

a word, with all its greenness,
goes into itself, transplants itself,

follow it

WAS NÄHT
an dieser Stimme? Woran
näht diese
Stimme
diesseits, jenseits?

Die Abgründe sind
eingeschworen auf Weiss, ihnen
entstieg
die Schneenadel,

schluck sie,

du ordnest die Welt,
das zählt
soviel wie neun Namen,
auf Knien genannt,

Tumuli, Tumuli,
du
hügelst hinweg, lebendig,
komm
in den Kuss,

ein Flossenschlag,
stet,
lichtet die Buchten,
du gehst
vor Anker, dein Schatten
streift dich ab im Gebüsch,

Ankunft,
Abkunft,

ein Käfer erkennt dich,
ihr steht euch
bevor,
Raupen
spinnen euch ein,

die Gross
Kugel
gewährt euch den Durchzug,

bald knüpft das Blatt seine Ader an deine,
Funken
müssen hindurch,
eine Atemnot lang,

es steht dir ein Baum zu, ein Tag,
er entziffert die Zahl,

ein Wort, mit all seinem Grün,
geht in sich, verpflanzt sich,

folg ihm
                    (*SP*, *GW* 2: 340)

"What stitches this voice?" The poem opens with a question, posed around figures of voice and of weaving. The voice both acts and is acted on, its thread stretching between "here" and "beyond." Out of sworn "abysses" emerges "the snow-needle," in Celan's lexicon almost an oxymoron: the snow of forgetting here joined with an instrument of rebinding, with voice itself. To weave, to speak, to remember: in these ways "you order the world."

Assertion in Celan, however, inevitably seems to require retraction. The world so promisingly emergent "counts as many as nine names, named kneeling"—nine, it seems, of the ten Sefirotic names whose letters form the world. The omission of the tenth suggests incompletion, which, in the following verse, becomes more severe:

> Tumuli, Tumuli
> you
> hill your way, living,
> come
> in the kiss.

The meaning of this passage is obscure. But within Celan's context, "Tumuli," funeral mounds, conjures the historical devastation of this century. Such historical trauma intrudes into the sequence of an ordered world, finally implicating all divine power. "The Lord of this hour was a winter creature," Celan writes in "On a White Prayer-Strap"; "what happened happened for his sake" (Der Herr dieser Stunde war ein Wintergeschöpf, ihm zulieb geschah, was geschah; *AW, GW* 2: 44). There he similarly speaks of "Spaltworte," split words, just as he speaks in "What stitches" of only nine names. History here figures as profound incursion, threatening to tear the fabric of creation and to garble its linguistic sequence.

Yet it is only in and as history that the articulate sequence can even take place. Celan's own language threads its way between the threat of such a shattering and a resistance to it. "What stitches" particularly resists dispersion, attesting the recuperative power of language. Through the "Tumuli" a "you" "hills" its way, above all as a "living" force, which the poet welcomes: "Come in the kiss." The poem's central stanzas then assert the continued power and presence of this "you" throughout creation. Like the 104th Psalm, it offers a roster of divine power and effect. The "you" appears through light, in water, through growing plants, among small creeping things: "A fin-beat steady, lights the bays, you drop anchor, your shadow casts you into the bush, advent, descent." "Liv-

ing creatures both small and great . . . all of them wait for Thee,"
says the Psalmist. And Celan writes, "A beetle recognizes you, caterpillars enweb you." The world, "the great globe," registers and
shows forth the mark of the Lord.

But at the poem's end, Celan reintroduces incompletion and interruption, in a further call for restoration, when every part may
again find place:

> soon
> the leaf knits its vein to yours,
> sparks
> must pass through,
> one panting breath long
>
> a tree is your right, a day
> it deciphers the number
>
> a word, with all its greenness,
> goes into itself, transplants itself,
>
> follow it

Three central kabbalistic images are invoked in this conclusion: the
tree, light, and language. Each of these, already well developed in
the *Zohar*, describes divine unfolding. In the Lurianic Kabbalah,
with its heightened sense of disruption, they acquire particular urgency. The world's disorder comes to be conceived in primeval and
cosmic terms: disruption occurred in the very process of creation,
indeed within the divine names; and the entire world-process becomes directed toward restoring that originary disorder. Restoration is here Celan's concern as well. First, within the Tree—and the
Sefirotic names are also branches of the Tree of God whose common root is the "Nothing," *Ein-Sof*—the link is reestablished between leaf and root through the "vein" that nourishes: "Soon the
leaf joins its vein to yours." Next, "sparks must pass through, one
panting breath long," invokes the Lurianic dispersion of divine
sparks, which must be regathered in the act of reinstituting order.
The "panting breath" then gathers together the imagery of light
with imagery of language, imagery confirmed through the numeri-

cal value of the letters—"it deciphers the number"—which is in turn realigned with the Tree: "A word, with all its greenness, goes into itself, transplants itself." The word at once returns to itself and, in so doing, engenders its transformation, now as restored world. Such linguistic restoration is another powerful Lurianic image: "The Tikkun [restoration] restores the unity of God's name which was destroyed by the original defect—Luria speaks of the letters JH as being torn away from WH in the name JHWH."[79] "What stitches" traces the path by which all the different divine manifestations rejoin, restoring and redeeming the world-order. It is the path toward which the poet points himself as well. Of the reblossoming "word" Celan writes: "Follow it."

This poem is among Celan's fullest efforts toward positive and productive order, continuous within experience as a linguistic and historical venture. As such, it refers to an ordering principle figured in tropes of the divine. But these tropes themselves reaffirm the historical world. As Buber also asserts: "The real communion of man with God not only has its place in the world, but also its subject."[80] There is no effort to transcend the world and its language, nor does language strain to penetrate the sphere of the absolute. Language rather both constitutes and represents the dimension of concrete and temporal reality as significant. Far from seeking to transcend these conditions, it instead insists that redemption take place within the activity of the temporal world—perhaps most radically expressed in the kabbalistic notion that God himself, because of the disorder in creation, has been exiled from himself, and that only human actions on earth can reconcile him to himself, restoring the letters of his Name.

The Trace of the Other

Celan's projection of meaningful order as the articulation of material language, especially in terms of the thematics of writing and of the letter central to kabbalistic language mysticism, opens his work toward contemporary theories of the sign. Such theoretical reflection has been undertaken, for example, by Winfried Menninghaus, who links Celan's "Sprachmystik" first to Walter Benjamin's philosophy of language, then also to Scholem's—which, according to Menninghaus, Benjamin also underwrites—and finally to Derridean sign-theory. Menninghaus argues that Celan brings "the mystical topos to an extensive and intensive reflection upon itself." He does so through, on the one hand, a use of "Name" in Benjamin's sense, and, on the other, a poetic "form-motivation" as "the union of signifier and signified" in a Derridean sense. This occurs through what Menninghaus calls a Derridean "erasure of semiological difference" between signifier and signified, which acts to "realise an 'indifference' of signification." As opposed to images of "vertically" directed signifier–signified relationships, Celan's work proposes "horizontal non-signifying signifiers," which Menninghaus specifies as its "mystical terminus."[81]

For Menninghaus, this mystical-theoretical impulse in Celan ultimately results in a severely self-referential poetics. Poems, instead of articulating meaning, become exempla of "non-instrumental language" that offer, in the end, allegories of metalanguage, indeed of sign-theory itself. Claiming that "all of Celan's poems realize in their form the breaking of instrumental reference," Menninghaus sees their "intentionality" as purely "metapoetic" and "metalingual," eliminating the "referential" aspect of language altogether. The 'name' is then "a self-signifying reality of the I and not only an arbitrary-instrumental reference."[82] Menninghaus, that is, adopts sign-theory as itself a "signified" which Celan's texts then represent. But this not only translates the poems into theoretical system, it also finally misreads the fundamental function of Celanian language. Theorizing the "Name" in Celan as "non-signifying presence," Menninghaus sees this as the center of Celanian linguistic mysticism, bringing him not only to what Menninghaus calls Derridean "indifference" but to "unio mystica" in the "inexpressibility of this (linguistic) indifference." The poetry thus conducts to a "not-said beyond the word" through a "distancing from verbal content" into pure "linguistic form."[83] The poetry becomes, as in other readings of Celan, an effort to transcend language, a union of signifier and signified as the transumption of the signifier into the signified.

Derrida's own discourse on Celan points, I think, in quite different directions. In "Schibboleth," what Derrida emphasizes is Celanian textual discontinuity and multiplicity as a commitment to particularity and historicity. Celan's writing offers the successive inscription of "irreplaceable singularity which is replaceable only by another irreplaceable singularity which takes its place without substituting for it." Derrida's own site for this irreducible singularity in Celan is the "date." Every poem is inscribed as dated, addressing itself to an integrity of moment. It acts as a "secret" that remains thus "withdrawn," not as "hermetic," but rather "like a date, heterogeneous to all hermeneutic totalization or radicalization." The poem, that is, asserts its resistance to transcendence and transumption. It insists above all on the particularity of its signifiers, not as representing any preconstituted meaning, but as articulating meaning only within and through its own component elements: "There is ciphered singularity which is irreducible to any concept, . . . a ciphered singularity in which multiplicity gathers itself."[84]

Derrida finally sees the "date" of historical specificity as the site of "encounter" and of "address": encounter as a nonmerging conjunction between discrete particulars; address as the very movement and possibility of signs.

What takes place in this experience of a date . . . is perhaps what Celan calls . . . the secretness of encounter; and in the word encounter two values come together without which there would be no date. . . . Encounter . . . suggests an encounter with the other, the other ineluctable singularity. What dating comes to is signing. To inscribe a date, to enter it, is to sign from a given place. . . . Addressing its date, what an address or discourse declares about the concept or meaning of the date . . . is to signify that it is, at the least, marked by its date, signed by it or re-marked in a singular manner.[85]

The date conjoins without effacing identity. Yet identity only occurs by way of such conjunction, which is therefore not static, but active venture. Derrida reiterates throughout the essay that the poem is what "reaches and leaves its mark on, and if it does not, at least calls to, the other. It speaks to and addresses the other." It is "the bearing of a word for the other, to the other or from the other."

The word of the poem is "given or promised, in any case opened, offered to the other," an act that, opening "the word to the other . . .
opens history."[86] The result is a linguistic movement at once disper-
sive and relative, interruptive and communicating: "discontinuity
and that which nonetheless gathers in the discretion of the discontinuous, that which gathers in the caesura of the relation to the
other, in the interruption of address."[87] The date comes to mark
heterogeneity itself, the unassimilable moment that inserts within
the structure of discourse the force of what can never be appropri-
ated by generalization. It remains ever other.

In pursuing this thematics of the date, Derrida is of course responding to Celan's own "Meridian" address. There Celan himself
traces a movement from the date to the address to the other. The
poem, he says, is ever "mindful of such dates," is always "the language of an individual which has taken on form" in "the present,
the here and now." But "precisely for that reason," and against all
pressure of silence, Celan, with astonishment, declares:

But the poem does speak! It remains mindful of its dates, but—it speaks,
to be sure, it speaks only in its own, its own individual cause. But I think it
has always belonged to the expectation of the poem . . . in precisely this
manner to speak in the cause of the strange . . . in precisely this manner to
speak in the cause of an Other—who knows, perhaps in the cause of a
wholly Other. (GW, 3: 196)

This appeal to the "Other" does not commit Celan to an absolute
world of absolute language as Peter Horst Neumann, for example,
claims, saying that "Celan's poetry strives for the language of the
absolute, the language of the 'wholly other,' and thus adopts the
difficulties of every mystical discussion, in which speech withdraws
itself in order to give way to absolute language."[88] The mystical
discussion that situates Celan's "Other" is not one of linguistic transcendence per se. It does not follow the trajectory from language to
silence that Derrida, in another essay ("How to Avoid Speaking")
describes as a Greco-Christian mode of negative theology. This
would pursue an "apophatic voyage" toward "immediacy of presence" in a logic that finally leads "to a union with God." The be-

yond Being of this apophatic designation, Derrida argues, remains in fact a being, although as "hyperessential mode," one that can ultimately be "unveiled" in a revelation toward which apophasis moves as "contact or vision, that pure intuition of the ineffable, that silent union with that which remains inaccessible to speech." In this Greco-Christian mode, then, negativity becomes a discourse of "reappropriation," as in Meister Eckhart, who remains directed toward "a certain signification of unveiling, of laying bare, of truth as what is beyond the covering garment." Negative theology here comes almost to oppose language mysticism. In "considering that every predicative language is inadequate to the essence, in truth to the hyperessentiality (the being beyond Being) of God," negative theology ultimately renounces language, committing itself instead to a silence in which "only a negative ('apophatic') attribution can claim to approach God, and to prepare us for a silent intuition of God." [89]

Derrida remains diffident in this essay regarding other possible stances toward the "other," declining to pursue his discourse into traditions other than the Greco-Christian. Nevertheless, he does imply the possibility of another negative theology: "The experience of negative theology perhaps holds to a promise, that of the other . . . not of this or that promise but of that which . . . inscribes us by its trace in language—before language." He marks this distinct negativity perhaps more explicitly when he alludes to a "thinking of difference" that is "alien, heterogeneous, in any case irreducible to the intuitive *telos*—to the experience of the ineffable and of the mute vision which seems to orient all of this apophatics." [90]

Celan's is distinctly such an "other" apophatics. The contours this may follow are perhaps clearer in Emmanuel Levinas, whose work, however, Derrida acknowledges. Levinas, in his own essay on Celan, contrasts the poet's use of the "other" with Heidegger's, which Celan also may evoke. Heidegger's impersonality of Being remains, according to Levinas, within ontological system, as against Celan's insistence on the personal, the particular, the immediate. Celan's is an address of "the for-other of the speaking of man speaking to the other, and not the speaking of Being which evokes a presence blossoming in the landscape." Rather than attempting "to speak the meaning of Being," or to "dwell poetically" within it, Celan is instead "in search of the Other . . . a significance older than ontology or the thinking of Being." This distinction of the particular from impersonality, address from ontology, Levinas refers in turn to Buber. Buber's categories are, he asserts, to be preferred to an "exegesis . . . that descends in majesty from the Black Forest in order to show poetry opening the world in Being. . . . The poetry of the poem will be the personal." Discourse, for Levinas as for Buber, is a matter not of ontology, but of ethics. He places Celan's language in such an ethical context, where it exists "prior to 'unconceal-ment.' . . . A language of and for proximity—more ancient than that of the 'truth of Being' (which it probably bears and supports), and the first of languages—response preceding question, responsi-bility to the neighbor—making possible through its 'for the other' the whole miracle of giving."[91]

The other here is never recovered into the same. It is forever beyond identity, an "infinite," in Mark Taylor's analysis, "that 'is' beyond essence and as such is otherwise than being and nonbe-ing."[92] It orients the speaker toward its irreducible otherness, at once a genuine relation and yet also a clear, untransgressible divi-sion. This double structure becomes the vital configuration of Le-vinas's discourse-model of ethics. The trajectory of address is the "trajectory of movement without return," and guarantees the pro-tection of the other from all appropriation, prohibiting exploitation and violence. Exactly in its otherness, the other retains its integrity against the incursions of the self, the same. Yet it remains in relation to the self, in the most personal sense—"the personal, from me to the other"—and does so specifically as discourse: to address the other is to assert both relation and difference. In Celan's trope in the Meridian speech, it is "a voice's path to a thou." In one sense, this path also is a movement of transcendence. Yet it is a transcen-dence that does not forsake the real for the absolute. It "leaves to the real the alterity which pure imagination erases," yet through its gesture as "poetic speaking outstretched toward the other," reality itself takes shape: "Things appear at last in the very movement that brings them to the other . . . in this offering, this giving, forms emerge and take on meaning." It is finally the shape not only of ethics, but of desire, of love, "in the for-other speaking to the other . . . signalling this very giving of the sign, in love speaking that love."[93]

The Meridian speech insists exactly on such distinctness of the "Other": that is its otherness. There is neither possibility nor desire to penetrate it. "The poem," Celan tells us in Meridian, "goes towards this Other, it needs this Other, it needs a vis-à-vis. It searches out and addresses it" (*GW* 3: 198). The Other is a beyond-the-self in every encounter with every irreducible particular, while the language of the poem is a trajectory that moves toward but never overtakes it: "Each thing, each person is a form of the Other for the poem, as it makes for this Other." This language, far from attempting an absolute speech, is one that Celan insists must "pay careful attention to everything it encounters" through "a finer sense of detail," a "concentration" he places in the particularity of "dates," indeed in the very "Wahrnehmenden" and "Erscheinenden," perceptions and appearances of phenomena as opposed to absolutes. The negative impulse can be called restraint or even contraction; the positive impulse Celan calls "Attention" (Aufmerksamkeit). Attention insists on the particularity that respects Otherness both in its difference and as orienting reference. As Celan adds, citing Walter Benjamin, "Attention is the natural prayer of the soul" (*GW* 3: 198).

For Celan the Other is beyond all specification; yet it is approached and above all addressed only in terms of specificity, particularity, individuality. The poem is "the language of an individual." "Only in this immediacy and proximity does it allow the participation of the Other's greatest particularity: its time" (*GW* 3: 198–99). The time of the Other: this near-oxymoron links transcendence with historicity, phenomena, differentiation. In Celan, the specificity of date is part of a continuing pledge to singularity—part of a refusal to incorporate, generalize, subsume, a refusal to dis-place from circumstances, from the particular and substantively immediate. But this devotion to the unassimilably singular and particular opens toward the strange and other. On the one hand, the Other remains beyond all discourse, removed from it as exactly what can never be penetrated or domesticated, never contained by identity. On the other hand, or rather, because of this, the Other exactly validates discourse, makes discourse possible as the mark of the irreducible, the sphere of a reality at once bounded by what it can never penetrate and essential within its own proper territory: a "verbal communication" that is not, Celan insists, "the abstract concept of speech," but is both mode and trope for concrete reality: "language become reality, set free under the sign of an individuation which is radical, yet at the same time remains mindful of the boundaries established for it by language, of the possibilities laid open for it by language" (GW 3: 197).

To see language reified is, then, to experience the world as ordered language. Beyond this linguistic world remains an Other that is inexpressible. But this inexpressibility makes possible the manifold creation experienced as (language) world. As in the founding Lurianic creation myth of divine contraction (*Tzimzum*), "God's self-contraction [makes] room for multiplicity," a process of "differentiation and separation" in which "relationship presupposes limitation."[94] Language-world is thus ordered in orientation toward, and bounded by, an Other that in remaining beyond language affirms and places the multiplicity of the present world.

This mode of signification recalls, in terms of sign-theory, not a "nonsignifying" unity of signified and signifier, but rather a notion of significance as emerging through the differential ongoing inscription of "signifiers"—what Derrida, following Levinas, calls a trace. "Every sign is a trace," writes Levinas in "The Trace of the Other"; "in addition to what the sign signifies, it is the past [*passage*] of him who delivered the sign."[95] Derrida, in his essay on Levinas in *Writing and Difference*, in turn cites Levinas's "The Trace of the Other": "We are in 'the Trace of God.'" What the trace asserts is a chain of signifiers that derive their meaning by referring not to a signified beyond themselves but to each other as members of an inscripted, differential order. Yet they do so as situated by an "other," with which they stand in relation "without intermediary and without communion, absolute proximity and absolute distance . . . eros in which, within the proximity with the other distance is integrally maintained." [96] With regard to Celan himself, Derrida speaks of poetry as inscribing "the multiplicity of languages . . . the migration of languages . . . the multiplicity within language, insignificant difference as the condition of sense in language." Such difference is at once "discriminative and decisive"; having "no meaning in and of itself," it is nonetheless "what one must know how to mark or recognize." [97]

Celan's writings are composed of such heterogeneous markings and recognitions of difference. The breaks and stops, interruptions and displacements, locate whatever meaning may emerge within a processional sign-inscription, with no release from textual space into some ideal territory beyond the signifier. Signs mean in relation to each other, as elements that never lose their discrete particularity, their unique historical situating. A Celan text is never subsumed by an encompassing concept. Its signs remain within the differences Celan's discourse refuses to elide, radically inscribed by way of specificity, juxtaposition, unrecoverable displacement: making each sign irreducible, and signification an ongoing project of finding, within the signifying chain, significant relationships.

The function, and the stakes, of this effort emerge particularly through reference to kabbalistic tropes of a linguistic reality. In the Kabbalah language, representing the temporal order of material phenomena, remains the proper domain not only of human relation, but also of relation to the divine as instituting the world of phenomenal order. The divine remains ever apart, other from all being. Yet the divine is also encountered in language, with the world itself constituted of the letters of the divine names. Religious significance is thus experienced within the world of signifiers—of temporal, articulated linguistic sequence, what Scholem calls the "self-differentiating word of the creation." [98]

In this, the traditional priority of silence over language is also in fundamental ways reversed. The divine as other remains beyond language, ineffable, and is designated therefore as Nothing. But this inexpressibility remains the mark of its final otherness, to overcome which is not the aim, and exclusion from which is not a failure. There is no effort to achieve, as Buber puts it, a "raising of the veil of the manifest, which divides the hidden from the real." [99] The sign of relation is here no longer silence, but language. As ineffable, the Godhead establishes and orients the sphere of linguistic activity. But it never fully subsumes language into silence as the mode of participation. The priority of silence as transcendence into the absolute and ineffable transforms into a ground for meaning as articulation in time, articulate time itself, a language-chain of the things of the world. This, then, is not the "apophasis" Derrida describes as one "that cannot contain within itself the principle of its interruption." Apophasis here instead asserts some radical, even originary break, but one that retains a kind of positive force: "a promise" that "will have always escaped this demand of presence . . . [but which] renders possible every present discourse on presence," so that even "silence yet remains a modality of speech." [100] Silence empowers speech, marks out the spaces for further utterance. It continues to represent an exclusion from Godhead, but not as sign of fall. Exclusion is instead the proper stance within creation, ennabling the utterance of creation to go forth. The ineffable institutes the letters of the world as unrecoverable distinction, yet as founding the world and as a positive orientation within it.

Creation from Nothing

Celan's is not a poetry of self-transcendence that takes itself beyond its own conditions. Nor is it a poetry of self-reference, a "speaking as detour, through which the poem tries to attain itself, to win itself," as Gerhard Buhr, for example, claims. [101] It is a poetry of trace: tracking, in imagery Celan himself repeatedly introduces, meanings through and across a world of temporal experience that yet speak toward what always remains beyond immediate experience, as its orientation, or hope. His are poems "of one who—as before—perceives, who faces that which appears. Who questions this appearing and addresses it. It becomes conversation." Yet this conversation is, as Celan adds at once, often "despairing (GW 3: 198). If Celan's is a poetry striving to trace significance within worldly experience, it is also a poetry of, and at, great risk. The trace it would pursue is unclear, elusive, distorted. Exactly because the meaning of experience remains temporal, within history, historical event deeply marks, challenges, even threatens it. The Other, which promises to anchor and orient, instead may itself be despaired of, erased in an overwhelming chaos of event. Celan also offers a series of figures in which Truth and Eternity are profoundly negative terms without conversion. "The truth" then is "tied up . . . from rubble" and evident only as a "high up blooming No in the crown" (Die Wahrheit, angeseilt an . . . von Geröll . . . oben erblühenden Nein—in der Krone; FS, GW 2: 138). The traditional other world of truth and eternity is deeply implicated in Celan by rubble, by destruction, by evil: "Eternity grows old . . . they ladle soup into all beds and camps" (Die Ewigkeit altert: . . . löffeln sie Suppen / in alle Betten / und Lager; FS, GW 2: 177). The eternal world is here penetrated by the history it has not redeemed. Or else it "holds itself in bounds" (Die Ewigkeit hält sich in Grenzen; SP, GW 2: 415), unavailable to a history it thus leaves bereft.

The absolute, if entirely beyond history, loses all force or meaning. Equally, without positive relation toward some ground for events, the world itself becomes, in Celan, unchartable. If Celan desires to render events as a trace of some orienting Other, the failure of this orientation results in trackless spaces, disorienting abysses. A "wordtrace" (Wortspur) comes to transport the "woundread" (Wundgelesene; AW, GW 2: 24). The divine fire guiding the Exodus in "Easter Smoke, flowing, with / the letter-like / wake in the midst" (Osterqualm, flutend, mit / der buchstabenähnlichen / Kielspur inmitten) becomes a "zerbissene Ewigkeitsgroschen," a bitten-apart eternity penny (AW, GW 2: 85).[102] All forward movement may halt, as "in the farthest secondary meaning, at the foot of the paralyzed amen-stairs" (In den Fernsten / Nebenbedeutung, am Fuss der gelähmten Amen-Treppe; ZH, GW 3: 77). Or, the trail becomes impossible to follow: "rained-over tracks, the small travelling-juggler-sermon of silence" (überregneter Fährte / die kleine Gauklerpredigt der Stille; FS, GW 2: 145). "Wrecked taboos" (Die abgewrackten Tabus) impel into a

border-walking between them,
worldmoist, on
a meaningchase, on
a meaning-
flight

die Grenzgängerei zwischen ihnen,
weltennass, auf
Bedeutungsjagd, auf
Bedeutungs-
flucht

(FS, GW 2: 168)

The world's "moisture"—tears, or perhaps merely events—makes life's journey into a hunt for elusive meaning. These texts do not so much track order as follow its disappearing trail. Celan crosses the trackless space of heavens whose traditional claims have been emptied:

The Higherworld—lost, the madjourney, the dayjourney.

Questionable, out from here
that with the rose in a fallow-year
homedeciphered, nowhere.

Die Hochwelt—verloren, die Wahnfahrt, die Tagfahrt.

Erfragbar, von hier aus,
das mit der Rose im Brachjahr
heimgedeutete Nirgends.

(FS, GW 2: 199)

Seeking for the trace of meaning, Celan instead traces mad journeys across unanswered questions. Yet even here, he leaves open the possibility for further meaning, "homedeciphered." The "year" is not simply barren, but "fallow," perhaps set aside, as in the biblical injunction, for a renewed dedication and flowering. And the "nowhere," here as elsewhere, is not so much ambiguous as ambivalent. It points equally toward two opposed Nothings. On the one hand, Nothing may be the transcendence of the divine, a transcendence that excludes the poet from its sphere. But this would not be the failure to achieve an absolute state. An absolute state is not considered appropriate as the goal of desire. "The absolute poem,"

Celan insists, "no, it doesn't exist, it cannot exist" (*GW* 3: 199). On the other hand, the Nothing may be nothing more than the empty spaces left by failed sanction, unavailable grounding, unanchored event.

This ambivalence impels some of Celan's best-known poems, as in the Holocaust memorial "There Was Earth in Them, and They Dug," where, after a caesura of "stillness" and "storm," the poet offers an ambiguous appeal: "Oh someone, oh none, oh no one, oh you" (O einer, o keiner, o niemand, o du; *NR, GW* 1: 211). Similarly, the iconic "Mandorla" translates the almond-shaped space that frames a divine figure into the blank shape of a question: "In the almond—what stands in the almond? The Nothing" (In der Mandel—was steht in der Mandel? Das Nichts; *NR, GW* 1: 244). The Nothing signals at once nihilism and messianism. It leaves open whether this negation is "negativity per se, nothingness or meaninglessness . . . an indication that at the center of being there is only randomness and chaos"; or whether, as in the Kabbalah, the negative is "intrinsically good . . . the creative origin and designing telos of all that is."[103] That the question ultimately addresses both poet and reader dramatizes not only what is at stake, but also the historical, ongoing process of decision.

Celan's juxtaposition of redemptive hope with despair occurs perhaps most famously in the poem "Psalm," which begins:

> No one kneads us again of earth and clay.
> No one incants our dust.
> No one
>
> Niemand knetet uns wieder aus Erde und Lehm,
> niemand bespricht unsern Staub.
> Niemand.

Creative origin or its denial: the poem traces a course through the spaces of Nothing, using the discourse of praise for doubt and reproach—or turning doubt and reproach back toward blessing:

> Blessed art thou, No One. For thy sake we
> want to bloom.
> Towards thee

Gelobt seist du, Niemand. Dir zulieb wollen
wir blühn.
Dir entgegen

(NR, GW 1: 225)

Such sacral language attempts to encircle and penetrate reality and experience, but it faces always the threat instead of engulfment and dispersion:

Go blind already today:
Eternity also stands full of eyes—
therein
drowns, what helped the images get
over the road that they came
therein
extinguishes, what also took you out of language
with one gesture,
that you let happen as
the dance of two words out of only
autumn and silk and Nothing.

Erblinde schon heut:
auch die Ewigkeit steht voller Augen—
darin
ertrinkt, was den Bildern hinweghalf
über den Weg, den sie kamen,
darin
erlischt, was auch dich aus der Sprache
fortnahm mit einer Geste,
die du geschehn liesst wie
den Tanz zweier Worte aus lauter
Herbst und Seide und Nichts.

(AW, GW 2: 45)

"Eternity" is transfixed by the "eyes" of Celanian memory and reproach. Rather than an engendering, productive force, it drowns "images" unable to cross the "road" of the past. Rather than unfolding as utterance, it extinguishes what would come forth as language. Eternity is here a site not of revelation, but of blindness. The history of "what you let happen" intrudes into eternity itself, which not only drowns and extinguishes productive force but is itself

258 Paul Celan and the Kabbalah

drowned and extinguished; not only blinds the eyes that stare into it, but is itself a blinded eye.

Still, "what you let happen" is figured as a "dance" of words. But it is a disjointed speaking. As in the poem "Unreadable This World," where "everything doubles," the words here are double rather than continuous, an obscure, disconnected sequence. "Autumn" recalls the moment of historical destruction, the season of Celan's parents' death. "Silk" is perhaps a figure for fine and valuable weaving, an accomplished textus this poem undoes in its own disjunctive sequence. Or, there may be some kabbalistic echo, such as Scholem ascribes to prayer as a "silken cord with the aid of which the mystical intention of the mind gropes its way through the darkness toward God."[104] (Celan elsewhere speaks of a "silk-covered Nowhere" [seidenverhangene Nirgend; ZH, GW 3: 74].) Here, too, there is a groping through darkness—but only to a "Nothing" that appears in all its ambiguity. It may refer to the "Eternity" of the poem's opening, but even so, in this poem this is hardly positive assertion. Peter Paul Schwarz, in discussing the paradoxes of Celanian negation, includes among its meanings "the dethroning of God through the Nothing of history."[105] For Celan, exactly because significance must be temporal and worldly and cannot be abstracted into a metaphysical realm, history can threaten it. The moment of "what you let happen" is one he cannot integrate into an ongoing pattern.

Yet, even here, the poem is cast as dialogue. The paradox of Nothing penetrates into the trajectory of discourse itself. Following the ambivalences of blasphemy, it continues to direct itself to a belief no longer fully tenable. Yet it remains address, a launching into language as the realm of human and poetic production, and toward a possible hope and significance. It is an address strongly marked by what Stéphane Moses calls "caesura," the "cutting of space and rupture of time [that] delimit a different kind of reality, through which absolute otherness can manifest itself."[106] The caesura in Celan is at once linguistic and temporal, structural and sacral. It is especially thematized in any number of the late Timecourt (Zeitge-

höft) poems, indeed in the very image of "timecourt," where the poet's "mouth / clambers up with late- / sense up there / in time courts" (Mund / das klettert mit Spät- / sinnigem droben / in Zeithöfen / umher). Through this site of interruption he tries to "touch you as a shadow" (als Schatten berühre: *ZH, GW* 3: 76). It is a site of interruption, of Nothing as a possibility both of orienting time by a transcendence beyond it, and of the disorder of mere emptiness:

> The Nothing, for our
> names' sake
> —they ingather us
> affixes its seal
>
> The end believes us
> the beginning,
>
> before us the masters that circled
> us with silence,
> in the unseparated, testifies
> the narrow
> brightness.
>
> Das Nichts, um unsrer
> Namen willen
> —sie sammeln uns ein—,
> siegelt,
>
> das Ende glaubt uns
> den Anfang,
>
> vor den uns umschweigenden
> Meistern,
> im Ungeschiednen, bezeugt sich
> die klamme
> Helle.
>
> (*ZH, GW* 3: 110)

The Nothing here, as in "Psalm," appears within a distinctively sacral, but reversed, rhetoric: not we for its sake, but it "for our names' sake." As in "Psalm," it is conjoined to a messianic gesture, an ingathering; and relation to it is in some sense affirmed: it "affixes its seal." But as in "Psalm," the positive orientation is no less marked by regression, dispersion, and retreat. The end and beginning seem linked, but in an oddly reversed direction, uncertain of a beginning rather than directing it. "Masters" is a word forever compromised in Celan by his use of it in "Deathfugue"—"Death is a master from Germany." Here it seems a double image of sage and silence, of a self placed or lost.

Is this a relation respectful of distance, or a distance that defeats relation? Such duplicity is inscribed throughout the final stanza as its fundamental structure. There, redemptive gestures are registered. "The unseparated," like ingathering, points toward hope of recovery and renewal, and perhaps specifically recalls the Lurianic vision of the letters of the divine Name once more rejoined. In this, it testifies to "brightness." But the brightness is "narrow," in a word that also recalls the gap between mountains (*Klamme*).[107] The testimony given is at the same time undone, the light asserted is also constrained.

Which of these impulses may prove the stronger is never decided finally. But the poem displays a consistent pattern of reversals that suggests that any decision must come from the world of creatures. The Nothing is invoked "for our names' sake"; it is our names that "ingather us"; belief by the "end" in the "beginning" depends in fact on "us." Even the "masters" stand before us, not we before them. And it is the brightness rather than "us" that is called to give testimony.

None of these reversals entails denial of the Nothing. On the contrary, they realize implications within the very designation of Nothing itself. According to Gershom Scholem, the ultimate Name

has no "meaning" in a special sense: The meaninglessness of the name of God indicates its situation in the very central point of the revelation, at the basis of which it lies. . . . There exists this element over and beyond meaning, but which in the first instance enables meaning to be given. It is this element which endows every other form of meaning, though it has no meaning itself. What we learn from creation and revelation, the word of God, is infinitely liable to interpretation, and it is reflected in our own language. Its radiation or sounds, which we catch, are not so much com-

munications as appeals . . . its communication and reflection in time. . . .
The fact that language can be spoken is, in the opinion of the Kabbalists,
owed to the name, which is present in language.[108]

It is exactly the restriction and limitation of the Name—its "meaninglessness," its nothingness—that makes way for the speaking of
others, that makes possible the speaking of others. In this sense, it
founds all language, which is directed toward the other of the Nothing in turn. The Nothing remains at once beyond and yet involved
within the act of discourse. It is the space, energy, and desire that
generate the trajectory of discourse, and that also penetrate within
discourse as interruption, rupture. This can be positive, the very
opening of creativity, in which the speaker participates with the
other to extend the world of creation. Yet it can also be negative,
traumatic, disruptive.

In Celan, these do not stand as static alternatives. Each is a call
to decision—in the poem, for the poet, and for the reader. Yet it is
a call specifically placed. Not negativity, not silence and the ineffable, but language remains the realm of poetic activity in Celan. In
this, Celan accords with a shift in value-structure itself, such as is
suggested by Adorno in *Negative Dialectics*: "One of the mystical
impulses secularized in dialectics was the doctrine that the intra-
mundane and historic is relevant to what traditional metaphysics
distinguished as transcendent."[109] Celan's appeal to the Kabbalah
marks such a shift to the "historic" from the metaphysical, where
the Kabbalah itself represents a departure from the dominant Western metaphysical tradition, an otherness from Western ontology.
Yet the configurations it proposes are by no means exempt from the
traumas of modernity, which become in Celan the traumas of language. Exactly because the divine is situated by way of discourse in
the temporal orders of phenomena and language, exactly because
of its historical involvement, the divine is itself vulnerable, at risk.
An ineffable Godhead establishes the sphere of, and orients, linguistic activity. Yet the ineffable may also cease to frame language and
instead threaten to engulf it. In situating divine activity in the temporal order of language, disruptions of that order can disrupt language and its relation to the divine. Such a possibility is suggested

in the midrash on *Lamentations* cited above, which concludes: "What does a human king do [when mourning]? asks the Holy One. 'He sits in silence.' He said to them, 'I will do likewise,' as it is stated, 'He sitteth alone and keepeth silence.'" What seems obvious, however, in a historical context remains radical in a mystical one. For this is not the fecundity of silence, not the silence that subsumes sequence into immutability. It is rather a disruption of sequence, a silence that realizes the negative possibility of Nothing without paradoxical conversion.

In Celan, this double possibility of positive and negative Nothing is pursued as an unfinished, unknown historical course, truly exposed in risk. His poems are not caught in static indecision. They instead offer a choice looking toward future action and future hope. It is a choice offered in the gaps opened within Celan's own utterance—an utterance pointing toward both the nothing which is not (the silencing of language) and the nothing out of which language can come forth; toward linguistic venture undertaken ever in possibility, but also ever in possible failure. Yet the act of dialogue, the pledge to enter into its historical trajectory, is itself a positive decision. It enters into the movement of discourse, to take part in history. The relationships of and within language can become disrupted, their source and direction unsure. The linguistic order that Celan in his poetry seeks can elude him, bringing his verse to the verge of silence in face of a silent Nothing. Nevertheless his verse strains against such silence. If his world, as he writes in one poem, is "The track of a bight in the nowhere," (Die Spur eines Bisses im Nirgends), he goes on: "You also must combat this, from here onward" (Auch sie / musst du bekämpfen, / von hier aus; *FS, GW* 2: 117). And in opposition to truth as only transcendent, he can offer his own poetics of immanent and temporal language:

> A Roaring: it is
> truth itself,
> taking its first steps
> among men,
> in the midst of
> metaphor-flurries

Ein Dröhnen: es ist
die Wahrheit selbst
unter die Menschen
getreten,
mitten ins
Metapherngestöber
(*AW, GW* 2: 89)

Celan attempts in his own "Metapherngestöber," snow-flurry
metaphors, not to attain to the ineffable, but rather to assert a generative relation to an absolute Other beyond his utterance. The concrete, the particular, the temporal—the historical world of human
activity—are insisted upon as the sphere of language and the mode
of creative endeavor, but also, therefore, as the site of historical
measure and possible defeat in silence. "Abstract, yet earthly," Celan calls this language in the Meridian speech, in which the poem is
"under way." He thus pledges himself to a linguistic movement
that, in pointing toward the other beyond it, strives to take shape
as an experience articulate and sacral, but always in the face of
genuine risk. Still, it is his hope that the Other, both distant and
proximate, other and accessible, may become, through language,
"a not entirely remote, a quite near Other" (*GW* 3: 196–97).

CHAPTER 7

Conclusion: Language Values

The imperfect is our paradise.
Note that, in this bitterness, delight,
Since the imperfect is so hot in us,
Lies in flawed words and stubborn sounds.
—Wallace Stevens, Poems of our Climate

✧

In *Philosophy in the Tragic Age of the Greeks*, Nietzsche offers his critique of metaphysics in the guise of philosophical history. Once long ago, at "the purest springs of Hellenism," Heraclitus boldly asserted the "justification of that which is coming-to-be." Denying "the duality of totally diverse worlds . . . he no longer distinguished a physical world from a metaphysical one." He proclaimed: "I see nothing other than becoming," and saw that "coming-to-be itself could not be anything evil or unjust." But then came Parmenides, who in a moment of "bloodless abstraction, unclouded by any reality" invented a world of Being. Coming-to-be is denounced as false and delusive; the Real is inaccessible in terms of the "manifold colorful world known to experience," which is "cast aside mercilessly as mere semblance and illusion." In this "un-Greek" moment was born the flight "into the rigor mortis of the coldest emptiest concept of all, the concept of being." And with the split into two worlds comes the "wholly erroneous distinction between 'spirit' and 'body' which, especially since Plato, lies upon philosophy like a curse."[1]

In this study, I have investigated ways in which the dualist structures Nietzsche here critiques continue to frame attitudes toward language, not least in literary contexts. They emerge in an ambivalence to language deeply rooted in the Western metaphysical tradition, where language is radically the sign of embodiment. An ambivalence to expression in words correlates with suspicion of time, multiplicity, and the body. The call to transcend words in turn represents the desire to rise above these conditions, which the divisions and sequences of words can never represent. The figure of language is thus metaphysically charged and takes its place within a scale of metaphysical values. Expression is suspicious and faulty; inexpressibility is transcendent and ultimate. This metaphysical evaluation carries over into literature, even when metaphysical issues seem remote. Eliot, Beckett, and Celan all, however, directly place their language-figures within just such religious and philosophical contexts. Each accepts language as representing material, temporal, historical reality, both in its own sequences and as an image for the sequential nature of the material world. But language therefore also acquires the equivocal status given to material-temporal reality within metaphysics: an equivocal status that Eliot, in embracing the tradition, reproduces; that Beckett, in critiquing the tradition, exposes; and that Celan, as against the tradition, significantly reformulates.

Eliot's own ambivalence to time and body has come increasingly to disturb readers. The figure of language, however, is no less ambivalent for him, despite the promise in the *Quartets* that it will convey a positive vision. Nor are his qualms merely his own. They are traditional, active from the philosophical outset, as Nietzsche suggests. Plato's *Timaeus*, for example, eventually forms a basis through Augustine for much Christian cosmology and theodicy. In it, the created world, as an expression of divine bounty, has positive value. But as unequal to and radically other from divine unity, the world also has negative value. And it is unity that remains the site of both truth and goodness. The tension implicit in this double valuation of world as at once positive and negative has been most acute in mystical movements such as those Eliot incessantly cites; and it extends to a mystical attitude toward language. Language in such mysticism represents time, body, multiplicity: the very conditions that define this world as apart from, and lesser than, ideal unity. Negative theologies therefore consistently strive, with other

assertions of radical ascesis, to transcend language, which they suspect as an inadequate medium for expressing truth and the Truth
of God. Instead, relations between created and transcendent realms
are expressed in negative terms that heighten their disjunction and
indeed opposition.

My discussion of Eliot establishes basic terms in the tradition
that Eliot embraced. I also try to show how, in embracing that tradition, he reproduces its tensions, ambivalences, and contradictions. The pursuit of unity shapes the *Quartets'* language practices,
both as overt theme and implicitly in its language theory and
stances. But the negativity of such transcendence can threaten to
empty the created world of meaning and value. It can make realizing the values of spirit and truth within the confines of historical
experience highly problematic. Transcendence then points to a
world so radically other as to entail the abandonment, rather than
redemption, of this one. Nietzsche calls this transcendence escape.
Two-world dualism, he writes in *Twilight of the Idols*, leads to the
desire to be "free . . . from the deception of the senses, from history,
from lies . . . and above all, away with the body." But this, he argues, empties the world and history of validity. The pursuit of unity
denies reality to multiplicity and change, but the world of Being
itself is nothing more than "an empty fiction." Of the philosophers
of being, he concludes: "Nothing real escaped their grasp alive."[2]

Beckett's work seems to me Nietzschean in its critical aspects.
Beckett, like Eliot, adopts the traditional terms of metaphysics, with
their implications for language. But Beckett takes these long-
established ideals at their word, in a reductio ad absurdum that
reveals their disturbing implications. His critique of traditional assumptions proceeds in part through their radical, parodic adoption.
This is especially the case in his treatment of language, in many
ways the obsessive center of his work. Beckett's knowing, self-
conscious use of theological and mystical material marks a steady,
elaborate pattern through his work. The very title of what is in
many ways his masterwork, *The Unnamable*, invokes one of the
most potent and pervasive terms of mystical speculation—one that
underscores the impulse to transcend language as the very heart of

the mystical undertaking. The short prose works of Beckett's later period continue *The Unnamable*'s relentless and inescapable meditations on language as these conjoin with its equally insistent and inescapable meditations on nothingness. These texts realize, to an especially pure and merciless degree, the condition in which the effort to escape and deny language can result. In so doing, Beckett's work questions both the positive value of ascesis and the negative value of language. Within his texts, inexpressibility comes to represent not linguistic paradox and transcendence, but linguistic suicide. Its negations are not transformative but tautological. Beckett's own negative project, however, also retains positive force, with language reemerging as the medium in which the life of the imagination takes place and endures.

The traditional ambivalence toward language as a perhaps unavoidable but always deficient medium is one to which both Beckett and Eliot respond. In this, they exhibit the pressure it has continued to exert as an assumption underlying literary discourse. The need to revise this inherited schema has become, however, increasingly urgent through the crises and disasters of this century. Paul Celan's work suggests important avenues for such revision, ones that cross with the critical thinking that has gained increasing force since Nietzsche. This is due not least to his sources in a tradition linked with, but in marked ways distinct from, the theologies that have dominated in the West. The Judaic and specifically kabbalistic contexts provide one central basis for Celan's treatment of language. These grant to language a significantly different place and status than do the metaphysical systems that frame Eliot and Beckett. Although also invoking terms common to negative theology, and also placing language within a mystical context, Celan's claims for language are not directed toward representing an ultimate state beyond temporal reality—which is not language's role—but toward establishing language as the proper mode for self-expression within the world of time and history. Negativity and silence are for him, as in other mysticisms, in some sense ultimate, designating transcendence and the divine. But this transcendence of language is also the founding of language, figured as significant created order. In this structure, language unfolds from a divine speaker who remains transcendentally hidden and other. But he expresses himself in his utterance, an utterance that is ultimately the world itself. Language is reified, granted an ontological status, while the other remains beyond ontological category. The term Nothing here retains the absolute distinction between God and world while nevertheless asserting them to be bound together. What links them to each other is exactly language. Silence represents not the possibility or hope of transcendence into an atemporal, spiritual world, but, on the one hand, the divine as beyond all predication; on the other hand, the space left open for linguistic address. Thus language, while it reaffirms the distinction between the beyond and the world, also asserts the positive relation between them. Although grounded in a transcendent realm, value does not reside there, but rather in the significant order of concrete things as linguistic utterance.

Celan's work remains ambivalent. Crisis in language for him correlates with crisis in the experience of history and time. Language continues to represent the temporal, material world; indeed, it does so in a particularly radical way, as the world's mystical fabric and instrument of creation, the very material out of which the world was and is made. But in its founding role within the world of history, language in Celan is also profoundly ruptured by historical trauma—trauma that remains for Celan, himself emerging out of the apocalyptic negativity of the Second World War, a pressing challenge to any creative possibility.

In Celan, ancient and contemporary language speculation converge. His work points from the Kabbalah toward reformulations of language theory at the center of much contemporary literary theory and philosophy. In the terms employed within contemporary discussion, his language structures place significance within the unfolding and differential relation between "signifiers" rather than in a "signified" above and finally beyond the concrete terms of language. They place significance within the conditions of difference that define our immediate experience. Language-meaning in Celan is therefore relational rather than hierarchical. It remains within the boundaries of phenomenal reality, constructing significance through orders within sequential, partial, multiple, and temporal experience rather than through their transcendence. Yet this differentiated order remains grounded in an absolute difference, in some sense the model for all the differences that remain the basis for orders among them, in some sense their orienting anchor as divine creator. The inaccessibility of this Other marks on one side a boundary that founds all orderly, and indeed moral, distinctions. On the other side, it risks a retreat beyond reference, a remoteness so profound as to lose relevance and force. Into this threat of abyss all orders could collapse.

The structures, and especially the value-scheme implied in the language theory of the writers studied here, have importance far beyond their individual poetics. For example, the demotion of language at issue in their work is confirmed by R. Howard Bloch as fundamental within the Christian metaphysical tradition. But he further exposes its sexualization and gendering. "An inadequacy of women to Being," he observes, "becomes indissociable from the inadequacy of words." The ideals of philosophy—"existence (substance), being, unity, form and soul"—are male, while women are associated with all the conditions that register failure of the ideal: "accident, becoming (temporality), difference, body, and matter." The same prejudice that elevates "unity, another word for Being, [as] the goal of philosophy because it is synonymous with truth" elevates the male and demotes the female, who "is relegated to the realm of matter." But this gendering exactly reproduces sign-theory. Woman is linked not only to body but to sign, has a role "indistinguishable from that of all signs in relation to the signified." There is a direct link "between the derivative nature of the female and that of figural representation."[3]

The inexpressibility topos, in other words, has broad cultural implications. The same impulse that demotes language as unequal to unitary truth finds expression in other systems that demote materiality, difference, and mutability, including traditional gendering. Conversely, an orientation toward history as the scene of language points toward a series of translocations of value to the immanent world of human experience. But this requires a more general rethinking of value-system and its sources. The kinds of revision this can prompt even in traditional metaphysical contexts is suggested, for example, by Hilary Armstrong. Armstrong sees the negativity central to Neoplatonism in a different light from the metaphysical one that in fact dominated its historical development. In his view, it could instead be construed toward

the end of two world thinking, in which the static intelligible or spiritual world, the living but immobile Divine Mind, is the superior archetype of this changing and imperfect world of ours. The only *kosmos noetos* which will survive in this way of thinking is a Heraclitean one, the ever-changing succession of created thoughts about the ever changing created world, in which we may hope and believe that we receive lights from the Good sufficient for our personal needs in our particular time and place, but not of a kind which we can appropriate and fix and demand that others should accept as unchanging universal truths.[4]

Here, Armstrong suggests how terms traditional to metaphysics and religion can be reconceived away from the fixed orders they traditionally asserted. He points away from a model of perfection which, as unchanging and immobile, negates the essential conditions of lived experience; and in this he also guards against the dangers of hegemony, of the claim to efface difference for a unity that thereby degenerates into an instrument of appropriation. In some sense, at issue is the whole philosophy of the One that has reigned more or less uncontested from the inception of Western culture in Greece. As David Novak remarks, "The demand for a return to pristine unity . . . must now be set aside or bracketed as a failed experiment."[5] A commitment to language would assert, in place of this ideal of unity, the positive value of multiplicity, mundane conditions, and history as the authentic realm of experience. Transcendence would in turn act as an Other at the absolute border of language, an irreducible limitation that also marks respect, relationship, and ultimately celebration of the multiplicity it makes possible and regulates.

In my argument here I have tried to explore the place of language within a critical rethinking of the tradition. The traditional attitude toward language as at best a concession to necessity, at worst a betrayal of truth, inscribes a profound retreat from the conditions that in fact define our experience—conditions that finally frame any attempt to make our experience concretely and ethically meaningful. This reflects a problematic relation between creation and transcendence, which Nietzsche dramatically exposed and which has since become increasingly explosive. It requires a revision in which language-theory plays a crucial role. In such a revision, a positive valuation of language would join with a negative sense of the limits of language, of what our language cannot express, which would still have a vital and necessary place. Language would then serve as trope for a positive skepticism, one that acknowledges the spaces we do not control. Unlike a traditional humility based in submission to a fixed, overarching rule, it takes shape as the acceptance of a negative boundary that leaves open and respects the world beyond ourselves as one we never fully possess. The negative boundaries of language then remind us of our own limitations, while its positive embrace calls us toward full responsibility within the realms of our action and of our utterance.

Reference Matter

Notes

᳅

Chapter 1

1. Curtius, p. 159.
2. "Mystical Speech," pp. 3–5.
3. "Samuel Beckett," p. 143. Ruby Cohn notes that Beckett calls a poem published in *New Review 1931–32* "Text" (*Comic Gamut*, p. 169). See also Perloff, *Dance of the Intellect*, pp. 142–44, on the relation between verse and prose in Beckett in their common use of "binary rhythms," rhymes, references, allusions, short sharp phrases, neologisms, contorted elliptical clauses, truncated syntax, repetition, archaism, and foregrounding of rhyme and metrical units, all finally tending, in her reading, "to express inexpressibility" (p. 143).
4. Cohn, *Comic Gamut*, p. 44; Bair, p. 327.
5. Bair, p. 308; Fletcher, *Novels*, p. 119.

Chapter 2

1. Jeffrey Perl offers a thorough and thoughtful discussion of Eliot's personal religious and philosophical development in *Skepticism and Modern Enmity*. Other discussions of Eliot's development include those of Harriet Davidson, John D. Margolis, Richard Shusterman, and William Skaff. See also Robert H. Canary's review of positions for and against Eliot's orthodoxy, pp. 220–28. Canary himself supports the view of Eliot as orthodox.
2. I avoid discussion here of the exact relation of Eliot's early work to

his postconversion poetry. I do see the attitudes and assumptions implicit in the early verse as projecting conditions for Christian belief, which are then accepted and urged in the later work, whether in syncretist or orthodox fashion. It is worth noting Eliot's letter of March 27, 1936, to Paul Elmer More that "what appears to another person to be a change of attitude and even a recantation of former views must often appear to the author himself rather as part of a continuous and more or less consistent development" (LPM, March 27, 1936).

3. Hay, pp. 98, 156–57.

4. Hay, p. 155. Hay is here concerned to correct earlier discussions by John Johnson Sweeney, Leonard Unger, and Louis Martz. See Leonard Unger, ed., *T. S. Eliot: A Selected Critique.* Yet Hay's own attempt to correlate Eliot's works with Saint John's "active" and "passive" stages only underscores how problematic her project is, since all of Saint John's stages include both active and passive phases.

5. Eliot's own choice of Anglo-Catholicism included his faith in it as normative and central within the tradition, reflected in, for example, the claim in "Thoughts after Lambeth" that "the Church of England can never be reduced to the condition of a sect" (*SE,* 338). As Donald Davie notes in "Anglican Eliot," "it was of the utmost importance to him that he choose what should seem to be not a sect at all but a national norm" (p. 186). This is not to overlook the particular and perhaps peculiar ground for Eliot's conversion, hinted at in his remark affirming Christianity's "necessity" rather than its practice ("Baudelaire," *SE,* 374) or his repeated concern with skepticism, as when he sees Pascal as "facing unflinchingly the demon of doubt which is inseparable from the spirit of belief" (*SE,* 363). Cf. the essay on Bradley: "Scepticism and disillusion are a useful equipment for religious understanding" (*SE,* 399). Earlier, Eliot had written that "doubt and uncertainty are merely varieties of belief," and that "to believe anything will probably become more and more difficult as time goes on" ("A Note on Poetry and Belief," p. 15). In a letter to Paul Elmer More (Aug. 3, 1929) Eliot acknowledges "the difficulty of a positive Christianity nowadays. And I can only say that the dangers pointed out, and my own weaknesses, have been apparent to me long before my critics noticed them" (LPM).

6. Hay, p. 154.

7. Underhill, p. 71.

8. Eliot insists, against Middleton Murry, that "what St. John means by the 'dark night' and what Mr. Murry means by my 'dark night' are entirely different things" (Clark Lectures 3: 11). In the Clark Lectures, Eliot generally prefers the "intellectual mysticism" of Aquinas to the affect

of John. Given in 1926, however, the Clark Lectures antedate the shift toward Saint John evident in *Four Quartets*.

9. Hay makes this point, interpreting the early work as "a descent without a foreshadowed sequel" (p. 7). Saint John's dark night represents periods of "aridity" in the process of emptying the self by nuns and monks already devoted to God.

10. Writers on the Eastern Orthodox Church like Vladimir Lossky point to just such personal passion as distinguishing between the Eastern and Western ethos of mysticism (*Mystical Theology*, p. 226). For an overview of Saint John's relation to Dionysius, and of Dionysius's relation to prior tradition, see Louth, pp. 184–90.

11. Eliot himself pointed out his use of Saint John's poetry in a letter to Professor H. W. Häusermann (see Häusermann, p. 109). Paul Murray undertakes a full textual comparison between Eliot and Saint John, pp. 89–95.

12. Harvard notes show that Eliot had read Dionysius and Saint John of the Cross at college. He also took a course in the history of ancient philosophy, and eventually, as an assistant professor of philosophy, taught a course on Neoplatonism. Cf. Valerie Eliot's "Biographical Commentary" to Eliot's *Letters*, where she documents Eliot's Harvard course work, p. xx. The Clark Lectures make numerous and learned reference to Dionysius and his Neoplatonist sources, as well as to a wide body of patristic, scholastic, and mystical writers, including John of the Cross, Augustine, Ignatius, and especially Saint Thomas Aquinas.

13. Cf. the translation by Andrew Louth: "The higher we ascend the more our words are straitened by the fact that what we understand is seen more and more altogether in a unifying and simplifying way" (p. 165).

14. Louth, p. 174.

15. Miller, *Poets of Reality*, pp. 161–62. Cf. David Ward, who argues that unity "is the urgent force behind Eliot's creative impulse" (p. 11).

16. Quoted from unpublished manuscript in Perl, p. 60.

17. Plotinus, *Enneads* 5.9.2 (p. 435).

18. Murray, p. 5; T. S. Eliot, "Rhyme and Reason," p. 503.

19. Gardner, *Art*, p. 162.

20. Hay, p. 155. Paul Murray also questions Hay's divisions, pp. 92–93.

21. Hugh Kenner's view that the timeless moment renders "irrelevant" the "waste sad time" of ordinary life hardly reveals a positive redemptive power (*Invisible Poet*, p. 257).

22. Hough, p. 114; Bornstein, p. 156; Spurr, pp. 89, 100.

23. Gerard, p. 126; Lynch, pp. 250–51. Sister Mary Gerard protests

that Eliot's is "the impersonal God of the philosophers, the God of the Neo-platonic mystic, not the personal Incarnate God of the Christian mystic." Father William Lynch complains that Eliot places his faith "not in the line and time of Christ" but in the "image and the goal of immobility, and that in everything he seeks for approximations to this goal in the human order."

24. Quoted in Murray, pp. 86–87.

25. Hay also emphasizes this precedence of negative over positive in Saint Thomas, p. 157. Vladimir Lossky argues that Aquinas, in making the negative way only a corrective to affirmative theology, betrays the true power and proper precedence of the apophatic way (*Mystical Theology*, pp. 25–26). Andrew Louth similarly insists on the precedence of apophasis: "Cataphatic theology, in that it affirms something about God, is clearly no less apophatic, in that our affirmations take us beyond what we can grasp" (pp. 162, 166, 172).

26. Gilson, *Christian Philosophy*, p. 120. Cf. *De Veritate* 2.1, ad 9; *Summa* 2.2, quest. 27, art 4.

27. See Louth, pp. 166, 172, 168; also Lossky, "La notion des 'analogies,'" p. 283.

28. That is, the negative way is "up," while the affirmative way of positive analogy is "down." See Lossky, *Mystical Theology*, p. 28.

29. Roques, pp. 169–70; translations from the French text are my own. Roques's study focuses on the Dionysian tradition as it informs the works of Hugo and Richard of Saint Victor (whom Eliot particularly praises in Clark Lectures 3: 8).

30. Roques, pp. 345–46, 356.

31. Finn Bille argues: "For the poet's task, neither human language nor its poetry is sufficient; neither contains adequate symbols nor sufficient rhetoric to communicate a mystical vision of existence" (p. 16). But this sets out to prove what in the poem is given, while proposing as a solution what remains a problem.

32. Hough, pp. 108, 114. Contrast Morris Weitz, who cogently presents the more common reading of Eliot that accepts rather than questions the poem's own premises: "To experience the Eternal, the 'still point,' is to transcend the temporal; it is to give up desire, action, and suffering; to rise up to God, but with no physical action; and to understand both the Timeless and the temporal for the first time" (p. 147).

33. Pp. 179, 227, 178. Leavis makes the further telling point that "Eliot is committed to discrediting the creative process he undertakes to demonstrate and vindicate" (p. 191).

34. As David Ward remarks, there is a strain between a poetry "lo-

cated in one way or another in time or in space," and "the experience which motivates it . . . [as] protected from the contamination of time and space" (pp. 223–25).

35. Miller, *Poets of Reality*, p. 161.

36. Kenner, *Invisible Poet*, p. 257.

37. A full explication of an Augustinian language model is presented in Kenneth Burke's *Rhetoric of Religion*.

38. Jacques Derrida, *Of Grammatology*, pp. 14, 8, 13. I have explored the theological implications of Derrida's critique more fully in Wolosky, "Derrida, Jabès, Levinas."

39. Mazzeo, pp. 187, 192. Mazzeo sees Augustine's as a Platonist "philosophical theology of silence."

40. Ferguson, p. 844.

41. Quoted in Mazzeo, p. 192.

42. Thomas à Kempis, p. 52.

43. *Cloud of Unknowing*, p. 95.

44. Roques, pp. 168, 347, 170.

45. Ibid., pp. 345–46, 356.

46. Ibid., 167–68.

47. Brisman, p. 579. Brisman refers his use of "trace" and the critique it signals to Derrida.

48. Murray, pp. 47–48, 51–53.

49. Michaels, pp. 182–84, 184, 190. References to *KE* are to pp. 132, 138, 161.

50. Perl, p. 70; cf. pp. 45–46.

51. Frank, pp. 10–14.

52. Michaels, p. 185.

53. Gardner, *Art*, pp. 54–55.

54. Ward, pp. 223–25.

55. Hay among others insists that Eliot never doubts "the reality of flux," seeing "the reality of time and also its providential movement toward the redemption of human nature" (p. 166). The question remains, however, to what extent time in Eliot is able to bring positive result in its own dimension, rather than serving as a negative means toward its own abrogation.

56. Roques, pp. 345–46, 356.

57. Bush, pp. 82–83. Bush here is citing remarks made by Eliot in his introduction to a translation of Valéry's "Le Serpent" as recognizing the "classicist" supremacy of pattern over feeling.

58. Spurr, p. 106; Hough, pp. 114, 110.

59. Hay, pp. 170, 179.

60. "United in the strife which divided them" may echo the Eastern liturgy of Pentecost: "The epiphany of the holy spirit has united the divided tongues of those who were parted in strife. . . . When he distributed the tongues of fire, he called all to unity." See Ernst Benz, *Geist und Leben.*

61. Gardner, *Composition*, p. 208. "The ground of our beseeching" is from Julian of Norwich's Fourteenth Revelation, and its substitution for the earlier "assent to death" makes good theological sense. There is in fact a historical continuity between martyrdom and the development of ascetic disciplines in monasticism. Andrew Louth sees the "flight to the desert" as offering a "white" martyrdom once the danger of "red" martyrdom faded with acceptance of the Church in the Roman world (p. 98).

62. Gardner, *Composition*, p. 219.

63. Gardner, *Art*, p. 184.

64. Gardner, *Composition*, p. 204.

65. *Cloud of Unknowing*, p. 3; Julian of Norwich, 13th Revelation, pp. 225–26.

66. Louis Martz offers this citation from *Confessions* as "expressing the central question of Eliot's later poetry" (p. 451). Since Martz's discussion, many commentators refer Eliot's construction of memory to Augustine.

67. Katz, "Utterance and Ineffability," p. 282. Katz's main interest is in demonstrating that mystics nevertheless "use language and through that contradict" their apophatic commitment (p. 284). I am more interested here in investigating the value commitment and ideal of this antilinguistic position, and the implications of the failure to achieve it.

68. Dörrie, pp. 34–35.

69. Smith, p. 298.

Chapter 3

1. Cavell, pp. 119–20.

2. Ibid., p. 124.

3. Perloff, *Poetics*, pp. 209, 207.

4. Ibid., 204, 201, 210, 211.

5. Kenner, *Samuel Beckett*, p. 125.

6. For discussions of translating/collaborating with Beckett, see Seaver; Bowles, pp. 1011–12; and Fletcher, *Novels*, p. 133.

7. Ruby Cohn, in *Back to Beckett*, pp. 58–59, collects Beckett's remarks on writing in French. Beckett says, for example, that "French had the right 'weakening effect;'" that "English because of its very richness holds out the temptation to rhetoric and virtuosity" as opposed to the

"relative asceticism of French"; and that he was "afraid of English because you couldn't help writing poetry in it." Compare Cohn, "Beckett and Self-Translation." For other discussions of Beckett on French see Ellmann, p. 100, and Fletcher, *Novels*, pp. 94, 113.

8. Hamilton and Hamilton, p. 188; Dearlove, *Accommodating the Chaos*, p. 107.

9. Descartes, *Discourse*, pp. 87–88, 99–100.

10. J. E. Dearlove's relegation of mathematical and scientific description to Beckett's later works is puzzling ("Last Images"). As Hugh Kenner has shown, the mathematical impulse is felt from very early in Beckett's work (*Samuel Beckett*, p. 132).

11. Derrida, "White Mythology," pp. 18, 25n, 25–26.

12. See Klein's discussion, 22–23, 50–51, 72–74.

13. Descartes, *Discourse*, pp. 88–89.

14. Descartes, *Philosophical Writings*, p. 165. See also Klein, pp. 198–200, and Kenny, pp. 233–34.

15. Cohn, *Back to Beckett*, p. 13.

16. After noting that *The Lost Ones* "at first seems to cry out for an allegorical interpretation," Brienza then dismisses allegory; but in doing so she dismisses the novella's allusive impulse as well. Fletcher finally sees Beckett's allusions as " a debunking of the whole act of literary creation" (*Novels*, p. 76).

17. Iser, "Pattern of Negativity," p. 2; Iser, *Implied Reader*, pp. 257, 267.

18. See, for example, the discussions in Koyre, *Metaphysics and Measurement*; Gilson, *Études*; and especially Burtt, *Metaphysical Foundations*.

19. See Klein, Merlan.

20. Quoted in Wolfson, 1: 118–19. Wolfson underscores that the method explains not only how to prove the existence of God but how "we can speak of God."

21. Hoefer, pp. 63–65, 69. Cf. Ruby Cohn, who argues that Watt is a "logical positivist" who "instead of accepting the inadequacy of names, explanations, observations . . . [marshals] experience into name, number, and logic" (*Back to Beckett*, pp. 42, 52, 55).

22. Federman, pp. 119–23.

23. Kenner, *Beckett*, pp. 104, 109; pp. 41, 142; p. 184. Kenner similarly argues for "mathematics as an impingement of system, and notably systematic forms of discourse, on experiences to which they seem inappropriate" ("Shades of Syntax," p. 28).

24. Hoefer, p. 66.

25. Chambers, pp. 152, 154, 156. Cf. Nicholas Zurbrugg, who sees Beckett's as a "poisoned variant of involuntary memory" when its "unity of images falls instead into contradiction" (p. 179).

26. Chambers speaks for many critics in describing Beckett's disappointed desire for "a principle of inner life—call it what you will: essence, self, personality or soul" so that "life as the pursuit of self becomes the endless, hopeless task of pursuing an infinitely receding something that has the characteristics of nothing" (pp. 155–56). Cf., for example, Cohn, *Back to Beckett*, pp. 73, 78.

27. Barnard, pp. 9, 32.

28. Federman, p. 23; Coe, "God and Samuel Beckett," p. 68. Compare Coe's discussion in *Samuel Beckett*, p. 17, where he sees Beckett's "true" self as "timeless and dimensionless"; "to allow the true self to escape, [it must] escape the tyranny of time." Also Knowlson: "All Beckett's characters are exiles excluded from the inner reality of the self, which if it exists lies outside of time and space" (p. 32); and Lawrence Harvey: "The myriad masks of temporal succession hide the permanent reality if it exists of the essential object. Concealed beneath the veil of its accidental surfaces, caught up in becoming, ultimate being escapes man" (p. 427).

29. Fletcher, *Novels*, p. 136; Abbott, p. 4; Bernal, pp. 190–91; Scott, p. 80.

30. Fletcher, *Novels*, p. 188; Federman, pp. 16, 14.

31. Robinson, pp. 17–18; Cohn, *Back to Beckett*, pp. 102, 112, 108; Dearlove, "Syntax Upended," p. 124; Hesla, p. 127; Chambers, pp. 155–56. Cf. Hannah Case Copeland: "The authentic self is beyond the reach of thought and language. Dwelling outside the limits of knowledge and language, the deepest self evades discovery through fiction" (pp. 181–82).

32. Wellershoff, p. 92. "Only he who has attained to his own identity, can be silent, only when thinking has reached reality, will it come to a stop" (p. 107). Cf. Mayoux, "Samuel Beckett's Universal Parody," where he describes the Beckett self as an inevitable "otherness" that "can never coincide with himself" (p. 80).

33. Thiher, *Words in Reflection*, pp. 81, 87, 82, 85–86, 87–88.

34. Perloff, *Poetics*, p. 200.

35. Schopenhauer, p. 358.

36. Kenner, *Reader's Guide*, pp. 30, 109; cf. 16–17, 70–73, 94, 97, 181. Kenner also compares the tired waiting of Estragon and Vladimir to Beckett's own countless waitings while working for the Resistance. John Fletcher, in *Samuel Beckett's Art* (p. 136) notes the relevance of Beckett's war experience, but most critics tend to dismiss the war's importance for Beckett: e.g., Michael Robinson "can't tell the importance of occupation"

(p. 132); Federman describes Beckett as secluded in an ivory tower (p. 48). The Hamiltons consider his work ahistorical (p. 33), with no relation to reality (pp. 40–41). Edith Kern concludes there is in Beckett "no personal confrontation with social problems" (p. 27).

Chapter 4

1. Landgraf, pp. 207–22. I would like to thank Jaroslav Pelikan for helping me locate many of the following theological sources.

2. See, for example, Lossky, *Théologie negative*, p. 89.

3. Cited by David Hesla, p. 63.

4. Hobson, p. 153; Kenner, "Shades of Syntax," p. 21.

5. Donna, *Despair and Hope*; *Augustinus Lexikon*.

6. Letter to the author, Sept. 9, 1985. Estragon and Vladimir's argument over the differing accounts of the scene of crucifixion recall Saint Augustine's in *Harmony of the Gospels*, book 3, chap. 17.

7. Augustine, "On the Gospel of John."

8. Fletcher, *Samuel Beckett's Art*, p. 145.

9. Mintz, p. 159.

10. Federman, p. 31; Harvey, p. 368; Robinson, p. 83; Mintz, p. 164. Also Cohn: "The mind alone is rich and graceful" (*Back to Beckett*, p. 5); Kenner: "Freedom within the mind" is "the only freedom toward which Beckett's clowns aspire" (*Samuel Beckett*, p. 18); Kostelanetz: "Murphy's is a quest for a valid asceticism" (p. 246).

11. Pilling, p. 33; Fletcher, *Novels*, p. 52.

12. Beckett certainly uses the figure of insanity in a variety of ways, including critically against obtuse rationalism. Yet to read him as urging psychosis as the ultimate achievement of interiority is to mistake his critique of interiority. Beckett is, moreover, profoundly sensitive to the pain of madness. He is careful to qualify Murphy's own idealizations of psychosis as Murphy's own: "The frequent expressions apparently of pain, rage, despair, and in fact all the usual, to which some patients gave vent, Murphy either disregarded or muted what he wanted" (170). Nevertheless, Harvey insists that "the artist must make contact with being, live as a madman" (p. 22). Fletcher speaks of "the insane as sincere and innocent and uncorrupted by the world" (*Novels*, p. 161). For Federman, Beckett's heroes "aspire to a state of intellectual irresponsibility, of lunacy" (p. 19). And G. C. Barnard makes the analogy between madness and Beckett's art the foundation of an entire study. Conflating psychotic withdrawal with beatific vision accepts a false syllogism that *Murphy* is questioning: inwardness is desirable; psychosis is inward; therefore psychosis is desirable.

13. Federman, p. 19; Fletcher, *Novels*, pp. 52, 51.
14. Hamilton and Hamilton, p. 52.
15. Harvey, pp. 367, 364; Barnard, p. 19; Fletcher, *Novels*, p. 86; Baldwin, p. 6. Baldwin expands: Knott is the "hiddenness of God" representing "an experience of an extratemporal reality"; Watt is a "quester who is a Christ figure, waiting patiently for union with divine spirit" (pp. 22, 86).
16. See Coe, *Beckett*, p. 39; Harvey, p. 352; Kern, p. 192. Robinson, p. 120; Hesla, p. 83; Harvey, p. 352; cf. Fletcher, *Novels*, p. 81.
17. Rabinovitz, p. 272.
18. Federman, p. 107; Robinson, p. 123; Hoefer, p. 69.
19. Cohn, *Comic Gamut*, p. 93; Hoefer, pp. 72–73. Harvey, p. 372.
20. Mayoux, "Samuel Beckett and Universal Parody," p. 78. This line of argument tends to result in what Ivor Winters has called imitative form, as is urged by Abbott, p. 129, and Finney, p. 73. Cf. Federman: Watt's is a doomed "attempt to explain logically a world that rejects all explanations" (p. 116). Also Coe, "God and Samuel Beckett": "Watt's reality of words disintegrates into fragments" (p. 77).
21. Kern, p. 7.
22. Robinson, p. 23; Chambers, pp. 155–56. Cf. Hoffman: Beckett "discredits the rational machinery for explaining God's ways" (p. 63).
23. Kern, p. 192.
24. Harry Wolfson discusses this distinction between scientific knowledge (episteme) or thinking (noesis) as against "vision" (1: 126). It is central to Wesley Trimpi's discussion of Neoplatonic representation in *Muses of One Mind*.
25. See Norman Gulley's discussion of the ways in which Plato's epistemology in fact presupposes the existence of the forms (pp. 31, 45).
26. Gulley, p. 40; Trimpi also discusses these gradations of knowledge (pp. 37–38, 202–5).
27. Gadamer, *Dialogue and Dialectic*, p. 105.
28. Gulley, p. 69. Compare the discussion by R. T. Wallis in "Nous as Experience," pp. 129–30; and Trimpi, p. 39. A. C. Lloyd remarks that it is a "philosophical puzzle what, if anything, such a belief [in nondiscursive thought] could mean," p. 261.
29. Cited by Trimpi, p. 39, from Aristotle, *De Mem.* 1.
30. J. Patrick Atherton notes that "the recognition of inaccessibility and unknowability of the predicateless unity or pure self-identity of the arche lay at the root of the entire Neoplatonic tradition" (p. 173).
31. The question of the degree to which Neoplatonism departs from or develops positions implicit in Plato is much discussed. See Findlay, "The

Neoplatonism of Plato"; Vogel; and various essays by Armstrong in *Plotinian and Christian Studies*.

32. Armstrong, *Plotinian and Christian Studies*, 22, p. 80.

33. Brehier, p. 134.

34. Gilson, *Being and Some Philosophers*, pp. 7–11.

35. Armstrong, *Cambridge History*, p. 238.

36. Wallis, *Neoplatonism*, p. 57. Compare Armstrong: "The infinite
in the first principle is an idea opposed to the normal Greek way of thinking, for which the good and the divine is essentially form and definition,
light and clarity" (*Plotinian and Christian Studies*, 5, p. 47).

37. For a discussion of this development from Pythagorean mathematics to Platonist and Neoplatonist metaphysics, see for example Findlay,
"The Neoplatonism of Plato," where he explains that "the measure itself
which produces essences and renders it manifest to senses cannot be identified with these essences" (p. 28). See also Findlay, *Plato*, pp. 185, 369;
Brehier, p. 134; Armstrong, *Architecture*, pp. 26–29.

38. Wolfson, 1: 115, 104.

39. Trimpi, pp. 107, 199, 210.

40. Armstrong, *Architecture*, pp. 29–35. Cf. Wolfson, 1: 122–23;
Trimpi, pp. 182–83.

41. Wolfson, 1: 125, 116, 120. Cf. H. Dörrie, "Formula Analogiae,"
on how negative theology develops from "those followers of Plato who
found it easy to renounce any possibility of comprehension or conceptu-
alisation in the realm of theology" (p. 35).

42. Iser, "Pattern of Negativity," p. 10.

43. Findlay, *Plato*, p. 58.

44. Augustine, *De Vera Religionis*, 1.l.c.39 (n. 79), PL 34. col. 154;
cited in Lossky, *Théologie negative*, p. 17.

45. Findlay, *Plato*, pp. 12–14.

46. Trimpi in *Muses* devotes much of his chapter on the "Ancient Dilemma" of knowledge as against representation to Plato's attempt in the
Sophist to accommodate a positive possibility of representation even for
what is not fully Being.

47. Wallis, *Neoplatonism*, p. 57.

48. See Findlay, "The Neoplatonism of Plato," on how we "can only,
by abandoning what is specific and individualizing in us, achieve a presence, coincidence, or contrast with such unity" (p. 28). The problem of
the status of the self in Neoplatonism has been much and variously argued. A. H. Armstrong in the *Cambridge History* presents a "negative self-
assertion" as the radical original sin causing the soul to fall into the world
(p. 238), although later, in "Gnosis," he argues for a more neutral value of

"self-assertion" and incarnation (*Plotinian and Christian Studies*, pp. 116–19). E. R. Dodds, however, affirms the negative value of self-assertion in the Pythagorean-Plotinian tradition, and links it in turn to Augustinian "audacity" as a self-love separating the soul from God (p. 24).

49. Trimpi, p. 179. Armstrong notes that while in Plotinus, "when we have completed our rational understanding of reality, we have to leave it all behind," at the same time "no religious man can afford to despise philosophy. . . . One may have to negate everything in the end: but one cannot negate it till one has understood it thoroughly" (*Plotinian and Christian Studies*, 16, pp. 13, 21). Cohn among many others makes this association with Wittgenstein (*Back to Beckett*, pp. 174–75, 43–44). Cf. Hesla, pp. 80–81; Robinson, pp. 122, 126; Hoefer, pp. 65–66. Beckett makes this same joke (*Murphy*, p. 188); he also refers to Augustine's ladder (*MP*, 120). Wittgenstein's, however, is far from the only philosophical context into which Beckett's language theory has been placed. A. J. Leventhal suggests the context of Gorgias of Lentini (p. 46). And of course Descartes remains central in many studies.

50. Kenner, *Beckett*, pp. 130–31.

51. Morot-Sir, pp. 38, 41. Morot-Sir reviews many of these critical discussions, dividing the various critical stances on Beckett into the "Cartesian" English and American schools as against "anti-Cartesian" French Existentialist readings.

52. For the first position, see Hesla, pp. 17, 36, 39; Federman, pp. 79–80; Coe, *Beckett*, p. 31; Fletcher, *Art*, p. 131; Morot-Sir, p. 69; Kenner, *Beckett*, pp. 31, 41, 50, 83–84; and Mintz, p. 160. For the second: Federman, p. 74; Pilling, p. 114; Cohn, *Comic Gamut*, p. 102; Harvey, p. 54; Hesla, pp. 78, 114; Morot-Sir, p. 67; Rabinovitz, p. 265.

53. Robinson, pp. 21, 87, 219–20; Kenner, *Beckett*, p. 61; Harvey, p. 41; Hoffman, pp. xi, 62–64; Federman, p. 119; Hesla, p. 79; Rabinovitz, p. 263.

54. See Gilson, *Études*, pp. 164–65.

55. Roy, pp. 11–12, 43–45 (citing letters to Mersenne from 1637 and 1639). Cf. Wallace Stevens on Pascal's view of the imagination as "the deceptive element in man, the mistress of error and duplicity . . . [that] indicates in the same way both the true and the false," *The Necessary Angel*, p. 133.

56. See Koyre, *Metaphysics and Measurement*, pp. 13–15, 40–43; Koyre, *Galileo Studies*, p. 94; cf. Gilson, *Études*, p. 199.

57. Trimpi, pp. 183, 191, 206.

58. Nietzsche, *Will*, sect. 522, p. 283; sect. 551, p. 296. Nietzsche, *Twilight*, pp. 482–83.

59. Paul De Man, "Rhetoric of Tropes," *Allegories*, p. 108.

60. Miller, "Theoretical and Atheoretical," p. 280.

61. Derrida, *Of Grammatology*, pp. 8, 13, 15. He goes on to remark of Nietzsche: "Reading and therefore writing the text were for Nietzsche 'originary' operations . . . with regard to a sense that they do not first have to transcribe or discover, which would not therefore be a truth signified in the original element and presence of the logos, as topos noetos, divine understanding, or the structure of a priori necessity" (p. 19).

62. Lossky, *Théologie*, pp. 22, 15, 17–18; pp. 42, 62.

63. Ibid., pp. 54–55.

64. Ibid., p. 55. Cf. the discussion of "Linguistic Dualism," in Chapter 2.

65. Atherton, p. 178.

66. Gilson, *Being*, p. 32.

67. Derrida, "How to Avoid Speaking," pp. 4, 41.

68. The difficulties involved in sorting out the orthodox Christian position from the heresies of Neoplatonism can be seen in the context of Eckhart, of whom E. R. Dodds writes: "When not defending himself against charges of heresy, Eckhart often writes in terms indistinguishable from those of Plotinus" (p. 88).

69. There are passages in Beckett's *Texts* that seem to me allusions to Augustine's *Confessions*. Cf. "Text 11," "It's forever the same murmur, flowing unbroken, like a single endless word and therfore meaningless, for its the end gives the meaning to words," with C 4.10. However, here as elsewhere, such allusive sources are more instinctive than demonstrable.

70. Beckett quoted in Driver, p. 22; Baldwin, p. 6. Cf. Champigny, on how "words kill words" in a "mystical tradition of via negativa" (p. 122).

71. Hamilton and Hamilton, pp. 51–52; Harvey, pp. 78–79; Fletcher, *Novels*, p. 229; Morot-Sir, pp. 84–86; Mayoux, "Theatre," calls Beckett a "Catharist choosing the way to annihilation" (p. 151). Cf. Hayman, p. 143, and Pilling, who calls Beckett a gnostic (p. 119). James Knowlson provides Beckett's notes from "Krapp's Last Tape" citing gnostic conflicts between light and dark, with an interesting note on "Ascetic ethics." Beckett's familiarity with the issue is here again evident, although, as always, with what intention is far from clear (Knowlson, pp. 45–47).

72. Hesla, p. 11; Pilling, p. 138; Federman, p. 7; Jacobsen, p. 24.

73. Kenner, *Beckett*, p. 62; Robinson, pp. 283, 28; Mayoux, "Beckett's Universal Parody," p. 78.

74. Scott, p. 17; Robinson, p. 206; Chambers, p. 160; Coe, "God," p. 77.

75. Mayoux, "Universal Parody," p. 81.

76. E.g. Hesla: "The unnamable's goal is silence, and to achieve his goal he must stop speaking of fictions, and speak only of self" (p. 127); Coe, *Beckett*: "The ultimate language of the self is silence" (p. 79); and Baldwin throughout.

77. Armstrong, *Plotinian and Christian Studies*, 21, pp. 110, 97.

78. Dodds, pp. 15–17.

79. Armstrong, *Plotinian and Christian Studies*, 21, p. 96.

80. Driver, p. 23.

81. Shenker, p. 3; Driver, pp. 23, 22.

82. Raymond Federman renders this "to make notice *me*," to show Beckett as "deliberately distorting the syntax" to emphasize the "me" (p. 14).

83. Shenker, p. 3.

84. Nietzsche, *Will to Power*, sect. 1, subsect. 12a, pp. 12–13.

85. Heidegger, *Holzwege*, p. 200.

86. Wallis, *Neoplatonism*, p. 115.

Chapter 5

1. Adorno, *Aesthetic Theory*, p. 443.

2. G. Steiner, *Extraterritorial*, p. 164.

3. Hamburger, p. 290. More recently, Thomas Sparr argues that modern art is essentially hermetic, with Celan his exemplar.

4. Ortega y Gasset, p. 42.

5. Chalfen, p. 114.

6. Lyon, "Introduction," p. 7.

7. Amy Colin, in her introductory chapter to *Paul Celan: Holograms of Darkness*, fully reviews the Celan criticism and its variety of approach. She underscores "the uneasiness of many scholars about how to find an adequate approach to Celan's poems and to place them in an appropriate context" (p. xviii).

8. Mayer, p. 77; Beese, p. 7; Alleman, "Zu Paul Celans neuem Gedichtband," p. 196.

9. Demetz, pp. 81, 83; Voswinckel, pp. 7, 18.

10. G. Neumann, pp. 199, 209.

11. Allemann, "Das Gedicht," pp. 266, 270.

12. Demetz, p. 81.

13. Janz, pp. 12, 323; Voswinckel, p. 155; Pretzer, p. 6.

14. Langer; Rosenfeld; and Steiner, for example in *Language and Silence*, all refer to Celan in the course of discussing the status of silence in the face of the Holocaust. See also Ezrahi.

15. Gadamer, *Wer bin Ich*, p. 60. The German text reads: "Nur dem angestrengtesten Lauschen bleibt dieser Gesang hörbar, diese Selbstaussage des Menschlichen in einer versandenden Welt, und nur in augenblickshaften Brechungen blitzt dem angespanntesten Spähen menschlich Geordnetes auf. Die krasse Grausamkeit der Schlussmetapher von Ohr und Auge lässt die beengende Dürftigkeit der Welt empfinden, in der Gefühl kaum noch etwas vermag."

16. Gadamer, *Wer bin Ich*, p. 15. Celan's visit with Heidegger has raised some controversy: cf. Hoelzel, p. 353; Schwerin, pp. 73–81.

17. Heidegger, *Being and Time*, p. 193; Heidegger, *Existence and Being*, p. 297; Heidegger, *Being and Time*, p. 387.

18. Adorno, *Aesthetic Theory*, p. 311; pp. 312, 444.

19. De Man, *Blindness and Insight*, pp. 183, 185.

20. Distel and Jakusch, p. 244.

21. Amery, pp. 17, 22.

22. Bettelheim, *Informed Heart*, p. 244.

23. Bettelheim, *Surviving*, pp. 65, 108.

24. Kahler, p. 65.

25. Sparr, pp. 66–67. Sparr sees the industrial imagery here only as referring to Germany's postwar "economic miracle," and not as implicating economy within the camp experience. He reads "Halljahr" as a negative "Jobeljahr," jubilee.

26. Arendt, pp. 136, 139.

27. Courtesy of Lillian Kahler.

28. Kahler, pp. iv, 46, 68.

29. Arendt, pp. 142–43.

30. Kahler, p. 76.

31. "Sachlichkeit . . . gegenüber den Lügnern und schwärmern, welche die schwersten, dichtesten, verantwortungsvollsten Namen leichthin und dämmerhaft, ohne die vollste Deckung durch greifbares Leben gebrauchen: gegen sie muss verteidigt werden, dass Allgemeines, Ewiges, Zeitloses nicht *besteht*, sofern es nicht aus unserm Hier und Heut und So, sich und unser Sein beglaubigend, entsteigt und dass nichts Macht auf uns hat, was nicht Macht aus uns ist." Courtesy of Lillian Kahler.

32. Kahler, pp. 187, 194.

33. Benjamin, pp. 241–42.

34. Adorno, *Negative Dialectics*, p. 365.

35. Jay, p. 177.

36. Adorno, *Negative Dialectics*, p. 361.

37. Martin Jay analyzes this kind of contradiction within Frankfurt

School Critical Theory with regard to the place of "Reason." Even as the School upheld German Idealist notions of reason as a utopian ideal, at the same time they wished to assert notions of nonidentity in resistance to the idealist value of identity and totality in order to admit historical-materialist reality into their system—without rendering it an absolute, metaphysical truth, as had occurred, they felt, within orthodox Marxism (Jay, p. 60.)

38. Adorno, *Prisms*, pp. 71, 24.

39. Amery, p. 12.

40. Quoted in Steiner, *Language and Silence*, p. 162.

41. Jay, pp. 155, 159, 154.

42. Levi, p. 45.

43. Quoted in Frank, pp. 138–39.

44. Steiner, *Extraterritorial*, p. 51.

45. Adorno, *Prisms*, p. 34.

46. "Weiss Man endlich wo die Barbaren zu suchen sind." Quoted in Glenn, p. 35.

47. Adorno, *Negative Dialectics*, p. 363. I do not wish to interpret Celan's suicide, which no doubt involved many factors. Yet his inevitably falls into place among other survivor suicides, such as those of Jean Amery and Primo Levi. Adorno repeatedly returns to this question of the possible claims of art, as balanced between consolation for and betrayal of suffering. See also Bersani on the compensatory claims for art. In Adorno's case, however, disappointment seems to be based in an almost Arnoldian faith in culture to save, a role Celan severely complicates.

48. Amery, p. 33.

49. Jung, pp. 65–66, 78; Steiner, *In Bluebeard's Castle*, pp. 54–55. Udoff pursues some of the distinctive features of the hell-analogy, p. 323.

50. Auden, p. 410.

51. Arendt, p. 143.

52. Arendt, pp. 155–56, 136.

53. Benjamin's remarks on war as "beautiful because it initiates the dreamt of metalization of the human body" has direct resonance for Celan texts (p. 241).

54. Auden, p. 85.

55. Cited in Demetz, p. 48.

56. Amery, p. 20.

57. Demetz, p. 49.

58. Burger, p. 18.

59. John Felstiner discusses Celan's German as mother tongue and also the language of murder in "Mother Tongue," especially p. 121.

60. Weinrich, p. 225. It has been suggested to me that the poem "Le Contrescarpe," which concludes with the word "Kristall," was written at the railway in Krakau that it also cites, on Kristallnacht.

61. Bakhtin, pp. 184, 75.

62. Derrida's "Schibboleth" makes this poem a center of discussion in ways that I pursue later.

63. Schäfer; Janz, p. 6; Pretzer, p. 21.

64. Janz, p. 200; Pretzer, p. 289.

65. Pretzer, pp. 63, 35.

66. Janz, p. 111; Pretzer, pp. 35, 142.

67. Pretzer, p. 63.

68. Amery, p. 8; Steiner, *Language and Silence*, p. 125. Steiner includes in this volume a number of essays on the political status of the German language. More recently, he has written specifically on Celan's use of German in "Das lange Leben der Metaphorik."

69. Weinrich, pp. 224–25. He associates this retreat with Humboldt.

70. Pretzer, p. 314.

71. Voswinckel, p. 214.

72. Brenkman, p. 108.

73. Arendt, pp. 167–68, 155–56.

74. Brenkman, p. 48; Morss, p. 45. Brenkman discusses various uses of the term *ideology*. For Adorno and Habermas it means "world-interpretation," whereas for Gadamer it means "subjective error," a "mis-interpretation of the world" against which some objective interpretation is assumed—a stance Brenkman considers ahistorical.

75. Kristeva, p. 304.

76. Bakhtin, pp. 82, 98.

77. Celan, "Conversational Statements on Poetry," quoted in Meinecke, "Einleitung," pp. 28–29.

78. Pöggeler, pp. 92–93.

79. Voswinckel, p. 10.

80. Heidegger, *Holzwege*, p. 199: "Wenn Gott also der übersinnliche Grund und als das Ziel alles wirkliche tot, . . . erweckende und banende Kraft, dann bleibt nichts mehr, woran der Mensch sich halten und wonach er sich richten kann."

81. Jonas, pp. 327, 332.

82. P. Neumann, pp. 7, 18.

83. Gadamer, *Wer bin ich*, pp. 101–4.

84. Pretzer discusses this poem, pp. 139–41.

85. Pretzer, p. 233; Janz, p. 38, cf. p. 169.

86. Aristotle, *Metaphysics*, 3.1.991a–991b.

Chapter 6

1. I take issue here with, for example, Alfred Hoelzel, who considers few poems to "explicitly reflect a Jewish sensibility," and feels that "the claim for kabbalistic influence derives primarily from Celan's documented interest in Jewish mysticism" (pp. 352–53). It is my argument, however, that the division between "Jewish" motifs and Celan's overriding linguistic interest is a false one. In this I also go beyond, or in a different direction from, both Barbara Wiedemann-Wolf and Amy Colin. In their studies of Celan's early Bukovinan contexts, they argue for a more sustained and pervasive Judaic interest in Celan, but mainly in relation to the Holocaust and to "Jewish suffering." Thus Wiedemann-Wolf sees Judaism as a "thematic center" of Celan's work after 1945, but mainly through imagery of death, of "deathlonging," of the "beloved" as the Jewish dead (pp. 253–54). Amy Colin proposes Celan's work as a "constant rethinking of the Holocaust, a questioning, and an identification with other disparate traditions within Judaism" (p. xx). She pursues this Judaic involvement, however, primarily through direct references, either biblical or historical, almost always centering around "Jewish suffering" (p. 133).

2. Chalfen, pp. 31–45. Celan's Judaic background is traditional rather than orthodox, and his own early relation to it seems rather indifferent. His grandparents, but not his own parents, were religiously observant. He received a Hebrew education for a few years at school and then through private lessons. Regarding the question of Celan's own research into Judaic backgrounds, besides rich internal evidence, Gershom Scholem answered, when I asked him, that "in order to understand Celan's Judaic background, read Scholem and Buber as Celan did." Celan also taught a seminar on Christian mysticism at the École Normale Supérieure.

3. Schwarz, p. 53.

4. Schulze, *Celan und die Mystiker*, p. 3.

5. P. Neumann, p. 40.

6. Schwarz, pp. 14, 17.

7. P. Neumann, p. 86.

8. Burger, p. 10.

9. Schulze, "Celan and the Stumbling Block," p. 71.

10. Buber, *Prophetic Faith*, pp. 58, 6.

11. Buber discusses this text in *Prophetic Faith*, p. 77.

12. Buber, *Prophetic Faith*, pp. 46, 6.

13. Buber, *Tales of the Hasidim*, 1: v.

14. Scholem, *Major Trends*, p. 349.

15. Glenn, *Paul Celan*, p. 93.

16. Meinecke, *Wort und Name*, p. 40.
17. Buber, *Prophetic Faith*, p. 29.
18. Voswinckel, pp. 62, 64.
19. Abelson, p. 127.
20. Ginsberg, 1: 3.
21. Scholem, *Major Trends*, p. 17.
22. Scholem, *Kabbalah*, p. 25.
23. *Zohar*, 1: 3.
24. Scholem, *On the Kabbalah*, p. 39.
25. Scholem, *Major Trends*, p. 216.
26. There can also be, interwoven through Celan's imagery, an intense sexualization, as in this poem, where the "bone-Hebrew" is "ground into sperm." The Shekhinah itself is a feminized, almost mythological figure. I am, unfortunately, unable to pursue such sexualized patterns in this study.
27. Buber, *Origin and Meaning*, p. 91.
28. Scholem, *Major Trends*, p. 89.
29. Levinas, *Totality and Infinity*, pp. 297, 69.
30. Buber, *Eclipse of God*, p. 90; Buber, *Way of Response*, p. 28; Scholem, *Major Trends*, pp. 221, 218.
31. Novak, p. 309; Scholem, *Major Trends*, p. 232.
32. Abelson, p. 127.
33. See, for example, Wolfson, "Halevi and Maimonides," in *Studies*, 2: 90, 114.
34. Scholem, *Major Trends*, p. 214; Scholem, *Kabbalah*, p. 112.
35. Scholem, *Major Trends*, p. 232.
36. Pelikan, 1: 230.
37. Maimonides, 1: 54; Novak, pp. 306, 301ff. Other terms Novak proposes for this distinction are "nonrelational priority and relational posteriority," "Deus absconditus and Deus revelatus" (303).
38. Pelikan, 1: 22.
39. Scholem, "Revelation and Tradition," p. 284; Novak, pp. 303–4: "The contrast between Rabbinic theology and Neoplatonic philosophy" emerges in that for Plotinus "relations can involve no reciprocity or mutuality"; Idel, "Reification," p. 50: "In Kabbalah the function of language differs from what we may have expected in a strictly Platonic universe of discourse . . . the possibility that the lower entity will affect the higher one is not accepted by Platonic or Neoplatonic thinkers." Katz discusses the tensions between a "dual inheritance" of Greek impersonality and Hebrew "covenantal relationship" ("Utterance," p. 281ff).
40. *Lamentations Rabbah*, 2: 17.
41. Cohen, p. 178.

42. Pelikan, 1: 53.

43. Buber, *Tales of the Hasidim*, 1: 236.

44. Scholem, *Major Trends*, p. 15; Scholem, "The Name of God," pp. 62, 60.

45. Meinecke, p. 23.

46. Scholem, *Major Trends*, p. 268.

47. Schulze, *Celan und die Mystiker*, p. 56.

48. Scholem, *Kabbalah*, p. 3; *Major Trends*, p. 123.

49. Katz, "Language, Epistemology, Mysticism," p. 34.

50. Buber, *Way of Response*, p. 36.

51. *Mekilta de Rabbi Ishmael*, 2: 224.

52. Idel, *Kabbalah*, pp. xii–xiii. Cf. p. 74; "Reification," p. 55: "The mentalistic and introvert mood that characterizes nonlinguistic mystical experiences seems to be exceptional in Judaism. Conceiving Hebrew as the perfect and the divine language, there was no reason to attempt to transcend, attenuate, or obliterate its use. Generating Hebrew was understood . . . not as a hindrance but as a mode of imitatio Dei. . . . If language is the main way to bridge the gap, or to communicate between God and man, it is the same vehicle that enables man to restore the connection with the divine."

53. Novak, p. 300.

54. Weber, pp. 279–80. For other references in Celan to Eckhart see Schulze.

55. Felstiner, "Paul Celan in Translation," p. 94, whose translation of the poem I use here.

56. Eckhart, "Von der Empfängnis Gottes in der Seele," in *Predigten und Schriften*, pp. 200, 202.

57. Ibid., p. 205; "Vernunft zieht Gott die Hülle seiner Güte ab und nimmt ihn bloss," *Predigten und Schriften*, p. 190; "Von der Empfängnis," p. 201.

58. Scholem, *Kabbalah*, p. 169.

59. Buber, *I and Thou*, p. 75.

60. Buber, *Way of Response*, p. 183; Buber, *Prophetic Faith*, p. 6.

61. Buber, *Origin and Meaning*, p. 193; Novak, p. 308; Scholem, *On the Kabbalah*, p. 35.

62. Buber, *Way of Response*, p. 104; Buber, *Two Types*, pp. 47, 129.

63. Levinas, *Totality*, pp. 207, 73. *Totality and Infinity* was first published in Paris in 1961, when and where Celan almost certainly came across it. Levinas himself wrote an essay on Celan, to be discussed later. In any case, Levinas speaks to and for the tradition in ways that illuminate Celan's writing.

64. Levinas, *Totality*, pp. 73, 66.

65. James K. Lyon carefully draws such distinctions between Buber's and Celan's uses of dialogue in "Paul Celan and Martin Buber," p. 115. Lyon generally argues for the importance of the dialogue form in Celan's work, above all as a structural principle even beyond the terms of the particular objects it addresses, which can vary.

66. Eckhart, "Vernunft," pp. 186–89.

67. Buber, *Tales*, 2: 179.

68. Buber, *Origin and Meaning*, p. 94; *Two Types*, p. 130; *Origin and Meaning*, p. 91; *Prophetic Faith*, p. 29.

69. Levinas, *Difficile Liberté*, p. 44.

70. Scholem, *Kabbalah*, p. 170.

71. Scholem, "Name of God," pp. 62, 59.

72. Ibid., pp. 75, 71, 167.

73. Ibid., pp. 166, 181, 175.

74. Dan, p. 128. Dan goes on to discuss how these general exegetical practices became incorporated and developed in kabbalistic exegesis. I more fully discuss the status of the letter in "Pharisaic."

75. Idel, *Kabbalah*, pp. 207–8.

76. Scholem, "Name of God," p. 165.

77. Ibid., pp. 71, 73, 189; *Kabbalah and Symbolism*, p. 40.

78. Scholem, *Kabbalah*, p. 100.

79. Scholem, *Major Trends*, pp. 214, 275.

80. Buber, *Origin and Meaning*, p. 94.

81. Menninghaus, pp. 22, 24; pp. 17, 24–25, 28.

82. Ibid., p. 34.

83. Ibid., pp. 46–47. Thomas Sparr also discusses Celan's poetic in "Derridean" terms, similarly interpreting it as antimimetic (p. 109), as language that is "non-instrumental" (p. 111) and thus essentially metapoetic. He sees the "essential feature" of the hermetic poem as deriving from a "tension between indecidability on the one hand and a referential structure on the other," a stasis that the poem encloses (p. 117).

84. Derrida, "Schibboleth," pp. 314, 327. Peter Szondi was perhaps the first to emphasize the importance of the date and of dating Celan's work.

85. Ibid., pp. 312, 313–14.

86. Ibid., pp. 327, 343, 345, 346.

87. Ibid., p. 309.

88. P. Neumann, p. 78.

89. Derrida, "How to Avoid Speaking," pp. 9, 10, 44, 45; 4.

90. Ibid., pp. 14, 11.

91. Levinas, "Being and the Other," pp. 19, 21, 17.

92. Taylor, p. 193.

93. Levinas, "Being and the Other," pp. 17–20.

94. Novak, pp. 310, 308.

95. Levinas, "Trace of the Other," p. 357. For a fuller discussion of the "trace" in Levinas and Derrida see Wolosky, "Derrida, Jabès, Levinas."

96. Derrida, *Writing and Difference*, pp. 108, 90.

97. Derrida, "Schibboleth," p. 323, 322.

98. Scholem, "Name of God," p. 165.

99. Buber, *Eclipse of God*, p. 162.

100. Derrida, "How to Avoid Speaking," pp. 11, 15.

101. Buhr, p. 87.

102. Amy Colin discusses this poem in terms of its Exodus theme, p. 141ff.

103. Katz, "Utterance and Ineffability," p. 289.

104. Scholem, *Major Trends*, p. 276.

105. Schwarz, p. 52.

106. Moses, p. 216.

107. Here as elsewhere Celan seems to be using an Austrian dialect base for his word choice. Perhaps this is due to his stay in Vienna in transit between Rumania and Paris, his single experience of actually living in a dominant German-speaking environment.

108. Scholem, "Name of God," p. 194. Scholem concludes this essay by naming as "the question of our times" whether we can still "hear the echo of the vanished word of the creation in the immanence of the world"—a question, he concludes, to which "in our times only the poets presumably have the answer" (p. 194).

109. Adorno, *Negative Dialectics*, p. 361.

Chapter 7

1. Nietzsche, *Philosophy in the Tragic Age*, sects. 5, 9, 10 (pp. 51–55, 69–71, 79–80).

2. Nietzsche, *Twilight of the Idols*, pp. 479–81.

3. Bloch, pp. 5, 10–11. Cf. Genevieve Lloyd, *The Man of Reason* (London: Methuen, 1984), for a review of the association between a female principle and the system of classical philosophy's inferior terms.

4. Armstrong, *Plotinian and Christian Studies*, 23, p. 84.

5. Novak, p. 314. Cf. Arlene W. Saxonhouse.

Works Cited

∽

Abbott, H. Porter. *The Fiction of Samuel Beckett: Form and Effect*. Berkeley: University of California Press, 1973.

Abelson, Joshua. *The Immanence of God*. New York: Hermon Press, 1969.

Adorno, Theodor W. *Aesthetic Theory*. London: Routledge and Kegan Paul, 1970.

———. *Negative Dialectics*. London: Routledge and Kegan Paul, 1973.

———. *Prisms*. Cambridge, Mass.: MIT Press, 1982.

Allemann, Beda. "Das Gedicht und Seine Wirklichkeit." *Études Germaniques* 25 (July–Sept. 1970): 266–74.

———. "Zu Paul Celans neuem Gedichtband *Atemwende*." In Dietlind Meinecke, ed., *Über Paul Celan*. Frankfurt am Main: Suhrkamp Verlag, 1970, 194–97.

Amery, Jean. *At the Mind's Limits*. Trans. S. Rosenfeld. Bloomington: Indiana University Press, 1980.

Aquinas, Thomas. *Summa Theologia, Basic Writings of St. Thomas Aquinas*. New York: Random House, 1972.

Arendt, Hannah. *Totalitarianism*. New York: Harcourt, Brace and World, 1968.

Aristotle. *The Works of Aristotle*. Vol. 3, *Metaphysics*, ed. J. A. Smith and W. D. Ross. Oxford: Oxford University Press, 1980.

Armstrong, A. Hilary. *The Architecture of the Intelligible World in the Philosophy of Plotinus*. Amsterdam: Adolf M. Hakkert, 1967.

———. *The Cambridge History of Later Greek and Early Medieval Philosophy*. London: Cambridge University Press, 1967.

———. *Plotinian and Christian Studies*. London: Variorum Editions, 1979.

Atherton, J. Patrick. "The Neoplatonic 'One' and the Trinitarian APXH." In R. Baine Harris, ed., *The Significance of Neoplatonism*. Norfolk, Va.: International Society for Neoplatonic Studies, 1976, 173–85.

Auden, W. H. *The Dyer's Hand*. New York: Vintage Books, 1968.

Augustine. *Confessions*. Trans. R. S. Pine-Coffin. Middlesex: Penguin, 1981.

———. *The Harmony of the Gospels*. Vol. 8 of *Works of Augustine*. Edinburgh: T. and T. Clark, 1873.

———. "On the Gospel of John." *Patrologia Latina*, vol. 35, Tractatus 33. Ed. J. P. Migne. Paris: Typa Catholica Migne, 1841.

———. *On the Trinity, Basic Writings of St. Augustine*. Ed. Whitney J. Oates. New York: Random House, 1948.

Bair, Deirdre. *Samuel Beckett*. New York: Harcourt Brace Jovanovich, 1978.

Bakhtin, Mikhail. *Problems of Dostoevsky's Poetics*. Trans. Caryl Emerson. Minneapolis: University of Minnesota Press, 1984.

Baldwin, Helene. *Samuel Beckett's Real Silence*. University Park: Pennsylvania State University Press, 1981.

Barnard, G. C. *Samuel Beckett: A New Approach*. New York: Dodd, Mead, 1970.

Beckett, Samuel. "All Strange Away." In *Rockaby and Other Short Pieces*. New York: Grove Press, 1981.

———. *Company*. New York: Grove Press, 1980.

———. *Le Depeupleur*. Paris: Editions de Minuit, 1970.

———. *Disjecta*. New York: Grove Press, 1984.

———. *First Love and Other Shorts*. New York: Grove Press, 1974.

———. *Fizzles*. New York: Grove Press, 1976.

———. *Ill Seen Ill Said*. New York: Grove Press, 1981.

———. *The Lost Ones*. New York: Grove Press, 1972.

———. *Malone Dies*. In *Three Novels*. New York: Grove Press, 1958.

———. *More Pricks than Kicks*. New York: Grove Press, 1972.

———. *Murphy*. New York: Grove Press, 1957.

———. *Proust*. New York: Grove Press, 1957.

———. *Stories and Texts for Nothing*. New York: Grove Press, 1967.

———. *The Unnamable*. In *Three Novels*. New York: Grove Press, 1958.

———. *Waiting for Godot*. New York: Grove Press, 1954.

———. *Watt*. New York: Grove Press, 1953.

Beese, Henriette. *Nachdichtung als Erinnerung.* Agora Verlag, Darmstadt (BRD) Lucasweg, 1976.

Benjamin, Walter. *Illuminations.* New York: Schocken, 1978.

Benz, Ernst. *Geist und Leben der Ostkirche.* Hamburg: Rowholt, 1957.

Bernal, Olga. *Langage et fiction dans le roman de Beckett.* Paris: Gallimard, 1969.

Bersani, Leo. *The Culture of Redemption.* Cambridge, Mass.: Harvard University Press, 1990.

Bettelheim, Bruno. *The Informed Heart.* Glencoe, Ill.: Free Press, 1960.

———. *Surviving and Other Essays.* New York: Alfred A. Knopf, 1979.

Bille, Finn. "The Ultimate Metaphor and the Defeat of Poetry in T. S. Eliot's *Four Quarters.*" *International Journal of Symbology* 3 (March 1972): 16–24.

Bloch, R. Howard. "Medieval Misogyny." *Representations* 20 (1987): 1–24.

Bornstein, George. *Transformations of Romanticism in Yeats, Eliot, and Stevens.* Chicago: University of Chicago Press, 1976.

Bowles, Patrick. "How Samuel Beckett Sees the Universe." *Listener,* June 19, 1958, 1011–12.

Brater, Enoch. "Still/Beckett: The Essential and the Incidental." *Journal of Modern Literature* 6 (1977): 3–16.

Brehier, Emile. *The Philosophy of Plotinus.* Chicago: University of Chicago Press, 1958.

Brenkman, John. *Culture and Domination.* Ithaca, N.Y.: Cornell University Press, 1987.

Brienza, Susan D. *"The Lost Ones:* The Reader as Searcher." *Journal of Modern Literature* 6 (1977): 148–68.

Brisman, Leslie. "Swinburne's Semiotics." *Georgia Review* 31 (1977): 578–97.

Buber, Martin. *Eclipse of God.* New York: Harper and Brothers, 1952.

———. *I and Thou.* New York: Charles Scribners, 1958.

———. *The Origin and Meaning of Hasidism.* New York: Harper Torchbooks, 1960.

———. *The Prophetic Faith.* New York: Harper and Row, 1960.

———. *Tales of the Hasidim,* Vols. 1 and 2. New York: Schocken, 1972.

———. *Two Types of Faith.* New York: Harper Torchbooks, 1961.

———. *The Way of Response.* New York: Schocken, 1966.

Buhr, Gerhard. *Celans Poetik.* Göttingen: Vandenhoeck and Ruprecht, 1976.

Burger, Hermann. *Auf der Suche nach der verlorenen Sprache.* Zürich: Artemis Verlag, 1974.

Burke, Kenneth. *The Rhetoric of Religion*. Berkeley: University of California Press, 1970.

Burtt, E. A. *The Metaphysical Foundations of Modern Science*. Atlanta Highlands, N.J.: Humanities Press, 1952.

Bush, Ronald. *T. S. Eliot, A Study in Character and Style*. New York: Oxford University Press, 1983.

Canary, Robert H. *T. S. Eliot: The Poet and His Critics*. Chicago: American Library Association, 1982.

Cavell, Stanley. *Must We Mean What We Say?* Cambridge, Eng.: Cambridge University Press, 1976.

Celan, Paul. *Gesammelte Werke in fünf Bänden*. 5 vols. Frankfurt am Main: Suhrkamp Verlag, 1983.

Chalfen, Israel. *Paul Celan: Eine Biographie seiner Jugend*. Frankfurt am Main: Insel Verlag, 1979.

Chambers, Ross. "Beckett's Brinksmanship." In Martin Esslin, ed., *Samuel Beckett*. Englewood Cliffs, N.J.: Prentice Hall, 1965, 152–68.

Champigny, Robert. "Adventures of the First Person." In Melvin Friedman, ed., *Samuel Beckett Now*. Chicago: University of Chicago Press, 1970, 119–28.

The Cloud of Unknowing. Trans. Clifton Wolters. London: Penguin, 1961.

Coe, Richard N. "Beckett's English." In Morris Beja, S. E. Gontarski, and Pierre Astier, eds., *Samuel Beckett: Humanistic Perspectives*. Columbus: Ohio State University Press, 1983, 36–57.

———. "God and Samuel Beckett." *Meanjin Quarterly* 24, no. 100 (1965): 66–85.

———. *Samuel Beckett*. New York: Grove Press, 1964.

Cohen, Jeremy. *The Friars and the Jews*. Ithaca, N.Y.: Cornell University Press, 1982.

Cohn, Ruby. *Back to Beckett*. Princeton, N.J.: Princeton University Press, 1973.

———. *The Comic Gamut*. New Brunswick, N.J.: Rutgers University Press, 1962.

———. "Samuel Beckett Self-Translator." *PMLA* 76 (1961): 613–21.

Colin, Amy. *Paul Celan: Holograms of Darkness*. Bloomington: Indiana University Press, 1991.

Copeland, Hannah Case. *Art and the Artist in the Works of Samuel Beckett*. The Hague: Mouton, 1975.

Curtius, E. R. *European Literature and the Latin Middle Ages*. Princeton, N.J.: Princeton University Press, 1953.

Dan, Joseph. "Midrash and the Dawn of Kabbalah." In Sanford Budick and Geoffrey Hartman, eds., *Midrash and Literature*. New Haven: Yale University Press, 1986, 127–39.

Davidson, Harriet. *T. S. Eliot and Hermeneutics*. Baton Rouge: Louisiana State University Press, 1985.

Davie, Donald. "Anglican Eliot." In A. Walton Litz, ed., *Eliot in His Time: Essays on the Occasion of the Fiftieth Anniversary of "The Waste Land."* Princeton, N.J.: Princeton University Press, 1973.

Dearlove, J. E. *Accommodating the Chaos: Samuel Beckett's Nonrelational Art*. Durham, N.C.: Duke University Press, 1982.

———. "'Last Images': Samuel Beckett's Residual Fiction." *Journal of Modern Literature 6* (1977): 104–26.

———. "Syntax Upended in Opposite Corners." In Morris Beja, S. E. Gontarski, and Pierre Astier, eds., *Samuel Beckett: Humanistic Perspectives*. Columbus: Ohio State University Press, 1983, 122–28.

De Man, Paul. *Allegories of Reading*. New Haven: Yale University Press, 1979.

———. *Blindness and Insight*. Minneapolis: University of Minnesota Press, 1971.

Demetz, Peter. *Postwar German Literature*. New York: Schocken, 1972.

Derrida, Jacques. "How to Avoid Speaking." In Sanford Budick and Wolfgang Iser, eds., *Languages of the Unsayable*. New York: Columbia University Press, 1989, 3–70.

———. *Of Grammatology*. Baltimore: The Johns Hopkins University Press, 1974.

———. "Schibboleth." In Sanford Budick and Geoffrey Hartman, eds., *Midrash and Literature*. New Haven: Yale University Press, 1986, 307–47.

———. "White Mythology." *New Literary History 6* (1974): 5–74.

———. *Writing and Difference*. Chicago: University of Chicago Press, 1978.

Descartes, René. *Discourse on Method and Meditations*. New York: Bobbs-Merrill, 1960.

———. *Philosophical Writings*. New York: Bobbs-Merrill, 1971.

Distel, Barbara, and Ruth Jakusch, eds. *Concentration Camp Dachau, 1933–1945*. Brussels: Comité International de Dachau, 1978.

Dodds, E. R. *Pagan and Christian in an Age of Anxiety*. Cambridge, Eng.: Cambridge University Press, 1965.

Donna, Sister Rose Bernard. *Despair and Hope: A Study of Langland and Augustine*. Washington, D.C.: Catholic University of America Press, 1948.

Dörrie, H. "Formula Analogiae: An Exploration of a Theme in Hellenistic and Imperial Platonism." In R. A. Markus and H. J. Blumenthal, eds., *Neoplatonist and Early Christian Thought*. London: Variorum Publications, 1981, 33–49.

Driver, Tom. "Beckett by the Madeleine." *Columbia University Forum* 4, no. 3 (1961): 21–25.

Eckhart, Meister. *Predigten und Schriften*. Compiled by F. Heer. Hamburg: Fischer Bücherei, 1956.

Eliot, T. S. Clark Lectures on the Metaphysical Poetry of the Seventeenth Century. Typescript. John Hayward Collection, King's College Library, Cambridge.

———. *The Complete Poems and Plays*. New York: Harcourt, Brace and World, 1971.

———. "English Poets as Letter Writers." *Yale Daily News*, Feb. 24, 1933, p. 3.

———. *Knowledge and Experience in the Philosophy of F. H. Bradley*. London: Faber and Faber, 1964.

———. Letters to Paul Elmer More. Unpublished correspondence. Princeton University Archive.

———. "A Note on Poetry and Belief," *Enemy* 1 (January/February 1927): 15–17.

———. *On Poetry and Poets*. New York: Farrar, Straus and Giroux, 1957.

———. "Rhyme and Reason: The Poetry of John Donne," *Listener*, March 19, 1930, 502–3.

———. *Selected Essays of T. S. Eliot*. New York: Harcourt, Brace and World, 1964.

———. *The Use of Poetry and the Use of Criticism*. London: Faber and Faber, 1975.

Eliot, Valerie. "Biographical Commentary." In Valerie Eliot, ed., *The Letters of T. S. Eliot*. Vol. 1, *1898–1922*. London: Faber, 1988.

Ellmann, Richard. *Four Dubliners*. New York: George Braziller, 1987.

Esslin, Martin. "Samuel Beckett." In John Cruickshank, ed., *The Novelist as Philosopher*. London: Oxford University Press, 1962, 128–46.

Ezrahi, Sidra. "'A Grave in the Air': Unbound Metaphors in Post-Holocaust Poetry." In Saul Friedlander, ed., *Probing the Limits of Representation*. Cambridge, Mass.: Harvard University Press, 1991, 259–76.

Federman, Raymond. *Journey to Chaos*. Berkeley: University of California Press, 1965.

Felstiner, John. "Mother Tongue, Holy Tongue: On Translating and Not Translating Paul Celan." *Comparative Literature* 38 (1986): 113–36.

———. "Paul Celan in Translation: 'Du sei wie du.'" *Studies in Twentieth Century Literature* 8 (1983): 91–100.

Ferguson, Margaret. "Saint Augustine's Region of Unlikeness: The Crossing of Exile and Language." *The Georgia Review* 29 (1975): 842–64.

Findlay, J. N. "The Neoplatonism of Plato." In R. Baines Harris, ed., *The Significance of Neoplatonism.* Norfolk, Va.: International Society for Neoplatonic Studies, Old Dominion University, 1976, 23–40.

———. *Plato: The Written and Unwritten Doctrines.* London: Routledge and Kegan Paul, 1974.

Finney, Brian. "Assumption to Lessness: Beckett's Shorter Fiction." In Katharine Worth, ed., *Beckett the Shape Changer.* London: Routledge and Kegan Paul, 1975, 61–84.

Fletcher, John. *Samuel Beckett's Art.* London: Chatto and Winders, 1967.

———. *The Novels of Samuel Beckett.* New York: Barnes and Noble, 1964.

Frank, Joseph. *The Widening Gyre: Spatial Form in Modern Literature.* Bloomington: Indiana University Press, 1968.

Gadamer, Hans-Georg. *Dialogue and Dialectic.* New Haven: Yale University Press, 1980.

———. *Wer bin Ich und wer bist Du?* Frankfort am Main: Suhrkamp Verlag, 1973.

Gardner, Helen. *The Art of T. S. Eliot.* London: Faber and Faber, 1968.

———. *The Composition of the Four Quartets.* London: Faber and Faber, 1978.

Gerard, Sister Mary. "Eliot of the Circle and John of the Cross." *Thought* 34 (Spring 1959): 107–27.

Gilson, Etienne. *Being and Some Philosophers.* Toronto: Pontifical Institute of Medieval Studies, 1952.

———. *The Christian Philosophy of St. Thomas Aquinas.* London: Victor Gollancz, 1959.

———. *Études sur la role de la pensée mediévale dans la formation du système Cartésien.* Paris: Libraire Philosophique J. Vrin, 1967.

Ginzberg, Louis. *The Legends of the Jews.* Vol. 1. Philadelphia: Jewish Publication Society, 1968.

Glenn, Jerry. *Paul Celan.* New York: Twayne, 1973.

Gulley, Norman. *Plato's Theory of Knowledge.* London: Methuen, 1962.

Hamburger, Michael. *The Truth of Poetry.* New York: Harcourt, Brace, Jovanovich, 1969.

Hamilton, Alice and Kenneth Hamilton. *Condemned to Life.* Grand Rapids, Mich.: Eerdmans, 1976.

Harvey, Lawrence. *Samuel Beckett, Poet and Critic.* Princeton, N.J.: Princeton University Press, 1970.

Haüsermann, H. W. "East Coker by T. S. Eliot." *English Studies* 13, no. 4 (1941): 108–10.

Hay, Eloise Knapp. *T. S. Eliot's Negative Way.* Cambridge, Mass.: Harvard University Press, 1982.

Hayman, David. "Molloy or the Quest for Meaninglessness." In Melvin J. Friedman, ed., *Samuel Beckett Now.* Chicago: University of Chicago Press, 1970.

Heidegger, Martin. *Being and Time.* New York: Harper and Row, 1962.

———. *Existence and Being.* Chicago: Henry Regnery Company, 1949.

———. *Holzwege.* Frankfurt am Main: Vittorio Klostermann, 1950.

Hesla, David. *The Shape of Chaos.* Minneapolis: University of Minnesota Press, 1971.

Hobson, Harold. "Samuel Beckett: Dramatist of the Year." *Theatre Annual* (London) 1 (1956): 153–55.

Hoefer, Jacqueline. "Watt." In Martin Esslin, ed., *Samuel Beckett.* Englewood Cliffs, N.J.: Prentice Hall, 1965, 62–76.

Hoelzel, Alfred. "Paul Celan: An Authentic Jewish Voice?" In Amy Colin, ed., *Argumentum e Silentio.* New York: Walter de Gruyter, 1987, 352–58.

Hoffman, Frederick J. *Samuel Beckett: The Language of the Self.* Carbondale: Southern Illinois University Press, 1962.

Hough, Graham. "Vision and Doctrine in *Four Quartets.*" *Critical Quarterly* 15 (Summer 1973): 107–27.

Idel, Moshe. *Kabbalah: New Perspectives.* New Haven: Yale University Press, 1988.

———. "Reification of Language in Jewish Mysticism." In Steven Katz, ed., *Mysticism and Language.* New York: Oxford University Press, 1992, 42–79.

Iser, Wolfgang. *The Implied Reader.* Baltimore: The Johns Hopkins University Press, 1974.

———. "The Pattern of Negativity in Beckett's Prose." *The Georgia Review* 29, no. 3 (1974): 1–14.

Jacobsen, Josephine. *The Testament of Samuel Beckett.* New York: Hill and Wang, 1964.

Janz, Marlies. *Vom Engagement absoluter Poesie.* Frankfurt am Main: Athenäum, 1976.

Jay, Martin. *The Dialectical Imagination: A History of the Frankfurt School.* London: Heinemann, 1973.

John of the Cross. *The Ascent of Mount Carmel, The Dark Night of the Soul, Complete Works of John of the Cross.* Trans. and ed. E. Allison Peers. Westminster, Md.: Newman Press, 1953.

Jonas, Hans. *The Gnostic Religion.* Boston: Beacon Press, 1972.

Julian of Norwich. *Showings.* New York: Paulist Press, 1978.

Jung, Carl. *Essays on Contemporary Events.* London: Kegan Paul, 1947.

Kahler, Erich. *The Tower and the Abyss.* New York: George Braziller, 1957.

Katz, Steven. "Language, Epistemology, Mysticism." In Steven Katz, ed., *Mysticism and Philosophical Analysis.* New York: Oxford University Press, 1978, 22–74.

———. "Mystical Speech and Mystical Meaning." In Steven Katz, ed., *Mysticism and Language.* New York: Oxford University Press, 1992, 3–41.

———. "Utterance and Ineffability in Jewish Neoplatonism." In Lenn Goodman, ed., *Neoplatonism and Jewish Thought.* New York: State University of New York Press, 1992, 279–98.

Kenner, Hugh. *The Invisible Poet.* London: Methuen, 1965.

———. *A Reader's Guide to Samuel Beckett.* New York: Farrar, Straus and Giroux, 1973.

———. *Samuel Beckett.* Berkeley: University of California Press, 1961.

———. "Shades of Syntax." In Ruby Cohn, ed., *Samuel Beckett.* New York: McGraw Hill, 1975, 21–31.

Kenny, Anthony. "Descartes on Ideas." In W. Doney, ed., *Descartes: A Collection of Critical Essays.* New York: Doubleday, 1967, 227–49.

Kern, Edith. *Existential Thought and Fictional Technique.* New Haven: Yale University Press, 1970.

Klein, Jacob. *Greek Mathematical Thought and the Origin of Algebra.* Cambridge, Mass.: MIT Press, 1968.

Knowlson, James. *Light and Darkness in the Theatre of Samuel Beckett.* London: Turret Books, 1972.

Kostelanetz, Richard. "Contemporary Literature." In Richard Kostelanetz, ed., *On Contemporary Literature.* Freeport, N.Y.: Books for Libraries Press, 1964, xv–xxvii.

Koyre, Alexandre. *Metaphysics and Measurement.* London: Chapman and Hall, 1968.

———. *Galileo Studies.* Sussex: Harvester Press, 1978.

Kristeva, Julia. "Psychoanalysis and the Polis." In *The Kristeva Reader.* New York: Columbia University Press, 1986, 301–20.

Lamentations Rabbah, Midrash Rabbah. Trans. A. Cohen. London: Soncino Press, 1961.

Landgraf, Artur Michael. *Dogmengeschichte der Fruhscholastik.* Vol. 3, *Die Lehre von der Sakramenten.* Regensburg: Friedrich Pustet, 1955.

Langer, Lawrence. *The Holocaust and the Literary Imagination.* New Haven: Yale University Press, 1975.

Leavis, F. R. *The Living Principle.* New York: Oxford University Press, 1975.

Leventhal, A. J. "The Beckett Hero." In Martin Esslin, ed., *Samuel Beckett.* Englewood Cliffs, N.J.: Prentice Hall, 1965, 37–51.

Levi, Primo. *Survival in Auschwitz.* London: Collier Macmillan, 1976.

Levinas, Emmanuel. "Being and the Other: On Paul Celan." *The Chicago Review* 29, no. 3 (1978): 16–22.

———. *Difficile Liberté.* Paris: Editions Albin Michel, 1963.

———. *Totality and Infinity.* Pittsburgh, Pa.: Duquesne University Press, 1969.

———. "The Trace of the Other." Trans. A. Lingis. In Mark Taylor, ed., *Deconstruction in Context.* Chicago: University of Chicago Press, 1986, 345–59.

Lloyd, A. C. "Non-Discursive Thought—An Enigma of Greek Philosophy." *Proceedings of the Aristotelian Society* 70 (1969/1970): 261–69.

Lossky, Vladimir. *The Mystical Theology of the Eastern Church.* Cambridge: James Clarke, 1957.

———. "La notion des 'analogies' chez le Pseudo-Denys l'Areopagite." *Archives d'histoire doctrinale et littéraire du Moyen Age* 5 (1930): 279–309.

———. *Théologie negative et connaissance de Dieu chez Maître Eckhart.* Paris: Librarie Philosophique J. Vrin, 1960.

Louth, Andrew. *The Origins of the Christian Mystical Tradition.* Oxford: Oxford University Press, 1981.

Lynch, William, S. J. "Dissociation in Time." In B. Bergonzi, ed., *Four Quartets: A Casebook.* New York: Macmillan, 1977, 247–53.

Lyon, James K. "Introduction." *Studies in Twentieth Century Literature* 8 (1983): 5–8.

———. "Paul Celan and Martin Buber: Poetry as Dialogue." *PMLA* 86 (1971): 110–20.

Maimonides, Moses. *The Guide for the Perplexed.* Trans. M. Friedlander. New York: Dover, 1956.

Margolis, John D. *T. S. Eliot's Intellectual Development.* Chicago: University of Chicago Press, 1972.

Martz, Louis. "The Wheel and the Point: Aspects of Imagery and Theme in Eliot's Later Poetry." In Leonard Unger, ed., *T. S. Eliot: A Selected Critique*. New York: Rinehart, 1966, 444–62.

Mayer, Hans. *Zur deutschen Literatur der Zeit*. Reinbek bei Hamburg: Rowohlt Verlag, 1967.

Mayoux, Jean-Jacques. "Samuel Beckett's Universal Parody." In Martin Esslin, ed., *Samuel Beckett*. Englewood Cliffs, N.J.: Prentice Hall, 1965, 77–91.

———. "The Theatre of Samuel Beckett." *Perspective* 11, no. 3 (1959): 142–55.

Mazzeo, Joseph Anthony. "St. Augustine's Rhetoric of Silence." *Journal of the History of Ideas* 23 (1962): 175–96.

Meinecke, Dietlind. "Einleitung." In D. Meinecke, ed., *Über Paul Celan*. Frankfurt am Main: Suhrkamp Verlag, 1970, 7–30.

———. *Wort und Name bei Paul Celan*. Berlin: Verlag Gehlen, 1970.

Mekilta de Rabbi Ishmael. Trans. J. Z. Lauterbach. Philadelphia: Jewish Publication Society of America, 1961.

Menninghaus, Winfried. *Paul Celan: Magie der Form*. Frankfurt am Main: Suhrkamp Verlag, 1980.

Mercier, Vivian. "The Mathematical Limit." *Nation*, Feb. 14, 1959, 144–45.

Merlan, Philip. *From Platonism to Neoplatonism*. The Hague: Martinus Nijhoff, 1953.

Michaels, Walter Benn. "Philosophy in Kinkanja: Eliot's Pragmatism." *Glyph* 8 (1981): 170–202.

Miller, J. Hillis. *Poets of Reality*, New York: Atheneum, 1974.

———. "Theoretical and Atheoretical in Stevens." In Frank Doggett and Robert Buttel, eds., *Wallace Stevens: A Celebration*. Princeton, N.J.: Princeton University Press, 1980, 274–85.

Mintz, Samuel. "Beckett's Murphy: A Cartesian Novel." *Perspective* 11, no. 3 (1959): 156–65.

Morss, Susan Buck. *The Origin of Negative Dialectics*. New York: Free Press, 1977.

Morot-Sir, Edouard. "Samuel Beckett and Cartesian Emblems." In Edouard Morot-Sir, Howard Harper, and Dougald McMillan III, eds., *Samuel Beckett: The Art of Rhetoric*. Chapel Hill: University of North Carolina Department of Romance Languages and Literatures, 1976, 25–104.

Moses, Stéphane. "Patterns of Negativity in Paul Celan's 'The Trumpet Place.'" In Sanford Budick and Wolfgang Iser, eds., *Languages of the Unsayable*. New York: Columbia University Press, 1989, 209–24.

Murray, Paul. *T. S. Eliot and Mysticism*. London: Macmillan, 1991.

Neumann, Gerhard. "Die absolut metapher: Ein Abgrenzungsversuch am Beispiel Stephane Mallermé's und Paul Celan's." *Poetica* 3 (1970): 188–225.

Neumann, Peter Horst. *Zur Lyrik Paul Celans*. Göttingen: Vandenhoeck and Ruprecht, 1968.

Nietzsche, Friedrich. *Philosophy in the Tragic Age of the Greeks*. Trans. Marianne Cowan. Chicago: Henry Regnery, 1962.

———. *Twilight of the Idols*. In Walter Kaufman, ed., *The Portable Nietzsche*. New York: Penguin, 1954.

———. *The Will to Power*. Ed. Walter Kaufman. New York: Vintage Press, 1967.

Novak, David. "Self-Contraction of the Godhead." In Lenn H. Goodman, ed., *Neoplatonism and Jewish Thought*. Albany: State University of New York Press, 1992, 299–318.

Ortega y Gasset, José. *The Dehumanization of Art*. Garden City, N.Y.: Doubleday Anchor, 1956.

Pelikan, Jaroslav. *The Christian Tradition*. Chicago: The University of Chicago Press, 1971.

Perl, Jeffrey. *Skepticism and Modern Enmity: Before and After Eliot*. Baltimore: The Johns Hopkins University Press, 1989.

Perloff, Marjorie. *The Dance of the Intellect*. New York: Cambridge University Press, 1985.

———. *The Poetics of Indeterminacy: Rimbaud to Cage*. Princeton, N.J.: Princeton University Press, 1981.

Pilling, John. *Samuel Beckett*. London: Routledge and Kegan Paul, 1976.

Plato. *The Collected Dialogues*. Ed. Edith Hamilton and Huntington Cairns. Princeton, N.J.: Princeton University Press, 1961.

Plotinus. *Enneads*. Trans. Stephen MacKenna. London: Faber and Faber, 1936.

Pöggeler, Otto. "Ach, die Kunst." In Dietlind Meinecke, ed., *Über Paul Celan*. Frankfurt am Main: Suhrkamp Verlag, 1970, 77–94.

Pretzer, Lielo Anne. *Geschichts- und sozialkritische Dimensionen in Paul Celans Werk*. Bonn: Bouvier Verlag Herbert Grundmann, 1980.

Pseudo-Dionysius the Areopagite. *On the Divine Names and Mystical Theology*. Trans. C. E. Rolt. London: Macmillan, 1920.

Rabinovitz, Rubin. "Watt from Descartes to Schopenhauer." In Raymond Porter and James Brophy, eds., *Modern Irish Literature*. New York: Twayne, 1972.

Rexheuser, Adelheid. *Sinnsuche und Zeichen-Setzung in der Lyrik des frühen Celan*. Bonn: Bouvier Verlag Herbert Grundmann, 1974.

Robinson, Michael. *The Long Sonata of the Dead.* New York: Grove Press, 1969.

Rosenfeld, Alvin. *A Double Dying.* Bloomington: Indiana University Press, 1980.

Roques, René. *Structures théologiques de la gnose à Richard de Saint-Victor.* Paris: Presses Universitaires de France, 1962.

Roy, Jean H. *L'imagination selon Descartes.* Paris: Gallimard, 1954.

Saxonhouse, Arlene. *Fear of Diversity.* Chicago: University of Chicago Press, 1992.

Schäfer, Hans Dieter. "Mystische Rede am Rande des Schweigens; letzte Gedichte von Paul Celan." *Die Welt,* August 6, 1970.

Schärer, Margrit. *Negationen im Werke Paul Celans.* Zürich: Juris Druck Verlag, 1975.

Scholem, Gershom. *Kabbalah.* Jerusalem: Keter, 1974.

———. *Major Trends in Jewish Mysticism.* New York: Schocken, 1973.

———. "The Meaning of Torah in Jewish Mysticism." In *On the Kabbalah and its Symbolism.* New York: Schocken, 1965, 32–86.

———. *The Messianic Idea in Judaism.* New York: Schocken, 1971.

———. "The Name of God and the Linguistic Theory of the Kabbalah." *Diogenes* 79/80 (1972): 59–80, 164–94.

———. "Paul Celan in Tel Aviv." *Neue Rundschau* 91 (1980): 256–259.

———. "Schöpfung aus Nichts und Selbstverschränkung Gottes." *Eranos Jahrbuch* 25 (1956): 87–119.

Schopenhauer, Arthur. *The World as Will and Representation.* Trans. R. B. Haldane and J. Kemp. London: Kegan Paul, Trench, Trubane, 1966.

Schulze, Joachim. "Celan and the Stumbling Block of Mysticism." *Studies in Twentieth Century Literature* 8 (1983): 69–90.

———. *Celan und die Mystiker.* Bonn: Bouvier Verlag Herbert Grundmann, 1976.

Schwarz, Peter Paul. *Totengedächtnis und dialogische Polarität in der Lyrik Paul Celans.* Düsseldorf: Pädagogischer Verlag Schwann, 1966.

Schwerin, Christoph. "Bitterer Brunnen des Herzens." *Der Monat* 2 (1981): 73–81.

Scott, Nathan. *Samuel Beckett.* London: Bowes and Bowes, 1965.

Seaver, Richard. "Samuel Beckett: A 1952 Introduction." *Merlin* 1, no. 2 (1952): 73–79.

Shenker, Israel. "Moody Man of Letters." *New York Times,* Sunday, May 6, 1956, sec. 2, pp. 3–5.

Shusterman, Richard. *T. S. Eliot and the Philosophy of Criticism.* London: Duckworth, 1987.

Skaff, William. *The Philosophy of T. S. Eliot.* Philadelphia: University of Pennsylvania Press, 1986.

Smith, Grover. *T. S. Eliot's Poetry and Plays.* Chicago: University of Chicago Press, 1956.

Sparr, Thomas. *Celans Poetik des hermetischen Gedichts.* Heidelberg: Carl Winter Universitätsverlag, 1989.

Spurr, David. *Conflicts in Consciousness: T. S. Eliot's Poetry and Criticism.* Urbana: University of Illinois Press, 1984.

Steiner, George. *Extraterritorial.* New York: Atheneum, 1971.

———. *In Bluebeard's Castle.* New Haven: Yale University Press, 1971.

———. "Das lange Leben der Metaphorik: Ein Versuch über die 'Shoah.'" *Akzente* 34 (1987): 194–212.

———. *Language and Silence.* New York: Atheneum, 1976.

Stevens, Wallace. *The Necessary Angel.* New York: Vintage, 1942.

Szondi, Peter. *Celan-Studien.* Frankfurt am Main: Suhrkamp, 1972.

Taylor, Mark C. *Altarity.* Chicago: University of Chicago Press, 1987.

Thiher, Allen. "Wittgenstein, Heidegger, the Unnamable, and Some Thoughts on the Status of Voice in Fiction." In Morris Beja, S. E. Gontarski, and Pierre Astier, eds., *Samuel Beckett: Humanistic Perspectives.* Columbus: Ohio State University Press, 1983, 80–90.

———. *Words in Reflection.* Chicago: University of Chicago Press, 1984.

Thomas à Kempis. *The Imitation of Christ.* London: Penguin, 1979.

Trimpi, Wesley. *Muses of One Mind.* Princeton, N.J.: Princeton University Press, 1983.

Udoff, Alan. "On Poetic Dwelling: Situating Celan and the Holocaust." In Amy Colin, ed., *Argumentum e Silentio.* New York: Walter de Gruyter, 1987, 320–51.

Underhill, Evelyn. *Mysticism.* New York: Noonday Press, 1955.

Unger, Leonard, ed. *T. S. Eliot: A Selected Critique.* New York: Russell and Russell, 1966.

Vogel, C. de. "The Neoplatonism of Plato and Platonism of Neoplatonism." *Mind* 62 (Jan. 1953): 43–64.

Voswinckel, Klaus. *Paul Celan: Verweigerte Poetisierung der Welt.* Heidelberg: Lothar Stiehm Verlag, 1974.

Wallis, R. T. *Neoplatonism.* London: Duckworth, 1972.

———. "Nous as Experience." In R. Baines Harris, ed., *The Significance of Neoplatonism.* Norfolk, Va.: International Society for Neoplatonic Studies, Old Dominion University, 1976, 121–54.

Ward, David. *T. S. Eliot: Between Two Worlds.* London: Routledge and Kegan Paul, 1973.

Weber, Werner. "Zum Gedicht 'Du sei wie du.'" In Dietlind Meinecke, ed., *Über Paul Celan*. Frankfurt am Main: Suhrkamp Verlag, 1970, 277–80.

Weinrich, Harald. "Kontraktionen." In Dietlind Meinecke, ed., *Über Paul Celan*. Frankfurt am Main: Suhrkamp Verlag, 1970, 214–25.

Weitz, Morris. "Time as a Mode of Salvation." In B. Bergonzi, ed., *Four Quartets: A Casebook*. New York: Macmillan, 1977, 138–52.

Wiedemann-Wolf, Barbara. *Antschel Paul—Paul Celan: Studien zum Frühwerk*. Tübingen: Max Niemeyer Verlag, 1985.

Wellershoff, Dieter. "Failure of an Attempt at De-Mythologization." In Martin Esslin, ed., *Samuel Beckett*. Englewood Cliffs, N.J.: Prentice Hall, 1965, 92–107.

Wolfson, Harry. *Studies in the History of Philosophy and Religion*. Ed. I. Twersky, 2 vols. Cambridge, Mass.: Harvard University Press, 1979.

Wolosky, Shira. "Derrida, Jabès, Levinas: Sign Theory as Ethical Discourse." *Prooftexts* 2 (1982): 283–302.

———. "Pharisaic." *Common Knowledge* 2, no. 2 (1993): 66–80.

The Zohar. Vol. 1. Trans. H. Speerling and M. Simon. London: Soncino Press, 1949.

Zurbrugg, Nicholas. "Beckett, Proust, and Burroughs and the Perils of 'Image Warfare.'" In Morris Beja, S. E. Gontarski, and Pierre Astier, eds., *Samuel Beckett: Humanistic Perspectives*. Columbus: Ohio State University Press, 1983, 172–88.

Index

᠗

In this index an "f" after a number indicates a separate reference on the next page, and an "ff" indicates separate references on the next two pages. A continuous discussion over two or more pages is indicated by a span of page numbers, e.g., "57–59." *Passim* is used for a cluster of references in close but not consecutive sequence.

Library of Congress Cataloging-in-Publication Data

Wolosky, Shira.
  Language mysticism : the negative way of language in Eliot,
Beckett, and Celan / Shira Wolosky.
        p.   cm.
  Includes bibliographical references and index.
  ISBN 0-8047-2387-7
    1. European literature—20th century—History and criticism.
2. Mysticism in literature.   3. Eliot, T. S. (Thomas Stearns),
1888–1965—Language.   4. Beckett, Samuel, 1906– —Language.
5. Celan, Paul—Language.   I. Title.
PN771.W65   1995
809'.04—dc20   94-19470
                                                        CIP